A REASON FOR EVERY SEASON

Memoirs of a Black
Superintendent in America

DR. PAUL E. COAKLEY

In loving memory of Paul Coakley Sr.

PALMETTO
PUBLISHING

Charleston, SC
www.PalmettoPublishing.com

Paperback ISBN: 979-8-8229-2629-5
eBook ISBN: 979-8-8229-2630-1

This is a work of nonfiction, some names and identifying details have
been changed.

Contents

CHAPTER 1
Sneaks, Rhymes, & Life

I am a sneaker connoisseur. As a kid I would meticulously clean my shoes after wearing them. Scrub them down with a toothbrush, warm soapy water, dry them with a hand towel, stuff tissue paper in the toe box and store them in their original boxes stacked in my closet. Today, those same sneakers I used to wipe down as a kid are called Retro's. They resell for hundreds, even thousands of dollars, sometimes five times what we used to pay for the same shoe. Most collectors of kicks say the boxes are important. I never cared much about the boxes, but kept them anyway, in case I ever wanted to sell them down the line, but I never did. Most sneaker lovers share a similar story of acquiring the kicks that they wanted but couldn't afford during childhood, my collection began vice-versa. A nostalgic mission to compile many of the sneakers that I was blessed enough to wear as a kid: Jordan 1s, 3s, 4s, Barkleys, Air Max, Air Force 1s (known on the east coast as uptowns), and even Flight 89s.

I came from what most would consider a Black upper-middle-class family, my parents both were educators, my father was the principal of Harriet Tubman Middle school and my mother a kindergarten teacher, they worked in the same district, Portland Public Schools, located in Portland, Oregon. They made the pilgrimage from down south to the west coast, from the small town of Gallatin, Tennessee approximately 30 minutes outside of Nashville, a town full of relatives, cousins, uncles, aunties and grandparents. As fate would have it, Portland Public Schools recruited them at an educator job fair in Tennessee, they took the chance at venturing out to Portland, Oregon. Both held advanced degrees, their friends were teachers, school administrators, pastors, and entrepreneurs.

The importance of education was instilled in me and my younger brother, Brian, at an early age, oftentimes my good grades were rewarded with a new pair of kicks. We'd hit the mall, but I liked shopping at the Nike Factory store on MLK Boulevard (then called Union Ave.) in North-east Portland most of all. In the 80s and 90s, the store was a hub located in the heart of the Black Community, and was Nike's first ever Factory Outlet in the world. The outlet came about through the efforts of Ron Herndon, a Black civil rights leader and community activist who was friends with my father. In the 80s Ron organized a protest of Nike with over 4,000 students in participation. Ron and many others were tired of seeing dollars leaving the Black community to line Nike's pockets. During those days Nike's workforce was 98% White. Herndon's efforts lead to the opening of the world's first ever Nike factory store, dedicated to diverse hiring practices, economic growth and access to Nike's resources at a discounted price. These Nike factory outlets are now located all over the country. In middle school, my good report card led to the purchase of the OG Jordan Bred 4s, a black nubuck basketball shoe, with black mesh cutouts, hard rubber wings on the side, a red Jumpman logo on the tongue, hints of red on the sole, with Nike Air highlighted in bold gray block letters on the back. In 6th grade social studies, I kicked my feet up on the desk leaning back in my chair for classmates to see them in all their glory, feeling as cool as Michael Jordan or Mars Blackmon, the fictional character created by Spike Lee in the black and white Jordan 4 commercials, "Is it the shoes? Money, it's got to be the shoes?" Mars asks Jordan. I told my classmate, "I got these for my grades."

So when I dropped out of college after the first quarter of my junior year, it came as a surprise to friends and family. The kid who came from a lineage of Black educators, just graduated from Gresham High School two years prior, a 95% White school, 2% Black, located in a small suburb east of Portland, the only Black male student in Honors English all four years in a row was throwing in the college towel. The first day of my ninth-grade year, I was stopped at the door of Honors

English by the teacher, Mrs. McNeal. "Excuse me, but I think you are in the wrong class," she said. "No. I'm in the right place, Paul Coakley, Jr. check your list."

After glancing at the list with a look of smug disappointment she said, "Oh, Paul. I guess you are in my class, have a seat." She quickly shifted her look into a smirking *we will see about* that face. I pulled my bright yellow Champion hoodie over my head, parking myself in the back of the classroom, tense, unsettled, seething...maybe I don't belong here I thought... it's evident that Mrs. McNeal doesn't want me here. After hearing what happened my parents' message was loud and clear. "You are Paul Edward Coakley, Jr., named after your father, you go into that honors class with your head held high and know that you are qualified. Whatever you plan to do, don't do it halfway. Give it your best! To make it as a Black man in America you've got to be extra good."

My grandfather was the first Paul Coakley, he ran his own barbershop in the 1960's, "Paul's Barbershop" located in Detroit, Michigan. That actually makes me Paul the third, but since my grandfather didn't have the same middle name, that made me a junior in my family. He died of cancer when my father was in middle school, but the stories passed down about him were larger than life. Like the time that he shot a man in the stomach while holding my dad's hand who was four years old at the time. Dad remembers a man confronting my grandfather and lunging towards him with a knife over a woman who had left him for grandpa. After the shots were fired, he called the police to let them know the man needed help, that he shot him in the side intentionally to graze him in self-defense.

As a kid, I listened to many stories from relatives about Detroit, and the riot of 1967, also known as the Detroit Rebellion. It all started when police raided a Black night club on 12th and Clairmount street arresting Black patrons and destroying club property. This racially charged event led to several days of looting, vandalism, break-in and arson, resulting in destroyed businesses, homes and properties. The Black people of Detroit like everywhere in the country were fed-up with the inhuman treatment that they were putting up with, especially at the hands of

3

police. The night club raid was the tipping point, Black folks wanted their respect by any means necessary. African-American entrepreneurs were writing "Black Owned" on the front of their business in hopes of surviving several anger-fueled days of riots. During all the action my grandfather sat boldly in his barber's chair directly in the front window of Paul's Barbershop with a sawed-off shotgun, his hand on the pump.

"I'm not putting up a Black Owned sign, everybody knows this is my shop, if they touch it, they're gonna find out what time it is!" he said loudly, shaking the shotgun in the air with his right hand.

Two days of fires, looting, thefts and vandalism Detroit looked like a warzone. Forty-three people were killed, firefighters hosed down burning buildings, over 200 police officers and federal troops were deployed to use extreme force and regain control of the city. When the riots ended Paul's Barbershop remained unscathed, and grandpa was back to giving the brotha's of Detroit fresh haircuts while sipping his cup of strong black coffee alternating drags of a cigarette with his left hand, while using the clippers to shape large, medium and small afros with his right.

My grandfather was 46 when he died, my dad could have easily been a statistic, a data point, a young black teen in need of a consistent father figure, on a pipeline to prison. Being the youngest of eight siblings, my grandmother Alvilda Fisher, sent him to live with his father's brother, Joseph Coakley and his wife Irene in Gallatin Tennessee. While Gallatin had its problems, it was much safer than Detroit, which was known as the crime capital of the world. The racism in the south was evident, transparent, open and in your face in most places, especially in larger cities in Tennessee like Memphis, Chattanooga, and Nashville, 30 miles north of Nashville sat Gallatin, a small county town with a Black side (referred to back then as the "colored side of town") and a White side, divided by a railroad track. Gallatin, like most cities in the Southern states, structured the city's layout on the Jim Crow laws. These laws were based on the "separate but equal" concept. Black folks stayed on their side of town and the White folks had no reason to leave their side. Each side also had its own history, culture and traditions. Physically, each side had their own stores, schools, salons, churches, restaurants, and drive-in theaters, so the separate part was accomplished. However, nothing about them was equal. Black families dwellings were all positioned on the older side of town, with aged buildings, businesses, and schools. Although Black schools and White schools were all part of the Sumner County School District, Blacks students received hand-me-down materials, out-of-date textbooks, rusted discarded instruments, second rate science materials, and used physical education equipment shelved by Whites coaches and athletes. Gallatin only had one movie theater, which was located close to the epicenter of town on the White side of the sidewalk. The main entrance and ticket booth was a Whites only entrance. Black people were "allowed" to cross the street and hurry past the White sidewalk and Whites only entrance into an alleyway, then stand in line under the "Blacks Only" sign to purchase tickets on the backside of the building. Once their ticket was in hand, they had to enter up the backstairs which led to the "Blacks Only" balcony fully encased with wire fencing. The more militant Black teens including my father didn't go to the movie theater, "until we can go through the front door and sit where we want, we won't go at all, don't spend your money there."

In small towns like Gallatin, high school happenings are a large part of the community's fabric. People filled the bleachers during sporting events, came out to see their kids' musical performance, and loved to watch the school's marching bands. In 1970, Union High School was thriving, an all-Black high school with a school leader that was well respected in the community, dedicated to supporting his students and staff, and who led by example with integrity and dignity. Principal John Malone, he stood approximately six-foot-one, with broad shoulders, mahogany skin. His crisply ironed white shirts, solid color ties, and well fitted suits gave him a distinct presence that demanded respect, even from White educators across the district. He didn't necessarily need to speak to get a student's attention, a serious look, deliberate gaze or deep stern exhale was enough to cease the banter or horseplay that happened in hallways, classrooms and cafeterias. Principal Malone had a Bachelor's of Science from Tennessee State University, and Masters from Fisk, a private historically black college in Nashville. During his time at Union, he built a strong team. The Union staff was a caring, loving group of educators, many grew up in Gallatin, the students were their family members, they taught to neighbors, cousins, nieces, nephews and grandkids. They spoke with parents about their students' attendance, assignments and grades at the grocery store, laundromat, barbershop, beauty salon and corner markets. They shared their academic and behavioral concerns with their student's guardians after Sunday services in church parking lots, family dinners and outings to the park.

Amongst the staff was Mrs. Dobbins the librarian, known for running a quiet library, making sure every student had books to read that would interest and challenge their reading ability, expand their knowledge, sharpen their skills, even during the summer. The business class was taught by Mrs. Jordan, who also graduated from Fisk. She held high expectations for all her students and would stay after school regularly to help those who struggled with assignments. My father's uncle and guardian Joseph Coakley, taught science at Union High, a slender veteran, who served in the US Army. He kept his hair brushed to the back, and kept a trimmed mustache. He was passionate about teaching biology, chemistry and physical science. Diligently, he kept a close eye on his nephew, my father Paul, who was in his junior year at the time. He knew that Paul had potential and would thrive with love and support. He was always talking about my Dad, "Paul could get along with anyone, it's hard not to like him. That booming voice and big smile wins everyone over. He's a real leader."

A kid from the murder capital serving as Union's Junior Class President, governed as chair and vice-chair of afterschool clubs and committees, and intermingled with Senior classmen like Principal Malone's son, Joseph (a life-long friend whom I refer to as Unk). Back then, Unk played power-forward for the Union High basketball team. Paul made the most of his time at Union High, a school booming with culture, connection, unity, pride and passion.

Brown v. the Board of Education's Supreme Court case prohibited the segregation of schools in 1954. Good old Gallatin dragged its feet on implementation for 17 years. Separation of the races hung in the balance for many reasons, fear of the unknown, racist acts of violence that would upset the cities sense of peace, as well as the fact that change can be hard, especially when those set to lead the change don't believe in the outcome, goal or reason for the change in the first place.

Everyone in Gallatin knew that at the end of the 1970 -1971 school year Union High would permanently close its doors. Black folks worried about their kids integrating into Gallatin High School with many of the same White students that used racial slurs in public, drove cars that displayed the confederate flag, and even a few that participated with their family members in the occasional late-night cross burning. Black students worried about losing their culture, comradery, identity and sense of belonging. Union staff worried about losing their jobs, their family's stability, their relationships with students, their identity as professionals. White folks worried about their kids mingling with Negro students, sharing facilities, space and materials, and being under the authority of Black faculty members. White students felt uneasy, afraid of the unknown, upset at the change that the next school year held. Many White staff expressed their frustration during district meetings where both staffs came together to plan for the upcoming school year. Union educators were met with unwelcoming looks and attitudes from Gallatin veterans teachers, educational assistance, custodians and coaches. A mediator from the state came to ensure that regardless of the hard feelings, the change was going to happen. Superintendent Daily, a middle-aged White man, and the Sumner County School Board had held out on desegregating the district for as long as possible. However, the mandate was clear, desegregate in the Fall or lose federal funding.

Principal Malone and Principal Herron were colleagues that talked often behind the scenes about how to best navigate the issues they were up against. The plan of dismantling Union High by moving the small Black student body and remaining staff into the much larger, all White Gallatin High was looming at the end of the school year. However, the two principals also faced many immediate challenges fueled by racial tensions, political pressure and running the day-to-day operations. Their schools had always been rivals even though they rarely competed against each other for a variety of reasons, the spirit of competition was thick in Gallatin, silent, unspoken, but there, Black vs. White, battle of the bands, battle of the cheerleading squads, battle for the best record in football, battle of academic performance and this year for the first time ever Union and Gallatin battled for the basketball state championship. A state championship rivalry that garnered national attention, by author Ken Abraham, in his book "More than Rivals" 1970 was a year to remember.

The desegregation of Sumner County School District took place in the 1970-71 school year. A year of change; that fall, Union High's doors remained closed, dark and vacant. Black students walked the halls of Gallatin High, attended classes, participated in the same clubs, teams and school events as White students. For any group of people, integrating into someone else's space sets up a dynamic of guests vs. owners. The wake of the desegregation process left Black staff demoted, demoralized, disenfranchised and disenchanted. Principal Dan Herron remained Principal of Gallatin High, while Principal John Malone was made one of two Assistant Principals. Of the new Gallatin administration, Principal Malone held a Master's Degree and more years of experience, except job placements weren't based on leadership or qualifications, solely skin color. A desegregation job placement was based on the unwritten rule... *if you are Black, get back!* But in the hearts and minds of Black students, families and community members, Malone remained their principal always and was revered as such.

As the Union staff members expected, many lost their jobs, the business teacher Ms. Fisk, the head basketball coach Cecil Scott, my dad's guardian uncle, science teacher Joseph Coakley, were laid off. Black staff at Gallatin High were few and far between, Mrs. Dobbins the librarian was amongst the survivors. Union students would smile at her and she'd always recognize them, ask what they were reading, giving them a grin or a wink when she saw them in the library. The crew of past Union students and staff, like most Black people in America, were resilient. Black Americans had been proving that they belonged their entire lives. In '71 Black Gallatin teens displayed their bounce back ability, elasticity to withstand challenges, the strength to overcome stress, upheaval and adversity. It was the type of strength that was built and sustained through generations. Amongst that resilient student body nobody proved to have more bounce-back-ability than my father, Paul Coakley the second. He moved with purpose, not only determined to graduate from Gallatin high school, but also to be a part of it, a peer, a friend, a leader. As Union's outgoing junior class president, he knew that his peers would look to him as they integrated into the much larger Gallatin High. Union teachers and community leaders would observe his attitude, demeanor, and work ethic. Uncle Joseph and Aunt Irene, his caregivers would say "we are depending on you Paul, you are carrying the Coakley name, make us proud, leave a legacy." A social-butterfly maneuvering amongst his peers both Black and White, he knew no strangers, didn't back down when he knew he was right. Exuding a natural swagger, he was deemed the nickname "Cool Paul" in the classroom, hallways, basketball courts and neighborhood. In his mind, the godfather of soul James Brown's "Say it loud" Otis Redding's "A change is gonna come" and Marvin Gaye's "What's going on" played like a soundtrack on repeat. Love, a fondness for his community that landed him a high school job at H.G. Hills - Gallatin's premier grocery store, where he was the town's first black cashier. Love, an attachment to his school peers (black and white) who voted him "most friendly" amongst his senior class. Love, a deep affection for his high school sweetheart, then known as Carlus Alexander, my mom who was two grades younger than him in high school. They met and dated a while before getting serious about each other back at Union high. She was a sophomore when she integrated into Gallatin High, which was no easy task for any Black female student.

Mom had to overcome additional challenges, not experienced by the majority of her Union high school peers. See, my mother had light skin. While having light skin's not unusual by any means for my generation or any generation that came after Generation X, for Boomers and Baby Boomers, colorism was real in the Black community. Throughout history, lighter skin has been viewed as superior to darker skin. This sad mentality of judging solely on skin color traces back to slavery. Around the world many countries use a caste system, where skin color plays a major factor in determining how beauty, power and success is perceived by the world. Due to this physical characteristic, she not only dealt with the racial injustices that all Blacks endured by racist Whites, she also endured verbal abuse, ridicule, jealousy, passive aggressive torment and cruelty from a small population of her own community, who set out to make her childhood extraordinarily difficult. A dark skin relative, neighbor or peer envious of her long smooth brownish-black hair and lighter shade of skin, making snarky ignorant comments and quips about her passing for White. By the time Carlus reached high school at Union, she had grown a skin thicker than most. Though she always had a sweet, kind demeanor, she developed an edge, a protective shield, the ability to stand up for herself at all costs. She wasn't the one to mess with, she knew who she was, strong, intelligent, loved, and she carried herself as such.

Born to a teenage mom, my grandma Mattie enlisted help in raising her. At the age of five she went to live with her great aunt, Miss Edna Mae Scott, who was a teacher. As Edna battled cancer she reached out to her neighbors for support. An affluent black couple known and respected in the community, the Gray's. The Grays had no children of their own, they raised Carlus, giving her a permanent home until she graduated from high school. The Gray's weren't affluent by today's standards, but for a young black couple in Gallatin in the 70s, they were. They owned a newly built one-story brick three-bedroom house with a large den fully furnished with a sofa and loveseat that sat in front of a large tv, a reclining chair that Mr. Gray would relax in while reading the newspaper. They also had a formal living room, which was unheard of for Black families during this time, filled with plush vibrant furniture and a classic black piano. Mrs. Gray would practice on the piano, singing songs, preparing for Sunday Service where she was the longstanding beloved church pianist at First Baptist Church of Gallatin. Off of the living room was a formal dining room with six oak chairs and an elegant dining table where they ate during holidays and special occasions. The Grays' home had a nice size kitchen with a dining area and a bay window that looked out on their farmland, they raised horses, cows, chickens and cattle. Mr. Gray could often be seen driving across his acreage on a riding lawnmower making his green field nice and even. Two freshly washed cars were parked evenly under their carport, the Oldsmobile Dynamic Celebrity two door sedan was used for Sunday driving to First Baptist Church where Deacon Gray served as an overseer, making sure the Church was in tip-top shape for Sunday service. The Buick Regal was for daily use, grocery runs, visiting relatives and driving to the many properties they own on the Black side of Gallatin, where they had long-term renters whom they had built strong ties to over the years. When their tenants struggled during the holidays or fell on hard times they would show them grace, help them land jobs, and provide them with holiday meals or presents for their children.

Mom spoke often about the Gray's, "they loved me as though they birth me into the world. They taught me life's lessons, helped me believe in myself, set goals and dreams." A reliable, family structure, with high expectations, true belief in one's ability to achieve, parents there to encourage you, listen and give you sound advice through life's adversities can make a huge difference in a person's future. For Carlus, she took full advantage of listening and learning from the Gray's, they were the type of people who blessed everyone they came in contact with in some way. They saw education as a key factor for Black Americans in reaching the American Dream, a message that led Carlus to graduating from Gallatin high school a year after Paul, and joining her high school sweetheart at the University of Tennessee in Knoxville. They soon were married and lived on campus in married housing while they finished college and acquired teaching degrees. I was born in Gallatin, Tennessee on June 23, 1976, Paul Edward Coakley, Jr. I was the third in a generation of Paul Coakley's everyone called me P.J.

To my surprise, my parents gave me grace when I told them I didn't want to return to college. "Well, if you are going to take 'a break' from college, you need to get a job" my parents declared. They knew I was no stranger to hard work. I kept jobs throughout high school ranging from grocery stores to hustling on the sales floor in retail shops that offered an hourly wage plus commission. During a few college winter breaks I worked at Macy's gift-wrapping presents, a life skill that my Dad ended up depending on every holiday. "Wrap these up for me dude, they're for your mom." I had developed a strong work ethic, I always kept some cash on me, I liked having money, and spending it as well.

My parents were tired of my mediocre grades, negative talk about Eugene, Oregon, and my complete lack of focus. Attending class consisted of tiptoeing into the auditorium mid-lecture after oversleeping, or sitting in the back when I was on-time, writing rhymes instead of notes, napping behind shades, or missing class altogether to watch three-hour mafia movies like Goodfellas, Scarface and Casino. Scorsese's influence led us to turning our three-bedroom apartment into a casino with weekly business hours, equip with a blackjack table, specified poker nights, plus a concession stand where we sold snacks at 3 times the cost of their value. You had to know one of us, or be vouched for to get in. LV, the most card savvy of us all ran the blackjack table, John held down concessions, I manned the door, checking in on the players trying to get them to bet big. Regulars like Beverly Hills Nick, a cool white boy that had been hanging with us since freshman year would ask, "What if I win? Do y'all have enough to pay me?" We were raking in a considerable amount per week. We always paid out the winners and had enough cash left over to split. Even if one guy did win, everyone else was losing. Like Ace Rothstein explains in the movie Casino, "the cardinal rule is keep'em playing and keep them coming back. The longer they play the more they lose. In the end, we get it all." We poured our blood, sweat and tears into the business, and our college buddies loved it. They'd come by constantly, losing their $5s, $10s and $20 dollar bills. Sure, they complained about the concessions, "I've been playing for three hours...you've got the nerve to charge five bucks for a hotdog." Their only other option was driving 6 minutes up the road to the closest convenience store, but being that most of them didn't have cars, we let'em gripe, eventually they coughed up the five bucks. We really didn't have many monthly bills; the casino money was mostly used to restock the concessions and for buying fresh clothes. We had neck breaking sneakers, fresh name brand hoodies, rugby shirts, starter jackets and velour sweat suits. We stood out on campus, got the attention of girls, building a following of unknown haters in the process.

While my life had turned into one big party, part of me felt ashamed, a sense of failure, like I wasn't college material, that I didn't belong or fit in. I wanted to quietly slink out, unnoticed and disappear. But that didn't happen, when I told my compadres that I was dropping out, the majority of them tried encouraging me to stay. It was a cold December when I packed my things, leaving my college friends behind. My roommate from sophomore year Jamar was the starting power forward for U of O's basketball team. The 6'3" dude bear hugged me "Bro you sure you aren't coming back? Things just won't be the same without you." I told him to take care of himself, "this college thing just isn't me" I replied.

Deep down, I never gave it my all, I wasn't focused. My main passion was rapping, or trying to make money. I had a backpack full of Source Magazines, a head full of rhymes, just waiting for any so-called rapper to test my skills. I wanted a record deal, not a college degree. I had been rapping since 8th grade, I hung with a crew called Ol' Dominion, a group of about 15 rappers from Portland and Seattle. In Eugene, I spent much of my time at the music store, right across from the University Bookstore, listening to the latest hip-hop album, or flipping through record crates. When I wasn't trying to get the cutest girl's number I was working on my craft - writing rhymes in a marbled composition notebook, entering freestyle battles, eventually doing shows at local dives with my buddy, John, who ended up being my actual roommate freshman year when the Shandog didn't enroll. We create a duo rap group called The Critics. We were gaining popularity around Eugene, even a bit in Portland, but I was on a mission to drop a solo album. On weekends, I'd make the two hour drive one-way from Eugene to Portland, a b-line to the studio...a basement of a duplex in NE where "Snafu" a beat maker and aspiring producer lived with his Mom. He was undoubtedly one of the best in the city, we linked up in high school, he also went to Gresham, where the 2% Black student population banded together like Voltron. Snafu saved up his cash, eventually purchasing an Akai MPC drum machine when I was in 10th grade. He played around with it until he figured it out.

Making beats that had everyone in earshot bobbing their heads back and forth to the baseline. I spent my time laying down vocals in the studio, pressuring him for my DAT tape, a miniature tape with beats that were performance quality. Once I got the DAT, I carried it everywhere just in case there was an opportunity to perform.

Thankfully, the three-bedroom casino was short-lived before anyone got into real trouble. One night it got overcrowded and out of our control. The same weekend we hosted a hip-hop show, the Ol' Dominion crew drove up as well as several partygoers from Portland. Friends helped us promote the show, passing out flyers and stapling posters to telephone poles. Shandog and a few dudes from my Gresham made the journey to Eugene to show their support. We assured the manager of the venue that we'd pack the place if he would give us 50% of the money collected at the door, he agreed. Despite the poor sound system, the show was lit, packed wall to wall with college kids, fly girls and a bunch of student athletes. After the show we opened the casino, but due to the number of out-of-towners our small potatoes wannabe Golden Nugget was overcrowded with the quickness. Due to the number of females in attendance we got sloppy, letting Beverly Hills Nick run the blackjack table, so we could mingle. The night was a blur which quickly came to a screeching halt when someone woke me out of bed curled up with a girl that had come to the show, notifying me that my parents were on their way. They had been trying to reach me for the last 40 minute.

I rushed to call them, mom was in hysterics, "are you ok? we got a call from the police, we will be there in an hour...someone stole your car. We have been trying to reach you!..." I surveyed the apartment; people sprawled out on the couch, laying on the floor, slouching in chairs, faces I knew, faces I didn't know. Garbage everywhere, half-eaten food, spilled cans, sticky wrappers, toppled over bottles, playing cards strewn about. LV, John, Shandog, LaBa, Ike-Boogie, my boy NyQuil and Dante helped me kick almost everyone out of the apartment. Then we started cleaning the place. We used large black hefty bags to cover our debauchery, Portlanders fled for their cars while saying their goodbyes. I used my voice like an invisible megaphone to get people out of there, mimicking "Lean On Me" principal Joe Clark, "hurry up and get out, and do it expeditiously!" I was a nervous wreck, but we put the place back in decent order, tossing giant garbage bags on the side patio for the time being. I went outside and stared at the empty parking space where I'd left my new 1995 blue pearl Honda Civic sedan my parents bought me after registering for college. They wanted me to have a safe and reliable car. Dad pulled his new burgundy Honda Accord into my empty parking space, they had already been to the police station. Mom followed behind him in my car, they saw the person who stole my vehicle and described him to me. After putting it together, I begged them not to press charges. It was a friend visiting from Portland who later claimed he woke me up and asked to borrow my keys to drive to Taco Bell, a conversation that never happened.

Dad was visibly livid but calm, he said, "Mom has your keys, you're not getting them back. I can't trust you." My parents saw the Shandog and a bunch of my high school buddies, none of which actually attended the college, they weren't amused. Mom gave me the silent treatment while sitting in the driver's seat of my car with the window rolled down. Before leaving she uttered three words, "PJ, this hurts." I could see the sadness, stress and disappointment in her eyes. "I'm sorry, Mom," I said. She quietly rolled up the window and closed her eyes. They made the trip back home in separate cars, Dad leading the way in the burgundy Accord while Mom followed closely behind in my blue pearl Civic, which took me three months to earn back.

"I got the homie's car took. Sorry dawg... you said I could drive to Taco Bell" said the overweight perpetrator concocting a quick lie. "Nah, dawg, I'd never give you my keys" I said... "you lucky we didn't press charges...when are you leaving anyway?"

Stuffed duffle bags and a car crammed to the max with personal belongings I hit the road, Jamar, looked at me, gave a fist pound saying "finish that album Bro, you got lyrics." I performed at Po-Hop, Portland's annual hip-hop festival. I was featured on local hip-hop promoter Idris "StarChile" O'Ferrall's debut album entitled Twist: Genesis Chapter 1. Idris was a childhood friend who I grew up with in the church. We met at Mt. Olivet Baptist Church back when we were in elementary school, we stayed connected from then on. He passed away at the age of 42 of lymphoma, but left a positive impact on the Portland music scene and was instrumental in establishing Portland's annual Hip-Hop Day. The song we made got a bit of local radio play. I remember driving, listening to the radio, hearing the song come on in my car, "yo, yo turn it up! turn it up!"

At the time, I didn't realize that Jamar's bear hug and fist bump wasn't just a "we will miss you" moment. It meant no more laughing over Jerome's appearances on the Martin show, the end of late-night pizza runs, no more snapping on each other's clothes or buck-teeth, no more holding down cafeteria tables to sit as a crew at breakfast, or freestyle over Jamar's beatbox. It was a fist pound that meant have a good life, it was nice getting to know you. That was the last time I'd see or speak to Jamar. I heard he went on to play for the Harlem Globe Trotter. While I recorded a lot of tracks, I never finished the album.

After dropping out of the University of Oregon, I quickly landed a job through a temp agency working for Nike, of course. The Nike Air sole Factory in Beaverton, Oregon to be exact. Oregon is the sneaker capital of the world, Adidas headquarters is located in Portland, and Beaverton is the home of the Nike World Headquarters. The Air sole Factory was about five minutes up the road from Headquarters, about a forty-minute drive from my parent's house, where I found myself staying rent-free after giving up my dorm room. Luckily, one of my closest friends from high school, Shannon, aka the Shandog, was hired before me through the same temp agency. He put in a good word which helped me land the job. The Shandog was my Aceboon, back when we were both accepted into the U of O we had planned to be college roommates. That plan abruptly halted when shortly before high school graduation he dropped the news on me that he was going to be a father. With a beautiful bundle of joy on the way he planned to stay back, get a full-time job, ready to be the best dad he could. In 1991, Ed OG & Da Bulldogs released a song entitled "Be A Father to Your Child," a responsibility that I saw several men from my community run from, the Shandog embraced it. I congratulated him on stepping up to be the provider for his family. Before leaving for college, I presented him with an outfit for his baby girl. He presented me with a framed poster of Janet Jackson posing on the cover of Rolling Stones Magazine, a gift that dawned my dorm room walls, and eventually the living room wall of the three-bedroom apartment that I shared with LV and John, until I packed to move back home.

There I was, back in Gresham, back in my parents' house, carpooling with the Shandog. We alternated drive days to save on gas, shooting the breeze during the commute. We worked from 5 pm to 5 am, the twelve-hour shift was no joke, but paid better than any job I had held in my 19 years of living. In a month, Nike hired both the Shandog and I from the temp agency. Nike employees had access to the employee store (or what we called the ES) where everything was 50 percent off. Saving money in those days became non-existent for me, we got paid every Friday. Once I got my paper check, I'd deposit it into my account, then sleep in my car in front of the ES waiting for the doors to open at 8 am. By 9 am I was walking out of there with a fresh pair of sneaks, a new outfit for the weekend, usually a jogging suit, matching hat, or a crisp t-shirt and basketball shorts to match my sneakers. I had Saturdays off, I dressed to impress on the weekend. The ES was also known for celebrity sightings, while shopping there we'd run into professional athletes, actors, and entertainers. Once, the Shandog and I met MC Hammer, who was 20 deep, he chatted us up while his posse of dancers, relatives and managers filled their shopping carts full of clothes.

The first month on the job we both started on the machines, a full day of sitting, lining up a tiny needle that when done correctly, blows up the Air sole that is placed in the bottoms of Nike's sneakers. You pull a handle that allows a metal rod to burn the needle hole, sealing the inflated Air sole shut. Approximately 1,800 air soles fill a box that is shipped off to another factory, completing a box for most people during a 12-hour shift was an accomplishment. But for me, that was child's play. I would put my headphones on blaring A Tribe Called Quest, and get into the zone. Honing in on my machine while the smell of dusty cardboard and burnt rubber filled the air. Vowing to complete more boxes than Shandog, anyone in the vicinity of my workstation, eventually competing with everyone on the factory floor. Don't get me wrong, the Shandog was no slouch, we're both competitors. "Man, your work ethic is crazy" is what the floor supervisor said after seeing me fill two and a half boxes with Air soles during a shift. My supervisor just happened to be a brotha named Carl, most of the supervisors were White males, the floor technicians were majority Asian, the Shandog and I ended up in Carl's section. Perhaps Carl requested we be with him, to take us under his wing and support us.

Carl was stocky with glasses, he wore a small Jheri Curl. This was the 90s, the era of low boxes and high-top fades. But Carl was cool, professional, calm and collected, after about three months of hard work he promoted me to shipping and receiving, which consisted of collecting the completed boxes of Air soles, then loading them on a conveyor belt, which travels into pods that go on trucks and planes to be shipped overseas. While the back of most Nike shoe tongue tags say "Made in China, or Vietnam" the air bubbles come from Beaverton. Shipping and receiving was easy for me to master. After that, Carl had me overseeing the orders of boxes that were to be shipped out, unfortunately there was no increase in pay, just responsibility. So when I saw a Floor Manager job posting in the Air Sole food court, I asked Carl what I needed to do to land the gig. "Paul c'mon man, that job requires a degree, you don't qualify." My work ethic, attention to detail and positive attitude didn't matter when it came to being a Floor Manager. Carl shocked me when he said he'd be glad if he came to work one day and I wasn't there because I went back to college. I sat in a rolling chair on the Air sole floor fuming, who does Carl think he is? You think I won't do it, you think I'm scared to go back...I've been putting in work in this factory for six months...I dwelled on his words over the weekend. They sunk deep into my soul. I knew he was right, but it took being told you are not qualified for me to realize that I wanted to finish my degree. On Monday, I completed my twelve-hour shift, snuck over to Carl's workstation, and left a note on his desk.

Dear Carl,

I appreciate everything you've done for me. Please accept this letter of resignation. I am going back to college. I hope you're not mad at a brotha. Hopefully, if everything is everythang, I can help out here during holiday breaks, maybe even in the summer. You can always reach me through Shannon.

Sincerely,
Paul

Returning to college shifted my life's trajectory, instead of going back to Eugene, one of the best moves I ever made was enrolling at Portland State University (PSU). I was more focused than ever, determined to raise my G.P.A. which was a measly 2.75, at the time. After one year, my G.P.A. increased to a 3.5, and eventually a 3.9. I was hitting the books hard, reading, writing and devouring assignments. I had something to prove, I was fueled by haters, non-believers, and people who counted me out, "he already quit once" they said.

As an attempt to determine my own success, in the summer of 97' I enrolled in college studies abroad, allowing me to visit Yokosuka, Japan coaching kids' sports camps on the US naval base. LV and I both decided to take advantage of the opportunity not only to receive 18 upper division credits over the summer, but also to collect a healthy stipend, free airfare, room and board and meals on the base. The camp consisted of basketball, golf, football, soccer, outdoor games, and swimming. Each camp counselor worked on a rotating schedule and ended up working their way through all the areas.

"Come on kid reach, you got this…" as I stretched out the 12' foot metal pole with the rescue hook on the end of it, laying on the concrete at the edge of the deep end of the swimming pool with my arms stretched out. Hooking him in the crook of the pole, pulling him to safety. Kids clapped and cheered, thanking me for my quick response. "You ok?, from now on you stay in the shallow end." Little Jason looked up and said "you saved my life, thanks" as he ran to the shallow end. One smart mouthed kid walked up to me about 5 minutes later and said, "hey...why didn't you just jump in?" "None ya!" I said, as he walked off. Covering up the fact that, like a bad stereotype, I never learned to swim. I couldn't wait for this two-week lifeguard rotation to end. In retelling the story of how I saved the kid during our end of the day counselor debrief, LV just looked at me and smiled. The only other person in Japan that knew my secret. He too carried the shame of the same Black stereotype.

I began using chopsticks, a life-long skill I often used during meetings held in a variety of Pan-Asian restaurants throughout my career. Living on the naval base was bittersweet, shopping at the commissary on the base helps stretch your dollar, most of the restaurants and cafeterias weren't half bad. Before coming to Japan I loathed eating white rice, but after a month on base I was hooked on it. It came with everything so you learn to like it or starve, chicken & rice, veggies & rice, egg with gravy & rice, and my military base favorite, ribs & rice. I got so nice with the chopsticks I could pick up one grain of rice at a time, "Yo check this out, man" I would say holding up a grain between my sticks. "So... everyone can do that here, but that is something back in Portland" LV would say laughing.

I picked up enough of the Japanese language to get by, and quickly found the emerging hip-hop scene. I won a rap contest by battling local artists, US soldiers stationed on base and Japanese dudes in Wu-tang t-shirts, baggy jeans and cornrows. The contest led to a hit on my Sky-Pager from the owner of Yokohama Bay Hall. I called him from the pay phone in the cafeteria, and was offered the opportunity to open up for Redman the following week.

I was on it, good thing I brought my DAT tape. The hall was lively, dark, packed, and hot. The two songs that I did got the crowd warmed up, although they had no idea who I was, they were supportive, bobbing their heads, swaying back and forth to Snafu's beat. LV was on stage as well, dancing and working the crowd like Diddy, while I spit rhymes clear and crisp into the microphone through the sound system making sure that listeners could catch every word. Then, the lights got dimmer and Redman's "Time 4 Sum Aksion" beat kicked in. Reggie Noble himself ran onto the stage smiling, dousing the hot crowd with bottled water, then handing me a water bottle to join in, an amazing moment.

Later that summer, LV and I met Charles Barkley, Shaq, and Mutombo after being introduced to them by Damon Stoudamire of the Portland Trailblazer and his cousin Antoine who was one of the homies I used to freestyle with in Eugene. Japan holds an event called the "Super Games" featuring fifteen NBA all-stars who pack the Tokyo Dome with fans by playing scrimmage games, taking photos and signing autographs. Dikembe blessed me with a signed jersey and Shaq gave his to LV.

I glanced sadly in the mirror after hearing the laughter in the barbershop, "I'm not paying you nothin!" I said loudly. It was the worst haircut I had ever received, a small barbershop on base with three Japanese barbers who mostly had soldiers as clients. My hairline was not only pushed back, but shaved completely off! Dudes sitting around the shop including LV were cracking up! Most of them had just got a fresh cut from the same barber that just scalped me. I watched him give LV a nice "Even Steven" using a one guard to cut the hair the same exact length all the way around, then he lined him up perfectly. Before getting in the chair, I ask him for the exact same thing. Why he picked me to mess up on, I have no idea. All I know is I wore a hat for seven straight days until the front of my hair grew back.

In my dorm, I met a brotha named O' who knew how to cut hair. "Le'me see, I hear you got jacked up over there" he said pointing in the direction of the base barbershop. I looked around, finding the coast clear, I removed my hat. "Damn! it's worse that I thought, but I can fix it" O' said and he did. "I'll have to cut your waves out, but they will grow back, just brush a lot... that's probably why he tore your head up," he said laughing, "they ain't use to waves over there, but me I'm from D.C., everybody got them round my way." I got my cuts from O' for the remainder of the summer, along with everyone else in our barracks. He had skills and only charged 5 bucks.

While getting a cut from O' we got on the subject of cards, he told LV and I about an annually spades tournament held on base every summer. Our ears perked up, "you Portland cats don't know nuthin bout bustin' spades" he said. LV smirked and I said "yeah right, I've been playing' since I was two." We entered the tournament with the quickness. Spades is a cutthroat card game that is a staple in many African-American households, it can be played in partners or solo. This specific tournament was partner play, the object of the game is to bid the number of "books" that your team will collect before the hand is played. LV was an all-around hustler, kind of a jack of all trades when it came to cards, so when he told me he could play, I had no doubt. I grew up on the game. My little brother Brian and I were always partners, we played against my parents, aunts, uncles, close friends, almost anyone willing to take us on. At the time, it was my true medium, similar to O' with a pair of clippers in his hand.

In the world of Spade "talking across the board" isn't referring to having a conversation at the table. It is specific to giving your partner clues that could influence the way they bid on the number of books. This type of talk is not allowed in the game of Spades, especially when you are playing in a cut-throat game with soldiers on a military base stationed 6,300 miles from US soil. However, LV and I pulled out all the stops, hand signals, eye contact, code words, gestures and movements that led to win after win. We beat the sistas on base from Florida that hung in a crew, we beat the brothas from Philly who wore shades during the game, we beat the Cali crew dressed like Snoop and the Dogg Pound, and we beat the breaks off the loud talking east coast dudes that wore Timberlands in 90-degree weather.

We found ourselves at the final table of the tournament playing against two Southern card sharks who kept toothpicks in their mouths and did a lot of smirking and mumbling. The tall one called himself Pretty Ricky, he and his partner didn't expect to be playing against a pair of college students from Portland. "What ya'll know about bustin' spades?" said Ricky. We stayed quiet, but in the midst of battle, LV jumped up from the table and said "this brotha reneged!" Reneging is when a player doesn't play the same suit of the card that led in the original hand - meaning that they can't play that suit because they don't have it, but later they play a card from the suit that they claimed they didn't have. The penalty for reneging is to award the other team three books. Spectators backed up LV's accusation, "yep he did, they're cheating, give up the books!" Instead, Pretty Ricky stood up and threw his cards in the middle of the table and said "these lil fools lying, man!," glaring at us before storming out of the mess hall where the tournament was held. Just like that the tournament was ours, while the actual prize was too insignificant to remember, the bragging rights lasted for the rest of our time on base.

About a week or so before the camp was over I got a phone call from my mom. "PJ, listen I'm calling to let me you know that your grandpa Gray passed away," she said sadly. "Your Dad and I are headed to Tennessee to help with the arrangements." "What happened?" I asked. "I don't know all the details, but when you get back home we won't be here, we wanted you to know what was going on." "Ok" I said feeling a knot in my stomach, "how is Nina? (the nickname I used for Mrs. Gray). "Not good" Mom replied before handing the phone to Dad. The news ended my Japan excursion early to get back to the States and possibly attend the funeral. LV left with me so I didn't have to travel the twenty-four-hour flight home alone in misery. The night before our flight back to Portland, we packed our bags, cleaned our dorm, and joined the camp staffers for the last bonfire of the summer. We said our goodbyes to colleagues and friends, most of which we'd never cross paths with again. The long flight back was quiet, my mind raced flashing through memories of the summer in Japan. But mostly I thought about Grandpa Gray, life-lessons he shared, laughs we had, quirky habits of his like clearing his throat before eating, his work ethic and his stellar reputation. I thought about my Grandma Nina, how she was coping with the stress of losing her husband, her lifelong best friend. What would she do? Would she stay in Tennessee, or move to Oregon? Would she continue to be a bright shining light in the lives of others, or slip into a personal deep dark depression? I had to get to Tennessee...Grandpa Gray was the first of many close relatives that I would lose. I felt like a vast piece of me was missing, a piece that would never be replaced. My life was a large puzzle laid out on a flat surface. The far end of the puzzle was unfinished but the past was tightly put together except for the holes that represented loved ones who passed away.

When I touched down in Portland, my parents were in Tennessee doing their best to console Mrs. Gray, relieving her of the burden of planning a funeral while grieving. Instead of coming back to an empty house, I stayed at LV's crib the first night back in the "world" meaning, the "States." As I unpacked, I found that my suitcase was missing my favorite watch, several Polo shirts, plus the autographed Mutombo jersey I was given at the Super Games. Lucky for me, the travelers checks I stashed in a hidden zipper pocket were still there. LV's bag also had missing items, including Shaq's jersey. Somebody robbed us while we were at the bonfire. I'm quite sure "Pretty Ricky" broke into our dorm to get his payback. I could picture him saying something like "I'm fixin' to teach these lil fools a lesson 'bout bustin' spades, man."

It was quite a summer, friends, foes, downtown Tokyo at night, Yokohama Bay Hall, playing cards, getting haircuts, meeting girls, a lot of conversation about sneakers, but most of all, I thought a lot about the kids, their needs, their talents, their goals, their dreams, their futures. While the experience highlighted my love for music, sports, and games, it also left me with a passion for working with children. Helping them smile when they don't feel like it, motivating them to reach their goals, challenging them to believe in themselves, working through problems, emotions, and the barriers of real-life. I realized what my parents and many other educators also realized…an opportunity. The opportunity to help others, kids, those that look like you, those that don't, kids that need you, kids that want help, those that don't, those that need to be challenged, those that struggle, all kids from a wide variety of backgrounds, ethnicities, and economic circumstances. My time at Nike fueled my desire to finish college, and my trip to Yokosuka ignited my passion for working with kids. I was ready to move forward with purpose. I was ready to become a teacher.

CHAPTER 2

This Is Not a Study of Animals

The Portland Teacher Program (PTP) was gaining notoriety across the city as a program dedicated to diversifying Portland Public Schools (PPS) educator workforce. It created a pipeline for teachers of color through a partnership with Portland State University. The PTP program not only increased a college graduate of color's opportunity to land a teaching position, it also provided a full ride scholarship for undergraduate students pursuing their teaching license. In turn, this would require PTP graduates to teach a minimum of three years in PPS. Failure to do so would result in paying back the scholarship. It was a grassroots effort, pumping out approximately twenty to thirty graduates a year. The only program in the city making a considerable effort to diversify the teacher pipeline across the district's eighty-one schools, one teacher at a time, it was quality over quantity. A breeding ground for many strong teachers of color who have changed the educational landscape across the city.

With my increased GPA, I applied for the program and was interviewed by the Director, a middle-aged Caucasian woman. She was known in the Black community as "down for the cause," "woke," or "for the culture." She'd sometimes wear a dashiki with an African headdress. After about 30 minutes of chit-chat with her, I was offered a full ride scholarship. To maintain the scholarship, I needed to keep my grade point average at 3.0 or above. Credit-wise I was a Junior, and after taking the required prerequisites for the teacher's licensure program, I'd have enough credits to graduate with a teaching license and a Master's in Curriculum and Instruction in just a year and a half. I found the brief stint at Nike didn't leave me too far behind, plus the 18 upper division credits I got from my summer overseas worked wonders. I continued taking classes throughout the summer between my Junior and Senior year so I could start the program right on track.

After Japan, LV returned to the U of O, while I began the teacher program at Portland State. We talked often, I updated him on the PTP program, the scholarship and my positive take on attending PSU. Soon, he graduated from U of O, and joined me in PSU's Master's program with a PTP Scholarship of his own. Portland State is located downtown surrounded by buildings, stores, and restaurants, amongst the crowded city streets. Our classes were delivered in a cohort model, allowing us to connect with students in the program throughout the year. Everything was smooth, until one day in our Theories of Instruction course the professor asked LV and I to stay after class. She instructed "split up amongst the class to share our cultural experience with others." "I'm cool, I'm here for me, not to teach everyone else," I replied. LV was quick, "lots of White students are sitting together, are you asking them to split up?" he asked. The professor was taken aback, dumbfounded, speechless as we left class.

Next, we're sitting in front of our PTP Director, the (not so) "woke" middle aged White woman, wearing a played-out dashiki, leering at us through her horn-rimmed glasses from a high seated burgundy leather executive's chair, perched over her tall wooden desk. "I hear you two are inseparable, you need to branch out and share your experiences with the rest of the cohort." "Are you serious, why?" I muttered. "This is not a study of animals," LV responded sharply.

The truth was, we had no problem talking or sitting with anyone in our classes. We got along well with the entire cohort. But this was no longer about being able to sit where we wanted, it was deeper than that. We were locked in a power struggle with the Program Director. How dare you two ungrateful Black students tell me "no" was the expression displayed on her face as she stared back at us. She wanted to break us, bend us to her will, as she'd done time and time again to many other PTP participants that came before us. Not happening, "this is America,

I'll sit where I want," I said. "Then I'll hold your scholarships until you learn how to play the game," she scolded. "You can't do that! We earn those scholarships, neither of us have below a 3.0" said LV. "Yeah, you act like the money is coming out of your personal bank account" I steamed.

Momentary silence … hearts raced, beating loudly … eyes glared, staring coldly … faces scowled, firmly clenched. She knew deep down, she didn't have the authority to pull our scholarships. She also knew that if she tried, it wouldn't stop there...my parents were well known educators in PPS, this could get ugly. "I thought you two wanted to be here, this is very disappointing!" she snapped. From then on, we had no choice but to cross every "t" and dot every "i". She held a grudge like nobody's business, just waiting for either of us to slip up, but we never did.

Most students found her to be a "champion for the cause," sure, her clothes, slang, and community connections spoke loudly. But after that day in her office, to me it was all a facade. A strategic chess move which allowed her to hold a position of privilege, power and influence over systematic decisions that impact the futures of people of color. While I can only speak about my own personal experience, I've heard stories of her wielding power as the program's director. Threatening students with scholarship money, limiting program participants' opportunities, discouraging them from venturing outside the city after they have fulfilled their three-year commitment to PPS. Even talking PTP alums out of taking on leadership roles or pursuing administrative licensure. She was very vocal that PTP graduates "were needed in the classroom." I took that to mean she believed teachers of color should not be in leadership positions. Don't get me wrong, this is not to say that the program wasn't of value. The program as a whole was very beneficial, creating a pathway to diversify the educator workforce, eliminate barriers to licensure, building a network of support for participants that will help to support and retain them in the field of education. Over the past 20 years PTP produced some of the best and brightest educators of color in the state.

The program began in 1989, the Oregon teacher workforce at the time was approximately 3% teachers of color. In 2020, Oregon's teacher workforce was estimated to be 11.7% teachers of color. It took three decades for these efforts to reach double digits. However, approximately 200 of these educators can be attributed to PTP, other increases in diversity across the state include individuals hired from out of state, based on individual district's recruitment efforts. Specifically in PPS, the PTP program made a significant impact in diversifying the teacher workforce. I sometimes wonder what kind of impact could have been made without gate keeping, limiting its participants to only serve in schools located in north and northeast Portland. One would only hope that non-profit programs and organizations with goals of increasing diversity and centering educational equity, would elevate the voices of people of color to identify strengths and challenges, remove barriers and roadblocks created by institutionally racist practices. However, PTP had no Board of Directors, no HR department, no complaint procedure, no internal audits, or participant surveys. It operated as a separate entity from the college and the district. The Director could easily manipulate participants. On the real, it was a program heavily influenced by the Director's own privilege, whether intentionally or unintentionally. There was no consultant or leader of equal power that could point out flaws, errors or blind spots.

Regardless of my program experience, on graduation night, I took the high road. In my one-minute speech I thanked my parents, colleagues, and Director for the opportunity to participate in the program. Then, I kept it moving, with no time to reflect, until now.

Once a PTP graduate completes the program and earns their teaching license, they're given a letter of intent from PPS. The letter guarantees the PTP alum a teaching position, an immediate opportunity to be interviewed for vacant positions, if a graduate wasn't selected by the start of the school year they would be placed in a vacancy by Human Resources. Being a PTP graduate lifted the weight of being stuck in the "pool." The giant teacher infinity pool where most resumes go to drown. An endless pit of thousands of boxes crammed with unread letters of interest neatly printed on cardstock paper. Rarely rising to the top of the pile for an actual interview let alone a job offer, unless you know someone, or had a letter of intent to be hired. Even PTP completers were nervous about interviewing. However, I was fairly confident that I would get an opportunity to work with a principal that I was familiar with. After all, most of Portland Public's Black administrators had known me since I was a kid. They were regulars at family cookouts, card games, birthday parties and holiday gatherings. I'd run into them at the mall, church functions, restaurants, the barbershop and grocery stores. They often would ask me when I was graduating or told me how proud they were of me for following in my parents footsteps.

As luck would have it, soon after I got my teaching license I got a call from Unk. He was my Dad's ace boon and the principal of Martin Luther King Jr. Elementary school in PPS. Unk and my dad were homeboys since Union High. Unk was from Gallatin, his father was Principal Malone, who remained a pillar in the town of Gallatin well after the desegregation of Union High School. Principal Malone continued to support students after the schools desegregated, seeing them through as they graduated at Gallatin High, where my father crossed the stage with the first integrated Senior Class. Unk was a year older than my Dad, so he finished his Senior year at Union. He was the starting power forward who played in the epic championship game against the Gallatin Green Wave.

My parents stayed in contact with Unk and his wife even after we moved to Oregon. They were best friends, all educators. Once my parents had settled into PPS for a few years, Unk and his family made the move from Tennessee to Portland just like us, based on my parent's recommendation, and immediately, we were family. I still call Unk's kids my cousins to this day even though we aren't blood relatives.

When the phone rang my father picked up, it was Unk. He and my Dad had a few laughs before handing me the phone "Doctor J!" Unk said. That was his nickname for me, which he later shortened to Docta'. "I hear you got your teaching license." "Yeah" I said excitedly, "well, I have three positions available at King; 5th grade, 2nd grade and 1st grade, what are you interested in teaching?" I explained that I was fine teaching any of those grades but I completed most of my student teaching in a second-grade classroom, and I was most comfortable starting there since I was more familiar with the curriculum. "Come on down to King tomorrow at 9 am so we can finish this conversation," he said. "Great, I will see you tomorrow, thanks Unk." I got off the phone and began preparing for my interview.

Unk was smooth, always dressed to the nines, with fitted blazers, summer suits, silk shirts, shining shoes or close toed sandals. On this hot summer day, he wore silky rayon pants and a matching shirt with a pattern on the front, although the shirt was mostly black, one side had four large tan squares zagging downward like a checkerboard. The school building had been constructed in 1926, before being renamed King Elementary it was formerly known as Highland Elementary. Composed of faded red bricks, drab gray concrete encased the front windows that towered above the school playground, which doubled as King Public Park. The red double doors at the main entrance seem to be recently repainted, above the entryway there was a rusted pink iron sign that said Martin Luther King Jr. Elementary School. I could tell that the letters used to be bright gold at one time, now the "M", and the "Jr." had turned from gold to black. The oxidized metal placard left a rustic old time Portland vibe, a historic monument with rich culture and character. The front windows displayed student work, book bins and asymmetrical blinds tattered and beaten by the summer sun, which hung low from years of wear and tear.

I parked my freshly washed dark blue Civic to the left of the main doors near the curb in front of the school. I took a deep breath, hopping out of the car wearing navy slacks, a white dress shirt, argyle tie, with black patent leather shoes. It was a rare sweltering day, Portlanders hardly experience humidity, although it was nothing like the heavy heat that leans on you in the south, for Portland it was notable... so hot that the school building doors were propped open with metal hooks and loops embedded in the concrete for occasional days like this. Days where no man would ever wear a long sleeve button down, tie and patent leather kicks unless they had an important job interview.

As I entered the school, Unk stood at the top of the short flight of stairs, "Dr. J, right on time." he said. He toured me around the building and asked me some questions, mostly about teaching. As we made it to the second floor, we stopped in the middle of the hallway, "here's your keys and this is your classroom," he pointed to the door. "Really? Wow, thanks Unk! What about the interview?" "You just had it, nice job, I like the way you answered those questions...go 'head and check it out, then swing by my office before you leave," he smiled, disappearing down the hallway towards the stairwell.

I nervously unlocked the door to my classroom...stood in the middle of the space and proudly looked around. Laminate wood grain manufactured desks with black undercarriages with built-in storage spaces to hold pencil boxes, notepads, trapper-keepers, loose snacks, overdue library books and daily writing journals. The room had a large white dry-erase board which was a big deal. It was the summer of 2001, classrooms across America were undergoing upgrades. Gone were the days of grima - the strong nauseating feeling one gets when hearing someone's fingernails scrap across an old school green chalkboard, goodbye to the days of chalk dusted teacher and students hands, soot printed dress clothes, fine powdery dander filled classrooms that hung in the midst and tickled our nasal passages. Unk has blessed me with a premier teaching space, larger than most, customized with a newly installed white board, a brand-new set of fine tip Expo dry erase markers, complete with two board erasers, a 4 oz spray bottle of whiteboard care cleaner sat prominently on the metal ledge mounted underneath.

I had arrived. A college dropout who overcame a multitude of negative Black male statistics landing amongst the ranks of those with a respectable career, I was Mr. Coakley. Given the opportunity to serve in the Black community, to work for a Black principal I trusted. I sat at my new desk reflecting on the years I spent in high school courtesy clerking at grocery stores, counting cans, collecting shopping carts, bagging groceries, loading them in trunks, mopping isles, and facing shelves were a thing of the distant past. I never understood the purpose of facing shelves, pulling products to the edge of the shelf in a straight row until a customer puts an item in their cart knocking the so-called "facing" back into oblivion. I even spent two days working at Wendy's - Day 1:

was watching training videos. Day 2: yelling I quit a few hours into my shift, after the manager made a stereotypical basketball reference about my speed toasting hamburger buns. I stormed out of the restaurant walking slowly up Division street thinking about Black folks struggles throughout history, even in the 90s overt and covert micro and macro aggressions were the daily reality of people of color in America. Vowing to never slang fast food again led me to trying a multitude of retail gigs, urban clothing establishments with names like DeeJay's and Mister Rags, places tucked in the corners of indoor malls. Department stores such as Macy's and Nordstrom's - where my hours were significantly cut after getting caught letting a friend benefit from my employee discount. Even Kitchen Kaboodle, a first-time home buyer's Mecca, known for its housewares, kitchen gadgets, cookware and cutlery. Kaboodle paid me 50 cents under minimum wage. Is that even legal? The rate of pay made the job feel like some form of modern-day slavery.

Still I was a hustler with a strong work ethic, I moved with pep, positivity, a smile. In these short lived jobs I stood out as a person that most managers liked. Some even asked me to stay after I gave my notice of leaving the job. Man please, there was no way I was staying. Those gigs were for buying the latest kicks, gas money and pocket change. Eventually, my summers were spent working at camps and afterschool programs as a Camp Counselor, Coach, Coordinator or some other title that began with a "C." Jobs that sounded somewhat important to the kids in a program but ranked you as a rookie in your experience and compensation. Although I was a "C" in title, I was fulfilled working with kids...teaching, solving problems and enjoying a summer full of activities, sports and day trips. It definitely beats toasting hamburger buns, while some middle aged bigot critiques your speed through stereotypical basketball similes.

In the weeks following my hiring at King, Unk inquired about two PTP alums that also recently graduated, my roll dawgs - LV and Rory. As part of the PPS "pool", we were a rare breed, three Black men all with Masters Degrees, all set on teaching at the elementary level. "I'm going to get all three of you," Unk said with a smile. LV was hired as a first-grade teacher and Rory was hired to teach fifth grade. It felt amazing to work in the same building as close friends I'd just graduated with. Rory was an older cat who seemed younger than his years, teaching was a second career for him. He'd been a mechanic many years before deciding to teach. His previous career made him one of those brothas with a rough edge to him, which proved beneficial working with older kids, plus he could fix anything. Always schooling us on the importance of home ownership, eating healthy and saving money. Rory was boisterous, energetic, loud and outspoken. He used to say "I don't have to be here, I don't need this lil' paycheck, I'm here because I want to be...I don't have to do anything but stay Black and die." His classroom was around the corner from mine, so every now and then I'd take my second graders to his classroom to read to a fifth grader or explain how they solved a math problem, the older kids loved it. My class of itty bittys liked hanging with the older kids, I guess it was a good way to build up your playground credibility.

School began on Tuesday, September 4, 2001, the day after Labor Day. My room sparkled, I spent Labor Day making sure that everything was in top shape for the arrival of my second-grade class. PPS serves more than forty-nine thousand students through its eighty-one schools spread across the city. Thirty-nine of those schools are elementary schools, approximately one hundred and twenty kindergarten classrooms, and of those I would hedge every dollar that none of them rivaled my mom's classroom at Vernon Elementary. It was like walking off the lot and stepping inside the showroom floor. When her principal gave parents the school tour they would always visit her room. It was vibrant, bright, immaculate, elegant, modern and up-to-date. Complete with colorful vocabulary word walls, bright bulletin boards displaying student artwork and journal writing, exhibiting her class's brilliance, hard work and perseverance. Bins, boxes and books neatly arranged in places to brighten the room were easily accessible to students. The classroom sparkled immaculately, even the area where students hang their coats and backpacks was constructed just so. Student's possessions correlated with the proper hooks and nametags.

So, when Mom offered to help me set up my second-grade classroom I took her up on the offer. She spent three days with me picking classroom materials, the same type of colorful book baskets, bins for math manipulatives, word walls cards, reading corner swag, and posters with motivational slogans like "believe in yourself, you're amazing!" We put in work, cleaning, scrubbing, dusting, vacuuming, placing and replacing, rearranging, organizing, assessing and revising, until my new classroom was on point. "I'm so proud of you" Mom beamed. "Yeah, you're Mr. Coakley now, this is your domain" said Dad, sprawled in my teacher's chair. The classroom was stuffy, Dad spent the day escaping work by running errands, bringing back lunch and giving feedback. He also spent a lot of time downstairs chillin' with Unk, or wandering around snacking on Corn Nuts, saying things like "yeah, you got it going on Dude."

School always began in the cafeteria, all staff and students in the same space for morning announcements. Students could grab breakfast, eat at a table, or sit in their teacher's classroom line on the cafetoranasium (a multipurpose space that triples as a cafeteria, gymnasium and auditorium) floor and wait for the bell to ring. It was a good way to provide a consistent routine, share announcements, ensure everyone had an opportunity to eat breakfast as well as socialize a bit before starting the day.

On the first day of school, I stood in the cafeteria holding a clipboard of my class list under a larger sign made of construction paper that said "Second Grade." I watched as kids entered the cafeteria with smiles on their faces. I introduced myself as they walked in, asking what grade they were in, trying to identifying my class. My students seemed excited to have a Black male teacher, they asked me questions like "do you know my parents?", "how old are you?" and "do you play sports?" We spent the day playing name games, touring the school, and practicing walking through the halls as a class. I talked about the class expectation from my reading chair while the students sat on the carpet listening closely. From the feel of the first day, I could tell it was going to be a good school year.

"How did you get your hair like that Mr. Coakley? It's tight!" a student asked one morning at the breakfast table. "I can teach you, but it takes time," I said. In high school, when I got my haircut low, it had ripples, ripples that gained the attention of girls. They would say things like "he's cute...his waves are making me seasick." I used to put a thin layer of pomade on the top of my hair and quickly brush it down, in no particular order. I wore a bald fade with waves on the top, patterned after my favorite rapper, Nas. He displayed his waves and bald fade on pictures inside the cover of his CD Illmatic, which I personally rank as the best hip-hop album in history. That was my first time noticing the hair style, I cut down my high-top fade and began wearing my hair low my Senior year at Gresham High School. It wasn't until college that LV said "you know, if you get a good brush, and keep brushing the top of your hair a lot you could get major waves. I have a friend with the same hair texture as you and his hair is super wavy. Also wear a stocking on your head when you sleep so your waves don't get messed up."

Since then, I have studied the wave game, own a collection of brushes ranging from firm to soft bristled. My bathroom drawers are filled with stocking caps, durags and sharp toothed combs. I've moved from using pomades to natural products, such as coconut oils and olive lotions. The quick brush down on the top of my head is a thing of the past. I let go of the bald fade and began brushing with a mirror to see the back and sides of my head. During my college years I worked on perfecting a 360 wave pattern that swirls at the crown of my head. I'd grab a large hand-held mirror, hold it in front of my bathroom vanity mirror, brushing for at least 20 minutes in a 360 wave pattern. 360 waves are when one's head is full of waves created in a pattern that starts from the crown, the starting point of where your hair grows. Over time brushing in the correct pattern of angles turns ripples into connections, waves that line up and connect create a 360 wave pattern on not only the top of the head but on the sides and back of the head as well. Brushing with a mirror helps with precision and the ability to assess the waves in the back of your head.

Waves that don't line up properly or crash into each other are called forks. Forks can be a real pain to fix, but it can be done through brushing regularly over time. Another key factor is the length of your hair, different textures look better at different lengths, for elite waves you need to understand your hair texture and the length that works best for you.

Waves are basically curls that have been laid down from brushing, there is a science to making them perfect. By the time I landed my teaching job I was a "waveologist" I could teach anyone to get waves, but most dudes just wouldn't put the work in, it takes consistency. For me, it was a symbol of pride.

As a kindergartener I remember being the only Black kid in my class. Classmates asked me why my hair looked like that? Why was it curly, or puffy? What did it feel like? Could they touch my hair? Why was my skin brown? Why was I different? I didn't have the answers at the time, I just knew that I didn't like people pointing out my differences. I wondered if being different was bad, was it something to be ashamed of? Was curly hair bad? I quickly found out it was something to be proud of. Black people have some of the coolest hairstyles and textures in the world, so why not take advantage of that. Difference is a good thing. In elementary school I had an afro, in middle school a high top fade, sometimes I had my barber cut designs in the back, like Paul Jr in block letters, another time I had the Jordan logo. In high school I rocked a bald fade with ripples, but ever since college I kept some variation of 360 waves. So, when students would say something like... your waves are tight, how did you get your hair like that? My response was always "thanks, I can teach you, but it takes hard work."

Less than two weeks into the school year, Tuesday, September 11, 2001 breaking news overtook every radio station on my morning commute. Cell phones rang, text messages flooded, the pace of the nation slowed to a snail's pace. Heavy hearts, deep sadness, overwhelming grief hung in the air as we entered the cafeteria. Principal Malone was centered on the auditorium stage, he shared the news of the terrorist attack on New York's World Trade Center, expressing his condolences before taking a moment of silence in the King Elementary Cafeteria. Teachers walked their students to classrooms. My kids sat quietly at their desks, tears, fears, questions...I sat on the large rickety radiator in front of my classroom windows, listening, discussing and providing what support I could muster as I thought about relatives, friends, families and the people of New York. Some of my students had loved ones that lived in NYC.

We realized that at times the world feels small, life is precious, short and not promised to any of us. A tragedy in one US city at the farthest point away from us can reverberate across the world, nation, state, city, even local household, impacting us on a personal level.

When the bell rang at the end of the day, we left the safety of our second grade classroom. We left as a family, connected, supporting each other through tragedy, contention and tough times. We were a family that cares, assists, pitches in and helps each other succeed.

LV's first grade classroom was on the main floor, its windows overlooked the playground. Right across from his room sat the curriculum closet, where the literacy materials were stored. King used a walk-to-read model, a skills based program where students are categorized by reading ability, teachers are assigned to teach a specific reading level and group. For 90 minutes a day, students leave their homeroom and "walk to" their reading group to receive targeted-instruction. King Elementary followed a curriculum called Success For All (SFA), which consists of larger boxes of basal reader books, with text ranging from Pre-Kindergarten to 6th grade vocabulary. The goal is for every teacher is constantly monitor each student's progress through fluency, comprehension, and vocabulary to regroup students based on their progress. If done properly, students should be increasing their reading ability and experiencing new teachers. Changing reading groups every cycle, challenging themselves as they move through the basal reader textbooks. I quickly got the hang of the curriculum, my students were making growth, progressing every cycle. I asked Unk if I could work with the lowest readers in the building for my 90-minute reading group. Non-readers, unfamiliar with the alphabet sounds, students who were beginning on basal number one. "Kids you are lucky to be in my reading group, because I am going to make you a reader" I would say. Then, I'd explain the importance of reading, how becoming a strong reader will make you better at math, writing, science and almost every other school subject. I'd share personal stories about my childhood struggling with reading, hating being called on during read out loud in elementary and middle school, but eventually overcoming that fear by spending a lot of time reading books for fun.

This became my passion, making non-readers into readers and struggling readers into stronger readers. I read novels out loud to my group, asking comprehension questions, articles about current events in the local news and asking reflections questions. Checking for their understanding, assessing their fluency on a regular basis, each student kept a journal to track the time they spent reading. We moved through basal readers and celebrated every time one was completed. We frequented the library, I'd help students check out books that sparked their interest while stretching their skills and abilities. My readers looked forward to our 90 minutes together, I would see smiles as they walked towards my room. I'd greet them at the door with a handshake or a fist bump, bop - bop. "Good morning, everybody ready to get to work?" I'd ask. Soon, parents began catching Unk in the hallway, cafeteria or on the playground, "Principal Malone, I want my son to be in Mr. Coakley's reading group. His cousin is in his group and he's really improving." Unk would grin, then say something like "that isn't exactly how it works Mrs. So-and-So, it all depends on what reading level your child is at and what group Mr. Coakley is teaching, but I'll look into it."

While conducting his rounds of teacher observations Unk came to my classroom to check out my SFA reading block. At our last staff meeting he told the teachers, "I'll be dropping in your rooms to observe. When I come in just continue teaching. I don't want you to stop your lesson, carry on as if I am not there." In my later years as a principal, I found that teachers who are nervous or unprepared often stop teaching when an administrator walks in the room. A few ask their students to stop what they are doing and welcome each "guest," sometimes the teacher walks over to meet the principal at the door to shake hands or greet them. There are a variety of methods to distract a principal from observing poor teaching. At any rate, I smiled when Principal Malone entered my classroom, I also continued teaching. Unk took a seat in a student desk behind my reading group, the kids were all sitting with their legs folded on the carpet of my classroom reading space looking up at me. I was reading from the novel "Tales of a Fourth Grade Nothing" by Judy Blume. Sitting in my large wooden rocking chair, asking comprehension questions, calling on students to share specific parts of the story. The chart paper next to my chair had a list of vocabulary words that we were working on for the week, words that were also in the novel. "Who can share the definition of the word "measly" and use it in a sentence?" I asked. Immediately, students' hands shot up! "How about someone I haven't heard from today…" With that Principal Malone said "Dr. Coakley", and got my attention, when I looked up he gave me a smiled and a thumbs up, then swiftly exited the classroom. Feeling proud of my reading group, I continued to teach.

The following summer I traded in my navy blue Honda Civic. A car only four years old that my parents covered the payments on until I landed a teaching job. Acquiring a car seven years older with a slightly higher car payment, a black 1995 Lexus GS 300. But why not, the mileage was low, the paint job flawless, the leather interior - peanut butter with dark chocolate carpet flooring. I kept it clean, waxed, tires shining, it was a head turning, neck breaking, ladies magnet. It rolled smoothly, nonchalantly, quietly gliding through the streets while the speakers from the 5-disc CD player in the trunk rotated through Jay-Z's The Blueprint, starting with the horns on track one. Swaying through all 15 tracks, before doubling back on my favorites. It took about twenty seconds for the changer to switch to the next CD, Nas's "Stillmatic." Sometimes you have to floss a bit, you only live once you know, fake it until you make it, this car was my way of letting people know I was on my way up.

I rented a small one-bedroom apartment about twenty minutes outside of Portland located in the city of Troutdale, adjacent to Mt. Hood Community College. I had a decent sized balcony that overlooked the parking lot of a newly constructed movie theater. The apartment was brand new, as the first occupant to live in the space I equipped it with the classic blaxploitation starter kit. A black leather couch, large tv, glass coffee table, glass kitchen table with silver legs, and black leather retro kitchen chairs to match. It was the crash pad, smash pad, barbeque layer, the homie hut, the honeycomb hideout, the place to prefunk before we slide out, hop in the Lex and ride out. 2002 - a good year to make big moves, do big things, a landscape for big dreams. A time to live in the now, care-free, nothing permanent, just a pit-stop to an unknown destination.

My third year at King, I had found my stride, well established with the students and parents, collegial with colleagues and connected to the community. I had moved from teaching second grade to teaching first grade. After looking at the progress that kids had made who participated in my reading group, the Literacy Specialist approached me about teaching in an even earlier grade to ensure that kids are exposed to a male teacher, build a strong foundation and have a positive start to their school experience. I was up for the challenge, my reading group would consist of a few advanced kindergartener's, grade-level first graders and some struggling second grade readers. My classroom was located on the first floor overlooking the playground. I methodically set it up again to incorporate a reading area, equipped with key materials I felt were beneficial for students to get accustomed to. When you love what you do, you can consistently perform at a high level, many achievements come naturally and your plans usually fall into place. I really enjoyed my job, that was evident to everyone that I came in contact with. King was my place, Principal Malone, my main man. A dude that I would follow, help and support when there was something that needed to be done. LV and Rory did the same, the three of us built a circle of success. Three guys that were determined to support each other in every way possible. We participated in site council meetings in the evening, fundraisers on the weekends, helping prepare for staff meetings, creating flyers, promoting performance for the King school choir, coaching and supporting new teachers, helping colleagues set up their classrooms, not because we had to, but because we ate, slept and breathed the King community. Motivation was our love for the school, the principal, the students, the parents, the culture.

For me, it was a state of mind, a 25 year old Black male, living in a state that was 2% Black, immersing himself in Blackness. My school, my barbershop, my corner store, my shopping mall, my small strip of neighborhood known as Alberta, that stretched from 6th street to 33rd was a thriving part of Black the community, my own slice of Heaven. The bliss of putting the suburbs in my rearview mirror and driving away until the buildings got smaller eventually vanishing. As I drive towards NE Portland, the landscape transforms, the pace quickens, people bustling on sidewalks, in and out of convenience stores and lounging at bus stops, their skin turning from White to Black and Brown. At an early age, I had become accustomed to being the sole "minority," the only Black person in a space, classroom, building, group, park, birthday party or team sport. Oregon's a place where one could go days, weeks, maybe even months without seeing another Brown or Black person's face outside of your family, or circle of friends, without intention. A place where people describe you by mentioning your race, a place where you are seen as the spokesperson for everyone that has a similar skin tone as yours. A place where you realize, "I better get my hair products while I'm in NE, cause' there's no way I'm finding them anywhere else." A place where you get racial profiled by police, mall security, grocery stores clerks, people make assumptions about your intelligence, work ethic and attitude based on stereotypes they'd seen on tv sitcoms and reality shows like "Cops" and MTV's "the Real World." A place where a teacher will ask their students to use the "flesh-tone" crayon to complete their self-portrait. But in the skin you're in, that crayon doesn't exist for you, it only works for your classmates. So, you take the brown crayon and angle the point, gently grazing it side to side lightly over your pencil lined sketch, because that's the best you can do.

Escapism came behind the wheel, commuting to work, clam. Everything felt right, until it didn't. Unk had been tapped by the district to lead Ockley Green Middle School in the Fall, the school that 5th graders leaving King fed into for 6th - 8th grade. It was a feeder middle school for many of the North and Northeast elementary schools in Portland Public. It was a larger school, yielded a larger impact, provided more responsibility, it was a great opportunity for Principal Malone. It was also a huge loss for the King community. I knew Unk and I would stay in contact regardless of school placement, we were family. Like the rest of the staff, I just hoped that King's next school leader would be a person that I could learn from. Someone that connected to our students, parents

41

and community like Unk had done. Someone that continued to make King a unique and special place.

Unfortunately, our hopes were dashed…the new principal was none of those things. I don't remember being a part of an interview process, or whether or not anyone had a voice in the selection of our new leader. Maybe she was transferred from another school in the district, or demoted from the district office. All I know is that the family feel, positive culture, school pride, staff morale, and parent involvement began quickly fading away in a few short months.

Before Unk left for Ockley Green he recommended me for the Aspiring Administrator Program, an internal PPS grow-your-own program that groomed school leaders for the principalship. I was accepted and enrolled in courses at Portland State to earn my principal licensure. In addition to the course work, one must successfully complete a 360-hour practicum. For me that meant 200 hours with the new principal at King Elementary, and 160 hours at the secondary level. I met with the new principal, Mrs. Vee, she signed on as my elementary level mentor for my practicum experience. I was still teaching fulltime and putting in addition hours deemed administrative experience. LV was also working on his administrative license and did the same. Ms. Vee agreed, taking full advantage of having two interns. That summer, we painted classrooms, office spaces, made photocopies for meetings, and organized textbook storage closets. Our days were filled with menial tasks, busy work that provided us with practicum hours that verged on the training that Daniel-son received from Mr. Miyagi in the first "Karate Kid" movie. An experience that leaves one pondering whether or not some deeper meaning or purpose would eventually reveal itself.

By the end of the summer, the purpose was clear, Mrs. Vee was an unorganized fish out of water, struggling to stay afloat. LV and I were buoys that she had latched onto, in hopes of navigating her through intentional and unintentional waves she was causing as an out of touch leader who struggled to grasp control of the ocean known as the King community. It was a rough practicum experience that stretched from summer to winter break. My practicum log yielded over 440 hours of time logged. My college advisor and I whittled it down to the hours that could actually be categorized as leadership experience which ended up being about 380 usable hours. It was good enough for me to move on to the next portion of the practicum requirement: Secondary school hours.

I was looking forward to breaking away from King for a while. Principal Malone was my mentor and the Aspiring Administrator Program allowed me to get a long-term sub, so I prepared my student's for the change. I talked to them, answered their questions, met with each of their parents and provided them with a written letter to be as transparent as possible about my plans. The responses were mostly positive, "I am so glad you are going to be a principal" or "I knew you would follow in your father's footsteps, he was my principal" or "the kids are going to miss you but they'll be alright." One parent who was rumored to be a dancer came into my classroom wearing an open blazer with nothing but a bra under it, just as I was packing up for the day. "I was just heading to the main office" I said as I B-lined it out of my classroom and into the main hallway. She followed me down the hall, "Kayana says you're leaving to be a principal" referring to the information her daughter had shared. Standing at least three feet away from her and maintaining eye contact, "It's just to complete a practicum to get my principal's license. The class will have a sub for about 4 weeks, but they'll do fine" I said. "Well we'll all miss seeing you around, maybe you should just be the principal here" she said as she looked me up and down and slowly walked down the hall. I briefly smiled at that thought of following in the Unk's footsteps. However, I quickly realized that I was in no way ready to take on the task in that particular moment. I chalked the comment up to the reality that things weren't going well, a mere glimpses into the frustrations of King parents.

My lesson plan book was detailed down to the minute, full of engaging activities, hands on math games, and writing assignments tied to art lessons. Each daily lesson plan was written in a way that was easy to follow, and provided a consistent routine for the kids. My plans had a heavy emphasis on literacy and math as well as options for the sub to choose from. My long term substitute was a King Elementary regular, Mrs. Walker, a tough older retiree who had a reputation for being strict, consistent and organized. While the kids respected her, many also feared her a bit. Mrs. Walker made sure that a teacher's classroom would be clean and everything would be in its place when they returned, no matter how long the leave. Using Mrs. Walker also meant that a teacher would be welcomed with open arms by their students when they returned. Ten hours a day, five days a week at Ockley Green was the plan, then return to my classroom in one month with 200 hours of secondary leadership logged and ready to present to the graduate committee.

I drove slowly down N Montana Avenue past the middle school, it was early, no students in sight yet. Another plain looking brick building, much larger than King Elementary, a bit newer, a light tan brick exterior with heavy forest green metal doors. I parked the Lexus in the back staff parking lot near the drab playground as Unk had instructed. Some playground, merely a grassy field with splotchy patches of green and light brown due to lack of water, it was a dry summer deprived of the usual Oregon rain. Near the side of the building was a tar driveway with a large US map painted on it. There were also a few tetherball poles and basketball hoops with new chain link netting to emphasize the new school year. I entered the building through the back staff doors, which put me inside the main office, near a wooden row of staff mailboxes. The school secretaries greeted me when I walked in. "You're Mr. Paul Coakley Jr, right? I know your father, I worked with him at Tubman" one piped up. "He looks just like his, Dad" said the other one. I grinned at the comparison, Dad's was a legend in the district, his reputation lent me immediate credibility with the office staff. "Welcome to Ockley, Mr. Malone is in his office over there to your left, you can head on in." "Nice to meet you both, thanks", I said as I headed toward Unk's door. "Dr. J! Right on time, looking sharp, I like that suit." Unk said.

Today Unk had on a heather gray double breasted suit with a crisp white shirt and a multicolored tie that highlighted the gray suit. We chatted in his office before taking the tour of the school, walking briskly through the halls, classrooms and quickly meeting the staff. We stopped in the cafeteria where students were entering to eat breakfast. In Unk fashion he smiled widely as students entered the cafeteria and headed for a table or the long breakfast line. "You will get all kinds of experience here, you'll definitely get the hours you need. Your number one priority is right here...I can't be in here every day and when I was out of the building last week we had a couple of food fights during lunch. Kids get to pushing and shoving in the lunch line, breakfast is pretty calm. Be in this cafeteria every day during breakfast and lunch, I want you to run this ship." I listened as I surveyed the cafeteria, "Ok, no problem!" I said. He introduced me to the custodians and security staff, "this is Mr. Coakley, Paul's son, this brotha's gonna be a principal, make sure you got his back." They all smiled, "yes sir, we will." I talked with the custodian and security staff and stayed on supervision duty with them after Principal Malone left. I also introduced myself to the educational assistants, cafeteria staff and anyone working in the lunchroom.

The first couple of days there was a lot of "who is you?" and "are you our new vice principal?" But on the third day, the student's got to know me, 'cuz on day three the honeymoon was over. The first two days I spent a lot of time observing the lunch line which seemed to run smoothly, eating at the tables was also fine. I was surprised to find that there was a food cart in the cafeteria as well, Pizza Hut. The school lunches were free, and students who brought lunch went straight to the tables to eat. The problem was the Pizza Hut line, which sold pizza by the slice, it was brought in to provide some variety for students. The cafeteria staff said not only was it taking away money from the school lunch program but it also caused a distraction. To students, it was for the cool kids, the who's who, proof that you weren't broke, if you had a slice, you had money. Kids would push and shove in the line, sprinting in the cafeteria to be first, or trying to cut the line by having a friend save someone's spot.

On day three the madness stopped, my detailed plan to fix the pizza line was crafted like a military plan to take over enemy territory. The plan came about after a comment my dad made about how to approach my practicum... "you'll be at the middle school for a month to get your hours, but the student's don't know that. You walk up in there and work your plan, like you're gonna be there a hundred years, that's how you fix that cafeteria!" So that was my approach, on day three I talked to the staff, "make sure everyone goes straight to the tables, no one gets food until after announcements." "Straight to the tables, have a seat" staff said to students as they entered the cafeteria. I used a mega phone I found in the office, "hurry up and find a seat, I need it quiet, the faster I can give you these announcements the faster it will be that you get your lunch. First of all, I have met most of you, I'm Mr. Coakley, some of you know me from King. Well I'm here now and it is a new day here at Ockley. From here on out, when you walk into the cafeteria you are going to do it calmly, anyone running loses 5 minutes of their recess break. That means you'll be sitting at an assigned table for the full lunch period. If you want to be able to choose where you are going to sit, walk! If you are cutting, holding a space in line or shoving in the pizza line, you'll sit at this table and be given a hot lunch from the cafeteria." A student giggled. "Terrance, is this funny? Sit right here, that is your spot for today's lunch. For you, Pizza Hut is out of the question!" Terrance frowned and moved to the table I pointed to and had a seat, wondering how I knew his name. "Anyone else want to join him? Now, let's enjoy our lunch. Walk to your place of business, and do it quietly…I should be able to hear a mouse walk on cotton (a saying I stole from my father) Thank you!" Quiet mumbles from students "He mean." … "Mr. Coakley don't play." There were also a few smiles. "He was my teacher." and a "right on Coke!" from the head Security Guard.

Besides a handful of students that lost time off the recess break which followed the lunch block, the new cafeteria protocol sailed along smoothly during my time at Ockley. I also got to respond to discipline referrals, meet with students and parents about issues, conduct teacher observations, meet with educators to provide feedback, present the middle school assessment data to the staff and discuss possible intervention strategies for struggling students. Practicum-complete, experience-solid, relationships-built, but all good things come to an end. My last day at Ockley Green I brought Principal Malone two slices from Atomic Pizza, a New York style joint not too far from the middle school. "Brought you some lunch Unk," I said. "This has been fun, I appreciate it." "Well, I'm glad you enjoyed it Docta" he said with a smile, before taking a wide bite of pepperoni. "What I want to know is… where did you get this pizza?" Unk said. "A little spot up the street," I replied. "Man, you should've brought me this every week" he joked. "Take care of yourself Dr. J, you did a nice job, we enjoyed you. Soon you'll be on your way to getting that administrator's license."

"Take care Unk," I said as I walked past the staff mailboxes and out the heavy forest green metal backdoors of the main office, surveying the splotchy greenish-brown grass field and shiny chain link basketball nets, before walking across the large US map painted on the blacktop of the parking lot to retrieve my car. I felt stronger, wiser, more confident in my abilities as a school leader. Thank you Principal Malone, you're the man!

I slightly cranked the volume as heavy drums, horns and snares reverberated my speakers. I dove out of the school parking lot, while the bass softly rattled my door panels.

CHAPTER 3

A Living Legend

Fresh from Murfreesboro, Tennessee, my father set foot in the halls of Harriet Tubman Middle School in Portland, Oregon as a new history teacher. He earned his Bachelor's and Master's degrees in education and his administrative license at Middle Tennessee State University. He was hired by a Black principal, Dr. Herman Washington, who attended the job fair in Tennessee and was impressed with the young man's confidence, charisma and leadership potential. The fact that Paul had his administrative license after his first three years of teaching showed that he was an ambitious go-getter.

Dr. Washington had served in Portland Public Schools for several years and provided a strong support system to my father. Having two Black male leaders at the helm of a school back then in Portland was rare. The Black community had high hopes for the future of Tubman and prior to dad's arrival influential Black community leaders like Ron Herndon and Joyce Harris, a long time Oregon educator, activist and co-founder of the Black Education Center, had advocated for years to put a new building in the Black community with the aesthetics, resources and programs to match existing schools in the predominantly White areas that surrounded NE Portland. After years of persistence, Tubman's staff, students and community were preparing for a transition in the fall. The school would be exiting the old red brick building and moving to a new building located at 2231 N. Flint Avenue, near the Memorial Coliseum and Moda Center (home of the Portland Trail Blazers), located right on the edge of NE Portland, just a hop, skip and a jump away from

Martin Luther King Boulevard. Dr. Washington was being promoted to the District Office in the fall, he encouraged my father to apply for the position of principal. Paul was visible, boisterous and had built strong relationship with students and parents. He easily made connections with community leaders and local organizations. Dr. Matthew Prophet, PPS Superintendent, took note of Paul's ability to enlist supporters and kept a close watch on Paul as a notable up-and-coming leader.

Paul Coakley was needed at Tubman. Washington's predestined strategy to identify his successor came to fruition, with just a year under his belt Paul Coakley opened the doors of the newly constructed state of the art Harriet Middle School, in 1981 as the school's Principal. The excitement of the new building uplifted the community, their new school leader stood out as caring and connected fish out of the Tennessee river's freshwater. He was loud, boisterous, energetic, passionate, direct, and assertive. A people champ, a new kind of leader had emerged, one that people flocked to, kids wanted to be around, and staff members wanted to be like. In a school of 800 students, he quickly learned the names of the students, parents, and community. Through his God given leader-ship abilities he built trust with his staff through dependability, visibility, accountability, personality, holding high expectations, and larger than life smile that showed his teeth, bringing out the smiles in others. He was a supportive leader who walked the walk and talked the talk. "Let's keep our building clean" he would say, picking up a piece of loose paper from the sparkling linoleum floor and tossing it in the trash, he won the hearts of his custodian who kept the floors shining and walls spotless. He was a man of slogans, sayings and phrases that he listened to on a regular basis growing up in the deep south, unheard by Portland ears. He lived in the classrooms and hallways, which won over his teachers and educational assistants. He always wore a suit and tie, with a voice that sounded like there was an invisible megaphone in front of him at all times. Students would smile as he commanded the space during passing time, "when that bell rings, have your face in the place, the place is the classroom!" or "this is a silent hallway...during this passing time I want to be able to hear a mouse walk on cotton." On the regular he could be found directing the flow of traffic in the narrow hallways where turquoise full size lockers took up a foot of space on each side, shouting "everybody stay to the right!" a life lesson for moving swiftly through crowded spaces.

He had a keen ability for solving problems, he never strayed away from tough conversations, he'd worked through issues head on, no problem was too large or too small. It was 1981, test scores across the nation were low, in inner city Portland, like most urban cities across the west coast, gangs and drug culture was at an all-time high

"When you walk in these doors, it's time to get to business" he would say loudly, "I don't want to see no saggin', no bangin' no nothin' leave that in the streets, in these doors everybody's under one gang, the Tubman Contenders and I'm the head of it" he said with a large smile.

The students showed Principal Coakley his respect, Tubman quickly became known as a "good school" providing a high-quality education and a safe learning environment. Harriet Tubman was one of the district's only magnet middle schools, a school that offered special programs and instruction that wasn't offered at most other middle schools in the city. Tubman Middle School had a heavy focus on science, performing arts and photography. Principal Coakley hired the best and the brightest teachers, the majority of the staff were educators of color, Black male and female teachers, Latinx and Asian-Pacific Islander educators, many who were passed over for jobs by their White counterparts until they saw a leader that looked like them and saw the potential in them to create the kind of staff the he had experience in Gallatin back at Union High School. The students were predominately Black, the school taught Black history, and multiple languages including Spanish, French and Swahili. Any student in the district could attend as long as they had transportation if they didn't live within the school boundaries. Due to the staff and school leader's positive reputation the enrollment grew higher every year, eventually the district put a soft cap on the number of students based on the building's capacity, somewhere around the 850 mark.

As an educator of over 20 years, I think a lot about institutional racism. The impact of slavery, segregation, and desegregation set Black

people in America so far back that today, we are still feeling the rever-
berations. As an educational leader, I have come to the conclusion that
the traditional K-12 system in the United States is created to regurgitate
similar results year after year. Pumping out a system of winners and los-
ers, graduates and dropouts, a system that tracks and sorts everyone into
categories that define an individual's life outcomes: affluency, middle
class, poverty and incarceration. Systems where approximately 70% of the
students meet the academic standards to graduate high school on time.
On the other side of this coin, 30% of the students were failed by these
systems. Multitudes of schools and districts consistently perform much
lower than that average 70%, even finding themselves in the lowest 5%
of schools in their state for academic performance. These bottom ranking
schools are usually filled with Black and Brown faces, from both larger
and smaller cities with dense minuscule zip codes, refrigerators devoid
of breakfast, where older siblings walk younger ones to school so parents
can work minimum wage jobs, night shifts and day shifts. Kids tossing
around in the mix of financial trauma, mental strain, marital drama,
financial struggles, living well below the poverty line, homes made up
of single mothers and absent father, neighborhoods where lives are taken
for wearing the wrong color on the wrong block, and cars spray bullet
and erase the lives of innocent bystanders, little children watching tv on
their living room sofas or sleeping in beds under cozy blankets at night.
Survival is real, goal number one isn't learning or homework and grades
scraped the bottom of one's list of priorities. Where cops harass, ticket,
beat, and cuff residents for D.W.B (driving while Black) and store clerks
hold pistols under cash register counters when children enter their corner
store to fulfill grandma's list of errands.

Dig a bit further to find teachers and school leaders with preconceived
notions, stereotypical beliefs about the students they serve and low expectations. Elementary school where fifth graders head to middle school
as non-readers without mastery of basic math but a good understanding
of how the system works. Exhibiting negative behavior will get you out
of doing the work you are frustrated with, a suspension will land you a
few days at home to relax.

Elementary school is the foundation to one's success in middle school and beyond, kindergarten and first grade are the building blocks to literacy, which impacts one's performance in every subject from reading and writing to math, science and even your overall feelings about school. Sixth, seventh and eighth grade are the "make or break" years, middle school can lead kids on a path to success or a pipeline to prison. In the 80's Tubman had found how to tap into something special, the potential, the hopes and the dreams of the students they served. The school's culture, identity and reputation became a catalyst for motivating students and staff to give their best inside the school's doors. Sure, like any inner city middle school it was not without its problems, but the staff took on the mindset that "it takes a village to raise a child." Each staff member regardless of title or position was responsible for every kid's success. Students saw teachers, leaders, coaches, secretaries and support staff that looked like them, related to them, knew their names, and were there to help them work through every stumbling block. Students had help if their family struggled to meet their basic needs at home, meals were sent home, alarm clocks and bus passes were provided, personal hygiene kits were distributed after teaching kids how to use them. Staff members even took students to wash their clothing if needed. Students felt seen, cared for, appreciated, even loved.

"We are in the business of building relationships, "Principal Coakley would say. "It is our job to do everything in our power to make sure our students succeed." As the school's principal he set the expectation and everyone worked to live up to that set of expectation. He saw his students as future leaders, doctors, lawyers, CEOs, business owners and professional athletes.

As a young Black male student attending middle school in suburbia, finding teachers willing to do everything in their power to ensure my success was a rarity. I remember three of them in my middle school and even less at my high school. I wasn't disliked by staff, nor did I have the "you will never amount to anything" experience from my teachers. My experience was different from the learning environment of students attending Tubman. The majority of my teachers provided me with an invitation to learn. An opportunity to sit at a desk amongst my peers, listen, read, take-notes, study, return completed homework and prove myself worthy and capable of being a student at that grade level. This invitation assumes that one is a grade level reader, one has strong study habits, one is motivated by grades, and one has the ability to seek help and answers to questions outside of class hours. It's a place where re-teaching or differentiating the content to meet each learner's needs is the furthest thing from a teacher's mind. I would go as far as to say that most of my teachers weren't actually teaching students, they were teaching content to students, similar to that of a college professor. This structure does not always work for students, is not effective for most students of color, and can be detrimental for Black male students specifically. This "invitation to learn" keeps many students that look like me at the bottom of the data pile for academics, graduation rates and college scholarship opportunities. It also keeps us at the top of the pile of discipline referrals, suspension rates, dropout statistics, special education programs and prison pipelines. "We've already covered that, you must not have been listening."

If we dig a bit deeper, we'll find that an invitation to learn, works for the majority of students. Those that come from the ideal traditional American family, a household understood to be the nuclear family made up of a husband, wife, children, maybe a pet. A classic 1960s - 1970s sitcom family like "Leave it to Beaver," "Dennis the Menace" or even the "The Brady Bunch." Homes where a family member is there to assist you on a daily basis with your homework, help you resolve issues with friends or siblings, keep you out of harm's way outside of school hours. Adults are never scheduled to report to work once a child arrives home. Dwellings where fridges and freezers are fully stocked, the stress of paying rents or mortgages is the furthest thing from a kid's mind, and all family members sit at the dinner table every evening to discuss their day at school or work. For many of my middle school peers, this family structure was similar to their experience at home, and they met or excelled the expectations set forth by an invitation to learn.

Now, let's dig on the other side of the sandbox, the side where students don't come from the "traditional" family structure, the side where many kids are just as responsible for helping obtain basic needs as the adults in the family. The side where parents sit down with their children and talk about how to respond if you are questioned by police, what not to do in a store because the clerk might assume you are stealing and pull that pistol from under the counter, the pathway you should take walking home to avoid passing the house with the confederate flag, what that flag means to you and your wellbeing. "I am off next Tuesday and we are going to sit down and go over your homework. When you get home, I'll be at work but you know how to reach me, there's some leftover spaghetti in the fridge if you want it, or some cash on the counter if you want to walk to Taco Bell but be careful, I love you" says single mom. For the handful of my Black and Brown middle schoolers and high schoolers in Gresham this was closer to some of their home experience. Especially the ones that struggled to prevail with a passing grade from an invitation to learn environment. For several family's safety and survival took precedence over grades. This was the experience of my peers, I watched it firsthand.

Lucky for me, I had the consistent family structure and support to push through the barriers that prevented success for umpteen peers that looked like me at my school. The same unwavering support students experience from the staff at Tubman, was what my younger brother Brian and I experienced at home. Our elementary years were filled with moments that built our resilience, our pride, our sense of being. Bounce-back ability building block moments listening, observing and immersing ourselves in rooms full of Black excellence. Black doctors, leaders, attorneys, pastors, teachers, superintendents, coaches, fathers, mothers and entrepreneurs. Shadowing Dad at Tubman as he worked the halls interacting with students and staff, smiling as he bellowed "2 minutes" while kids rushed to their classes. Watching him enter the gym doors while future college and NBA players hooped in the hot, crowded middle school gym during PE. He called for the rock and sank a three-pointer from the corner, which was his only shot he made with consistency. With amazement, kids would say "Mr. Coakley you want to play?" "Nah I'm in a suit, I'll leave it to y'all, I don't want to get all sweaty" then he'd quickly exit the gym. Sitting in my mom's classroom on my days off and watching her teach with math manipulatives, asking open-ended questions while the little kids raised their hands high hoping to be called on.

Educational researcher John Hattie spent years studying influences and the effects they have on student achievement. As one may assume, influences such as suspension and expulsion have a negative effect on achievement. While afterschool programs and hands-on learning have a positive effects. However, the influence that yields the most positive impact is something that called *collective teacher efficacy.* In laymen's terms it's a staff's collective belief that every student can achieve regardless of race, gender or socioeconomic status. Hattie explains that it's more than a growth mindset, once a staff collectively believes, they intentionally pour into each and every student by teaching, re-teaching, monitoring growth and making adjustments until they've reached every student.

By the time I had reached middle school, my parents had washed over my brother Brian and I with the collective teacher efficacy of the Black community and sent us into our predominantly White schools with it. I wasn't searching, longing or in need of the staff's efficiency, I knew my worth, my potential, my inner strength and my ability to be whatever I wanted to be, and where my support system came from. I was proud of my history, my family, my culture, my hair, and my appearance. I was comfortable in my own skin, it was evident in the way I moved though Gordon Russell middle school in Gresham, Oregon. At this point in my life I was used to navigating school, classrooms and almost everywhere imaginable as the only Black male in the space. I could do it without assimilating, without feeling uneasy or uncomfortable, I just didn't look forward to it. I spent much of my time outside of school at Tubman, attended summer school there my middle school years just for fun, it was a place that I loved to be. Many of my close friends were there, life-long friends like LV and Ike-Boogie, dudes I had known since sixth grade, stayed connected to through high-school and college, and continue to be in my small inner-circle of friends that I trust and frequent with. At Russell I moved through the space with a sense of purpose, confidence or swag that stuck out like a sore thumb. A kid in a system but not of the system, disconnected while associated, motivated as a student while unmotivated by my school, not necessarily wanting to be there, but needing to persist enough to continue to move forward.

The Search Institute is a research firm that has spent over 70 years conducting studies on the success of students, their findings prove time and time again that when children have at least one strong connection to at least one caring adult they are more likely to engage in school, feel connected to the school's culture and experience more academic success. And while my attitude and disposition to my surroundings portrayed "I don't need you are anyone vibes," I had a pre-existing friendship with my middle school PE teacher, Coach Ron Hudson. That excited me, sustained me, grounded me and at times carried me through my toughest part of K-12: middle school. He was the only Black male teacher I had from kindergarten through 12 grade, he was also my best friend Marques father, he was even my next door neighbor for a while, a play Uncle, someone close as family that you grew up with, who has basically known you your entire life.

When my parents made the move to Oregon, the first place we lived was a split-level rental house in a cul-de-sac in Troutdale (a small city) on the backside of Gresham. While Troutdale hadn't seen many Black families, adjacent to our house to the right was a row of ranch style duplexes angled on a diagonal line, and in the first house was Coach Ron Hudson, his wife Angie and his son, one year younger than me, Marques. They had moved up from Sacramento a year previous and Ron landed the gig as the PE teacher at Gordan Russell. Lucky for me my parents picked a house in a neighborhood close to the only other Black boy around my age. We met in the driveway as we moved in, and became fast friends. Marques reminded me of the countless cousins that I would play with back in Gallatin, I probably reminded him of his family in Sacramento. We were play cousins, friends as close as family, just like relatives. They were people that held seasons of your life together like glue. Maybe without them that specific portion of time in your life would have been more sullen and insignificant.

Marques made the small Troutdale cul-de-sac feel like home, the relatives and friendships I left behind were a little less hard to bear. We ruled the neighborhood on our big wheels, racing and pulling the plastic brake lever to spin out to a screeching halt. We built tree forts and threw mud pies at attackers, hid behind shrubs covered in the debris of burnt orange bark dust holding our walkie-talkies "hurry up you have to report to base" I would say. We called each other "LaBa," short for little brother. "What's up LaBa?" ... "Hey Dad, can LaBa come to the store with us?" We also had the everyday childhood disagreement, "fine I'm not going to be your friend anymore."... "Me either." But thirty minutes later, we had forgotten about whatever led to the argument and we're back on big wheels laughing and racing. We told all the kids in the neighborhood that we were cousins and soon we thought we really were, only realizing it was an exaggeration when our actual relatives came to visit.

During this time, our mothers were both expecting, "you are going to be a big brother, dude" Dad would say. Ron would say "Marques and Jaybird, you set a good example for the little ones, you're big guys." Soon we both had little brothers, Brian and Marques's brother Nicholas. Over time they also had their play cousin moments of inseparability, fond memories of family cookouts, birthday parties, sleepovers, family outings and driveway basketball competitions.

As the neighborhood grew, so did the diversity of the cul-de-sac, an interracial couple with a few kids, a large family from Saudi Arabia with many children - heavy accents and the propensity to throw loud parties that went until the wee hours of the night every weekend. Even Unk and his family end up residing at the edge of the cul-de-sac for a period of time. Unk, Ron and Dad, a three man crew that held down that small suburban circle, making it a space filled with pride, laughter, fun and memories while being surrounded by all that comes with being the 2 percent minority in a majority White city. Outside of our neighborhood a person of color could go days, even weeks without seeing another person that looked like them.

Coach Hudson stood 5'9" with a fit muscular build, as a kid he reminded me of Sugar Ray Leonard. He wore shades, tank tops, athletic shorts and a small afro cut and edged sharply. Like my father he was also loud, boisterous, and had a blustering voice from years of coaching. Marques and I could hear our dad's talking and joking with each other from a block away, "Coke, what's up Brotha?" he would say to my Dad. "Nothin' much Hud!" my Dad replied. Over the years, Hud's afro turned into more of a Lionel Richey type fade that was cut low on the sides and evenly rounded on the top and back part of his head, without a hair out of place. Coach Hudson gave everything 100% of his attention. He tended his own yard, it was immaculate - no weeds, evenly cut, mowed, water regularly for optimal greenness and edged to perfection. His red and black 1969 Plymouth Road Runner and white old school Monte Carlo stayed washed, waxed, shined, vacuumed with gleaming tires from foam Armor All. He would wake up early and wash his cars in the driveway. "When you get your ride, hand wash it Jaybird, the car wash scratches your car" Hud would say. He treated his house the same, his carpet always had fresh vacuum lines, glass freshly windexed and collectible antiques placed just so, to the point that he could tell if something had been messed with. "Who's been in here? That bird doesn't point that way, it goes south. Who messed with my stuff?" I enjoyed the level of precision and high standards that he held himself to. He also did the same on his job. He took the time to connect with students, showing patience, grace and providing motivation, encouraging best efforts, and helping kids work through issues.

As my fifth grade year came to an end, my Dad made it clear that despite my request, I wasn't going to Tubman. "It's tough having your father as your principal, also we don't live in the district. You're going to Russell, but you'll be with Hud." Hud was the bright spot for me as a look toward middle school, and he lived up to all my unrealistic expectations. He was my own personal hype man, support system, accountability officer and caring school connection wrapped in one. He was the epitome of 70 years' worth of research conducted by the Search Institute proving that one adult can make the difference in a student feeling connected to their school, positively impacting the trajectory of their academic success.

In middle school I maintained a 3.0 or above grade point average, played basketball and football, dealt with discriminatory acts driven by race in addition to all of the challenges, pressures and stresses that comes with being a middle school student. As I think about educational systems, districts and schools, I hope that every student has or had a Coach Hudson, someone safely guiding them through uncharted waters, turbulent times while strengthening their confidence, character and competitive spirit as they learn and grow.

June of '89 marked the summer before my eighth grade year. I attended Self-Enhancement Inc (SEI) summer school, which was held at Tubman Middle School at that time. Shortly after his arrival to Portland my father linked up with two brothas that had plans for running a one-week summer program focused on helping students academically and socially, while holding basketball as the focal point of engagements. It gave students the opportunity to hoop in a safe environment, learn about sportsmanship and work ethic. The program provided breakfast and lunch and every student was given a t-shirt with the slogan "Life without education is a long shot." Above the slogan at the top of the shirt was a basketball hoop in the distance with a cloud at the post of the hoop, zoomed in on the lower part of the shirt were two hands holding a basketball, ready to launch a super deep three. The SEI logo t-shirt represented reality, not everyone was going to the NBA. My dad loved the logo and slogan. When adults asked boys what they wanted to be in the future, the majority of us as sixth graders would say we were going to the NBA. While the Tubman gym did have a few NBA success stories, like Tyrell Brandon, and Damon Stoudamire, the 5'10" guard known as Mighty Mouse, the percentage of NBA greats were few and far between. Dad and I'd watch their games, he'd bragged, "I had both of them, they were both quiet kids with good grades, they'd be in the gym everyday schooling 8th graders, when they were 6th graders…they had a raw talent that was incredible." Others played college ball, some played overseas, with hopes of going to the league at some point. But for the majority of us, including myself, our hoop dreams were short lived, proving that life without education would be a long shot.

The SEI program began at Tubman Middle School in 1981, dad's first year as principal. Connecting with the founders and leaders of the program in year one of its conceptions as a thought partner, helping the program come fruition only further strengthened Tubman's reputation for success. Tony Hopson Sr. and Ray Ellis Leary were young up and coming community leaders back then. Each went on to be success stories, influential and beneficial to students' lives in a variety of ways. In the 80's they were the duo that championed the expansion of SEI, each year the program grew in popularity, size and participation. SEI's ability to motivate Black students was a force to be recognized and celebrated. My father being the good Dad that he was, made sure I was a part of it.

Initially, the program was a summer program, but eventually business foundations and corporations began funding it much heavier based on its successful reputation. By the time I participated it was a full year around program. Participants would attend summer school at Tubman, the morning was three periods of academic classes and afternoon was co-curricular activities. A point system was used to track students attendance, positive behavior and grades, the top 100 point-getters took a field trip at the end of the summer to Thrill-Ville USA, an amusement park located in Turner, Oregon with more than 20 rides. That summer I was in the top 5 point-getters. At an end of the summer assembly, the list of the top 100 students was displayed on a big screen using an overhead projector, and there I was Paul Coakley Jr (PJ) listed at number four. I sat in the front row and smiled at my father who was standing on stage as Ray read the names of each student and their number of points. When my name was read Dad winked at me and gave a large smile showing his teeth.

Turner, Oregon is approximately an hour commute from Portland. On the last day of camp, we loaded charter buses and spent the sunny summer day on roller coasters. Participants were split by teams and while our SEI shirts had the same graphics, they varied by color. Our coordinators, high school counselors responsible for a group of camp attendees, made sure we stayed together as a group. That summer I was on team aqua, and made sure I wore kicks that matched my shirt and also wouldn't get scuffed up easily in the amusement park - Nike Air Wildwood ACG, cream and gray with the aqua check and black toe box. I also had a fresh haircut, shades, and kept finding cute girls to go on rides with. Being a top point-getter felt great, it meant that I was one step closer to the ultimate SEI goal, earning the jacket. In my mind only the smartest, coolest and well accomplished brotha's had the jacket. To earn the jacket, you had to be on the honor roll your entire 8th grade year, and be one of the top 10 SEI point-getters at the end of the summer. I'm not sure what year SEI began giving out jackets but a few high school participants had them, your hustlers, kids that exhibited a combination of drive, smarts and street savvy… I was one of them, longingly wanting that jacket.

In sixth and seventh grade my GPA always hovered around a 3.0, but I took on my 8th grade year with a new motivation. Determined to get a 3.5 and stay on the honor roll all year long, letting nothing deter me from getting my jacket. In every class I was on time, on task and on a mission. A covert operation unbeknownst to any of my Gordan Russell peers, which was fine by me. A switch had been turned on, it was go time. With every week I moved with more purpose, visibility and vigor, checking in with teachers about assignments, talking with basketball and football coaches and teammates. My best ever sports seasons happened that year, growth spurts combined with the weight room plus daily practice. My grades were meeting the mark, first quarter 3.5, second quarter 3.6… Coach Hudson kept me accountable, "nice job Jay! You're staying on top of your grade, you're always smiling, that's what a positive attitude does for you." I had found myself… young, Black, intelligent, with the ability to navigate in and out of White spaces without backing down, taking a back seat, or feeling less than, I was fearless. Fearlessness combined with the ability to set goals, plus the determination to achieve them, separates the leaders from the followers, the ordinary from the extraordinary, the doers from the talkers.

In eighth grade I realized that my ability to operate on this perceived "higher level" came as second nature. People took notice, my teachers, coaches, school administrators, students, teammates and especially girls. However, the zone I was in allowed me to have fun while maintaining or increasing my grades and taking care of my responsibilities. I always woke up early, that was my time to get things done, reading, writing, planning out my day, setting up short term goals, and prioritizing my strategy. Looking at due dates and assignments and creating my visual roadmap for success. This allowed me time with friends and family after school, outside of team sports. My SEI coordinator would check in with me at the end of each grading period and get a copy of my report card. "I see you Coke!" he would say. Third quarter. 3.65, fourth quarter I ended the year strong with a 3.7, my best middle school report card ever. So close to perfect but my grade in Home Economics dropped from an "A" to a "B" after batter ran down the face of the student next to me after trying the short stack of pancakes I made for my class final. Oh well, it made for a good laugh.

I had checked all the SEI boxes - making the grades to remain on honor roll every quarter for the full eight grade year. "We are so proud of you," my Mom said. "You did it dude, that's what I'm talking about. Just remember it's not time to lighten up, it's time to tighten up! Now you've got to represent at summer school" Dad said. All that was left was ensuring a spot as a top 10 point-getter by the last day of summer school, a goal that I could reach in my sleep. While many students dread the idea of summer school, for me it was the place I wanted to be. Back amongst diversity, students, teachers, leaders, coaches and coordinators. I was about the business of working hard, crushing assignments and tasks, helping others, assisting staff, asking questions, improving my B-ball skills, and helping everyone on my camp team succeed - this summer I was on team orange. We had bright orange t-shirts with the SEI logo of a hooper's hands preparing to shoot at the basket in the clouds. This summer the slogan was printed in black block letters on the back, "Life without education is a long shot." On feet I wore Bo Jackson's orange and blue Nike Trainer SC, they hit just right with my team colors. Each day I'd strut into my summer school classes with vigor and confidence, displaying a large smile and some sort of handshake, pound or dap for staff and teammates. Representing number one of six SEI's standards, a list of expectations of conduct that participants were to know and live by.

"At SEI we greet each other with a smile and a handshake to strengthen the relationship between us" was number one.

Summer school ended in the blink of an eye. I had secured my spot in the top 10, moving from number four the previous summer to number two. At the number one spot was my close friend, John aka Punchy, who attended Tubman, and was well liked by all. We became friends in sixth grade when my Dad partnered us together on my visits to Tubman, "PJ, you're shadowing John today" he said. We sat next to each other in the front row of the awards assembly. "I got you by 12 points," John said with a grin. "Barely" I laughed. The top 10 list was displayed prominently on the overhead projector. SEI staff took to the stage, "This has been a great summer, today we are recognizing 10 students, not only do they know the SEI standards, they live by them! They've gone above and beyond expectations, maintained at least a 3.5 GPA all year long and remained in the top 10 two summers in a row! They do things without being asked, they are quick to help others when they need it, and they have proven themselves as leaders. Clap it up, give them a round of applause, they deserve it! The students in the auditorium clapped and cheered. My father who was standing on stage clapped loudly, straight faced, with his lips pursed tightly pinched together, glaring silently as his eyes scanned the auditorium.

"At number 1 with 265 points, give it up for John Slaughter!" said the assembly announcer. John smiled widely, walked across the stage, shaking hands with the announcer. He turned toward SEI leadership and was handed a black varsity jacket, with the word John embroidered in white on the front left side. The soft black leather sleeves looked smooth as butter. The back dawned a large patch with the SEI logo in white puffy varsity style knitting, with red stitching surrounding the patchwork. John held up his jacket to the audience showing off the back, he exited stage left as we all cheered. I sat on the edge of my seat with my hand clasped tightly. The announcer piped up, "alright, this next brotha on the list earned 253 points, he stayed on honor roll and he always greets people with a smile and a handshake, give it up for Paul Coakley Jr!" I hopped up out of my seat and made a b-line toward the announcer as campmates applauded. I shook his hand, "Congratulations, unfortunately we can't give you a jacket because you don't live in the district, but we are proud of you, and we want to recognize you for your hard work" said the announcer.

The applause stopped, I heard a few kids blurt out "damn!" and "that's cold!" I froze and glanced at my father, he made eye contact with me as he stood in silent anger. Little did I know that he had gotten into it with SEI staff that morning after they notified him of this technicality or excuse, but it was out of his control. I turned toward the announcer who had his hands stretched. I shook it quickly and went back to my seat. "They did you dirty" John said as I slouched in my seat watching the remaining 8 point-getters receive their jackets. Tuning out the applause I sat in silent reflection, clapping loudly, straight faced, with my lips pursed tightly together, glaring silently as my eyes scanned the stage.

For the many things that Principal Paul Coakley was to the community and his student's, I observed those charismatic displays of leadership first hand on my visits to the school's he served in throughout his career. Yet to me, he was so much more than that…he was a good Father. The guy who asked me for help putting up Christmas lights and wrapping gifts every December. A Dad who exhibited his patience when he taught me to drive, learn to ride a bike, play basketball, and begin to shave. A proud parent that never missed my brother and I's extracurricular activities. He was a planner of family vacations, showing interest in our likes and dislikes. A man who would express his disappointment in you when you mess up, but his frustration came from a place of love. In the same breath he'd fight the world for you if someone tried to harm you, or treated you with disrespect. "For you, I'll fight a Buzzsaw, man! I'll walk through Hell with gasoline draws' on before I let somebody get to you. I won't go down without a fight. There's gonna be some furniture movin" he'd say. The day of the jacket debacle there was some furniture movin'. The furniture was in the form of heated debate as he expressed his feelings about how I was treated.

To mend fences, the SEI staff blessed my Dad with a jacket. The same jacket the 9 pointer-getters received, with the word Coakley embroidered in white on the front left side. "Look what I got" he said to me when he arrived home. "SEI gave me this jacket, you can wear it anytime you want" he said. I tried on the jacket, which drooped over me like an oversized blanket. I took it off and handed it back to Dad. "No thanks, Dad. This is your jacket, you earned it, and besides...I'm over it" I said with a grin.

CHAPTER 4

The Smartest Brotha I Know

Like most kids, I bounced from one pipedream to the next before figuring out my "why," my calling, that thing I was born to do. Some never find it, for me it was a series of testing out options, changing course and tapping into real world experiences before finding the quintessential pathway that brought me food for the soul.

Be that as it may, there are also kids that are born with a clear vision, a razor-sharp focus, a reason they're aware of for why they came into this world. While the children I describe may be rare, I know they exist because my younger brother Brian (otherwise known as "B") was one of those people. Five years my junior, at an early age we all knew that Brian planned on being a doctor. Different from most, he didn't "want" to be a doctor, he "planned" to be one. As a first grader, he told classmates, relatives, neighbors and friends "I'm going to be a doctor when I grow up." He spoke his dreams with the kind of confidence and conviction that only comes from years of experience and success, as a family - we believed in his plan.

Throughout elementary school Brian naturally exhibited the traits of a good doctor. He was a good listener and strong communicator. He not only listened for understanding, he took mental notes, asked clarifying questions, was thoughtful and reflective in offering advice. Adults would chuckle at the reality of them taking serious consideration to the council of a seven year old. Wise beyond his years, his curiosity led him to accurate diagnosis, even when it took a bit of research. One sweltering summer day of playing in the sun in tank tops and shorts I noticed his lower shoulders and arms looked blistered and raw. "B, you've got a bad rash," I said. "That's not a rash, that's acanthosis nigricans" he said factually. I fell to the grass rolling around in side-splitting hilarity as tears uncontrollably poured down my face from extreme laughter. For years to come I teased him about it, bursting into his room as he studied, my fists held to my sides like Batman, in my best superhero voice, announcing "That's not a rash, that's acanthosis nigricans!" He'd respond unamused with a monotone, "man please, I'm trying to study."

Like most geniuses in the making, Brian had childhood moments where his high level of intelligence got him into trouble. Like when he was eight and he told a group of teachers at Mom's school that Santa was actually just kids' parents. He shared that he knew exactly what he was getting for Christmas because he found where his gifts were hidden in the house. He continued to dig the hole deeper, describing each present that he spied. This of course frustrated my parents to no end. He suffered the natural consequence of not having anything to be surprised about on Christmas. "We didn't get you any additional gifts, there are no surprises under the tree for you. You already know what you are getting, since you searched the house and took the joy of surprising you away from us" said Mom. That was the last time B decided to play Columbo on holidays.

"B" navigated the game of life like a season of Survivor - "outwit, outlast and outplay." Every now and then we'd have dinner out. Mostly, after Sunday Service, usually at Red Lobster, a family favorite. It was packed with churchgoers in their Sunday's best attire, button up shirts, ties, suits, sports jackets, ladies in bright colorful dresses with large fancy hats, gigantic bows, sizable flowers and hefty pendants. As we waited for a table, Dad would growl "C'mon fellas, follow me to the restroom." We knew that a fatherly lecture was coming, the men's bathroom was our usual pit stop where Dad laid down the law to Brian and me. Although I received the lecture, the speech was heavily intended for Brian. He tended to listen to Dad's sermon, and then intentionally do the opposite. "Now look here!" Dad said, "I don't want to spend a bunch of money, so you two need to order off the kids menu" his eyes bulged with intensity as he stared down at both of us. "Do I make myself clear?! That'll keep the cost down." We'd nod in agreement.

Once situated and ready to order, Mom always ordered first, Dad last. "Get whatever you want, Carlus" stated Dad. Followed by me ordering something off the kids menu, one of three choices: popcorn shrimp, chicken tenders or the go to for most kids, fish and chips. B always ordered after me, without looking in Dad's direction he'd make direct eye contact with the waiter "I'll have the Admiral's Feast" he'd said bravely. An item that definitely wasn't on the kids menu. The Admiral's Feast was a platter of deep fried goodness, shrimp, bay scallops, clam strips, fried flounder and two sides. My father's eyes were as large as saucers. "Are you sure B? That's a lot of food" Dad said, flabbergasted by his youngest son's disobedience. "Oh, let him get what he wants, Paul…get whatever you want baby" Mom quickly replied. So, Brian doubled down, "I'll have the Admiral's Feast with mashed potatoes and steamed vegetables" he stated with even more conviction than before. Dad cut his eyes at me, holding in his anger as he steamed. I clenched my teeth holding in my laughter. "I'll take a large bowl of clam chowder," Dad said, sounding defeated. "That's all you want Paul?" asked Mom. "Yep." The old man had lost his appetite, wanting to snatch B by the collar, but couldn't. "Wait 'til we get home" he muttered under his breath. This was a regular occurrence, Dad always followed the dinner with a serious consequence. Brian was a highly intelligent kid, making a conscious decision "I'll take the food and the consequence" he told me when I asked him why he did it. "You're a different breed" I laughed.

B was highly driven, "I plan to attend Harvard" he proclaimed in elementary school. He researched what it took to get accepted into Harvard, then began to work towards the goal. In sixth grade, his science teacher assigned a project that sparked Brian's interest and passion - building a structural model of an atom. He came home that particular Friday with a list of materials he hoped to collect to assemble the project. Styrofoam, paperclips, construction paper, rubber cement, paint, brushes, and a bunch of ins and outs to represent the number of protons, neutrons and electrons. My parents as dedicated educators drove us all over town that weekend collecting the items on Brian's list. They stayed up late Sunday night helping him hold pieces in place, as glue dried to Styrofoam and paint hardened on cut out cardboard. They even drove him to school so he didn't need to lug his project on the bus and risk being damaged. He got out of the car beaming with pride, project in hand. A student from his class remarked "Good morning Brian, is that your atom? Wow, you know it's not due for another six weeks!" From then on, my parents asked the question "when is it due?" anytime he asked for help with an assignment.

Nonetheless, he was a beast when it came to studying and completing assignments, earning a 4.0 every quarter from 6 - 12 grade. He once got a B+ on a midterm grade in PE, he scheduled a meeting with the Principal and PE teacher to challenge the teacher's grading policy. "You're not going to mess up my chance of going to Harvard, based on subjective grading. Where's your data?" he said, questioning the PE teacher. While my parents were always ready to advocate for either one of us, Brian, didn't need the additional back up, "I'm not letting this happen, it's not right" he persisted. "Dude, it's a B+ and it's a midterm grade, you're all fired up over a B+" I chuckle! "If I deserved a B+ I'd accept it, but I don't, and I won't!" He went into the meeting like a defense attorney prepared to explain his plea of not guilty or deserving of a "B+." When the meeting concluded the PE, teacher changed his grade to an "A." The teacher left the meeting in a state of deep reflection, wandered out of the main office. Had he been grading students subjectively all these years? Halting high schoolers dreams, goals and aspirations based on their ability to run a five minute mile or complete twenty clean push-ups. As far as I know, that coaching conversation with B might have been the nudge the veteran PE teacher needed to announce his retirement at the end of the school year. That same conversation may have motivated Brian to keep pushing, the will, determination and drive to see light at the end of a long tunnel. "I was right, he changed my grade," he said to me with a smile, "I knew I didn't deserve it!"

One bright morning in mid-June Brian crossed the stage as Gresham High's first Black Valedictorian with a 4.0 grade point average and plans to attend Harvard University in the Fall. Most of the Black and Brown faces sparsely representing Gresham's student population got bogged down in the education system. B didn't live in that system, like most of the students of color that came after him and before him, including myself. He moved freely through it, hovering above it, sometimes working around it, shaking off the barriers of institutional racism and exclusionary practices, making his way beyond each and every situation. He attended school not like a student but a staff member, someone with a job to do. His pay wasn't monetary, he was paid in "A" grades. For some of us, graduation is a means to an end, for Brian it was the culmination of his K-12 experience. A season that had ended, a completion of a short chapter. It was a time for leaving behind the feeling of being the only Black speck in all White spaces, classrooms, hallways and afterschool clubs. The days of elderly neighborhood haters cracking jokes about his dream of attending Harvard were long gone, "hello Brian, how are you doing in school?...do you still want to go to Haa-vuud!?" ... the hater would say in his worst Boston accent. Gone were the days of me busting into his room to interrupt his study session with my superhero impersonations. Memories of ordering off the adult menu and facing the consequences were far behind us. Every family member and relative from Michigan to Tennessee, and further corners of the deep south beamed at Brian's accomplishments. For graduation dinner we went to a local steakhouse of his choosing, "Get whatever you want, Baby," Mom said. "Yeah, eat up guys, it's time to celebrate!...You remember when he was little, I'd tell this knucklehead to order off the child's menu..." Dad said with a laugh, nudging me in the side with his elbow.

My third year as an elementary teacher all pathways afforded me the opportunity to experience the joys of homeownership. Credit unions flooding my apartment mailbox with first time home buying opportunities for educators. It was the season of low interest rates, little to no money down deals. While my apartment living phase yielded me some lifelong memories, the rent that I paid each month was hard earned cash I'd never see again. No equity being made, no return on investment, no property to sell at the end of the lease. LV purchased a home during our first year of teaching. He was always kicking knowledge about the importance of home ownership. "It's like putting your money into an account, because over time the value of your home will increase as you pay down the loan you're building equity that you have access to later" he explained. I heard the same information from my folks several times throughout college. But as a product of YO! MTV Raps, I opted for a small apartment and bought a Lexus GS 300. When I signed my teacher's contract, I couldn't wait to ditch the Honda Civic, which in my mind was my college car - it was almost paid off by the way, thanks to my parents, I could have stacked a ton of money by going a few years without a car payment. But as soon as I got a job my mind was made up, I wanted a vehicle like the ones rappers highlighted in videos.

Everyone loved the Lexus, but the car payment took away a bit of its luster. A vehicle much too nice for a carport, and after a crazy ex-girlfriend, using the term "girlfriend" loosely, threatened to "key" my car, I began paying an additional hundred dollars a month for a single car garage located way on the other side of my apartment complex. Walking the full complex to park safely, BBQ's at LVs spacious crib, annoying neighbors, rent increases and a change the apartments management, prompted me to search for a home. Dad accompanied me to the Credit Union where I banked, the *Portland Teachers Credit Union*. We left the credit union with my pre-approval letter.

A few years prior my parents had sold the childhood home B and I grew up in on the edge of Gresham. The house represented our K-12 years. A peaceful neighborhood, reminiscent of bike rides to friends' houses that extended throughout the subdivision, where neighbors knew each other by name, most family BBQs would had a smattering of neighbors dropping in from Dad's invitation to "come on through and make yourself a plate." There was Herb and LeAnne, a few Bill's and Donna's, Margaret, Moe and Bob, with more than a handful of Doug's and Debbie's. While we were the only Black family in the neighbor-hood, everyone loved my parents, so much so that they even knew their friends, Hud and Unk, their spouses and children were always there. It was an era of sports fans, cookouts and summer vacations. Politics weren't talked about much, guys would help each other with home projects like building a larger deck off the back of a neighbor's house, or installing a basketball hoop in the driveway while splitting a six pack of ice cold Budweiser. When my parents moved to Happy Valley, a suburban metropolitan area, larger homes with offices and bonus rooms, picturesque views at high elevation, the old neighborhood felt the loss of their presence. Their new home had a breathtaking view of Mt. Hood, it also had a three car garage, which was unheard of in the old neighborhood. They'd moved from 1,800 square feet to well over 3,500, leveling up, times were changing.

While looking for homes LaBa would roll with me, I'd drive the Lex through the back hills until we reached the million-dollar homes nestled around Persimmon Golf Course. Slowly driving through the private community looking at estates with Spanish tiled rooftops, manicured lawns, large front facing balconies and circular driveways with luxury cars. "I'm gonna have a crib like that one day," I would tell him. "Let's get outta here before they call the cops Fam!" he would say, as we received looks of fear from homeowners as we drove past. "I'll settle for a starter home now, until I build some equity, then flip it for something larger," I said gazing at the golf villas. "Man, you buggin,…let's go." said LaBa.

After looking at a variety of starter homes I settled on a brand new daylight house. The kitchen, living room, master bedroom and half bath was on the main floor, and there was a lower level with two small bedrooms, a den and a bathroom. It was located in my old neighborhood where a dead end full of blackberry bushes had been removed, expanding into a winding street with about twenty newly built homes. I liked the idea of living in familiar surroundings, being the first to live in a newly built space, all while generating equity to level up like my parents at some point in the future. While many teachers were purchasing homes with no money down deals, I hadn't established enough credit history to qualify, so I needed to put down 5% earnest money to seal the deal. Money that I didn't have, which was about 10 thousand dollars…my hope was dashed.

I sat with my Mom in the living room of their new house on the plush large cream couches with giant support pillows, "we want you to get that house, so your Dad went out today and put down the earnest money you needed" she said. "You can't do that, it's a lot of money" I said. "Life isn't all about money, someday when we're older we might need your help, don't forget about us" Mom said, reaching out for a hug. I hugged mom tight as I thought about all of the times my parents put their faith into me, many of which I disappointed them, I better not mess this up.

When I moved in to my new place, I rented one of the downstairs rooms to LaBa. Not only was his rent money helping me offset my mortgage payment, but two years living in a house with your childhood best friend was a time of classic memories, from weekend BBQ's and poker tournaments with dudes wearing clear green visors and aviator sunglasses. It also highlighted the fact that we were no longer the carefree kids from the cul-de-sac. We had responsibilities, both of us setting alarms, waking up every day heading off to work, me to my classroom at King. LaBa worked downtown at his Uncle's factory warehouse. During the busiest months of the year we were like two passing ships sailing in different directions, rarely on the same schedule headed to the same location. After two years, LaBa moved, friendship still intact, into his girlfriend's apartment where he spent the majority of his time.

B graduated from Harvard in May of 2002, the graduating class held an assortment of future lawyers, doctors, Wall Street tycoons, writers, entrepreneurs and A and B list celebrities. He landed his medical residency at Oregon Health Sciences University (OHSU). I was elated that he was moving back home. He moved in to my place, occupying LaBa's old room, which was the largest of the two downstairs bedrooms. When B moved in it felt like no time had passed. We were siblings, both proud of each other, connected through a blood bond, childhood experiences, and a deeper understanding of who we were regardless of time. I made a few trips out to Boston during B's undergraduate years, hanging with him and his Harvard crew. During his freshman year I visited for about a week, chilling with his roommates, crashing in the dorms, attending the events and letting people assume I was a student on campus. We hung at Pinocchio's Pizza & Subs at Harvard Square, a tiny building with white brick and uncomfortable aluminum chairs. I'd order a large Sicilian for the table, we'd crowd around the square linoleum table laughing, joking and scarfing down cheesy squares of goodness on flimsy white paper plates. On my last night we hit Harvard's Hong Kong Restaurant & Lounge, located right across from campus. It brought the old school feel of Chinatown to the square, the bright red signage with Chinese characters, along with the music blaring filled the streets with energy. The bottom floor was full of patrons sharing family style dishes of sesame chicken, broccoli beef and garlic noodles. While the upstairs door was guarded by two Black bouncers wearing red polo shirts with Hong Kong embroidered in white. College students and Cambridge locals danced to the top 100 hits on the hardwood floor under blue, red and green strobe lights. While couples sat in dark leather booths sipping on scorpion bowls, a large tub of alcohol, juice, orange slices, ice and multiple straws.

B's Harvard crew consisted of six Black men from all walks of life, hailing from DC, Chicago, Indianapolis, Los Angeles, Baltimore, and of course Portland. It was a crew unsuspecting of what comes to mind when you typically think of Harvard. Regular guys, hardworking, driven and motivated. Each different in their own way, but connected in many other ways, not just as Black men but also with personal traits that Brian exhibited, all intellectual forces to be reckoned with.

By connecting with the crew through visits to Harvard, I joined them in Las Vegas for a spring break weekend. B and I stayed at the Mandalay Bay, others were spread out all over the strip, based on whatever vacation package, connection or travel deal made sense. Regardless of distance, we'd meet up every day at a central location and hit the restaurants, casinos, pools, and nightclubs. The vacation culminated at the Rum Jungle Nightclub at Mandalay Bay where I ended up in the VIP area. After trying to walk into the VIP area and being asked for ID, I showed the bouncer my Oregon driver's license. "You're the guy that works for the Trailblazers" said the bouncer. I grinned and gave him a fist bump, next thing I know I'm in a roped off upper balcony with Sir Mix-A-Lot and his posse of Seattle-based partygoers. Ed Lover and Dr. Dre made a guest appearance. B spent a large portion of the night herding cats. Working to reassemble the crew, wandering the club, scanning face under flashing lights, bumping shoulders as nineties hip-hop blared through the speakers. All of us disappeared on solo missions, deep in the abyss of the Rum Jungle. Epic memories, stories, and strong friendships were forged. As I spoke with the guys I knew B was in good hands, each of them genuinely real, supportive, trustworthy, dependable, there were no haters. As his older brother, I'd looked out for him since childhood. Now attending college across the county, I didn't have to worry about him as much. We were family - immediately connected, those are the type of friends worth fighting for. I have some of those types of friends, from all walks of life, but my circle consisted of several who didn't take the college route. I lost contact with many of them over the years. A handful of them are my closest friends to this day, LV, Ike Boogie, Jones, and the Shandog. Rest in paradise to my main man Vann, who died way too soon.

My last visit to Harvard was the week before graduation. The campus was full of visitors, bustling relatives rolling hard shell suitcases with cameras around their necks, students transporting regalia in plastic covers. Crowds of people waiting to take photos in front of the Johnston Gate, one of Harvard's many entrances - constructed of two large pillars made of coarse handmade red brick, black rod iron gates that come to a point at the center of the arc. Others draped themselves around a statue of John Harvard, in their burgundy and cream collegiate sweaters with an embroidered "H," or sweatshirts with "Harvard" in arched lettering boldly displayed across their chests in white trim. In less than 48 hours, commencement would take place on Harvard Yard, amongst the historic dormitories, large oak, elm and maple trees display flags from the school each undergraduate group represents, located smack in the middle of the dark green manicured Ivy League lawn. Two days later, we were in the midst of the pomp and circumstance listening to speeches given to the undergraduates by the president, provost and deans and specified facility members, proud family and friends anxiously looked on, waiting for their graduates name to be called. I stood next to Uncle Bobby, my Mom's younger brother who drove up from Nashville to support B's greatest accomplishment to date. My parents crouched in front of us in Harvard lawn chairs they purchased from the bookstore. I held the program tightly following the announcer as he read every graduate's name clapping loudly for each of Brian's crew, waiting for his name to be called, "Let's go B!" I said loudly. Our circle of family members piped up with applause for a quick second, "You the man, B!" Dad yelled turning slowly, swiping a tear from his cheek with his index finger, "you the man" he softly repeated.

In high school Brian was consumed in his school work, focused and vigilant. He was a model for the cliché "you can accomplish anything you put your mind to." He dreamed big, a Black man carving his own pathway to academic and professional success regardless of how the system was set up. He knew what his dream was and how to reach it. If you didn't believe in him dream, he didn't get discouraged, he'd just erased you from his dream.

CHAPTER 5

Let Your Pain Be Champaign

With my administrative practicum completed, I was ready to submitting my application and receive an official Oregon Administrators License. However, Portland Public had its own internal processes, additional hoops to jump through, hurdles to ascend over and obstacles to remove. For people of color roadblocks were multiplied to the fifth power. Not only was there the dreaded "pool" where administrators of color applications were tossed into the deep water to drown hopes, dreams, and goals of leadership positions. There was also the "unwritten requirement" of completing the Aspiring Administrator Program, PPS's internal vetting process. A program that took the internal educators who'd earned their administrator credentials and were highly recommended by leaders in the district into a yearlong boot camp run by the HR department. Word on the street was "without this program, you'll never become a principal in PPS." Unk and others encouraged me, LV and a handful of other up-and-coming leaders, to join the Aspiring Administrator's program to get our foot in the door. I had come this far, another hurdle was nothing, let's do it! I saw it as an opportunity to meet central office administrators, principal's across the district, build relationships, learn from leaders' experiences, while being groomed for a principalship in the future.

While my colleagues from Portland State were applying for jobs as assistant principals and landing positions in districts situated just outside of Portland like Gresham, David Douglas and Parkrose, I specifically placed my hopes on working as a leader in PPS. It was where my connections lived, where my learning and growth took place, where my support system was built. Not only did I love working in the Black community, I was also observing firsthand what my Dad was going through as the first Black Principal of Gresham High School (GHS).

It was the classic suburban tale, a school district with intentions of recruitment, retention and a plan to diversify the leadership since the student body was becoming more diverse each year. As part of the graduating class of '94, when I attended, GHS had a handful of Black and Brown faces, less than twenty students who I knew by name. When Brian graced the stage as valedictorian in '98 that number had grown closer to fifty. Fifty faces walking the halls and classrooms making much of the staff uncomfortable, students they found more difficult to connect with. Many of whom held English as their second language, others they felt were threatening, possibly gang related based on stereotypical assumptions that followed students of color. There were a few students that made the athletic coaches smile, Black kids that moved from PPS, known as top-tier athletes, basketball and football stars, future NFL draft picks or NBA players. The coach's job was to keep them out of trouble, ensuring they're grades were "good enough" to step on the court or field. "I'm being recruited by Gresham, their Assistant Superintendent reached out to me" said Dad to Mom and I. "They say I'm just what they are looking for, the student body is becoming more diverse. They're suspending Black and Latino kids left and right, I'd put a stop to all that. Kids need a principal they can relate to" he justified… "it's a salary increase, but I'm fine right where I am, at Roosevelt."

Gresham-Barlow recruited Dad from PPS while he was serving as principal of Roosevelt High School. He'd become known across the state for turning schools around. He'd coined the use of the phrase "On time, On Task, On a Mission" to increase daily attendance and morale. The district did its due diligence in recruiting Dad to the High School Principal position, not only offering him a healthy increase in salary, giving him tours of the district's facilities, the superintendent offering him carte blanche on leading the building in the way he saw fit to increase student outcomes. He was transparent with PPS, meeting with

HR staff, notifying them of the offer. He also told them his heart was with Roosevelt, even if they couldn't match the offer, if they got close he would stay. No counter offer was made, they told him "best wishes."

After being treated expendable, he set his sights on going to Gresham. There he quickly found that a system of support for a leader making long term changes was non-existent. Transitioning into Gresham High was no easy feat, the previous high school principal was promoted to the district office, becoming his direct supervisor. A fatal misstep or a nail in the coffin for anyone taking on a new leadership role depending how you look at it. During my high school years, Dad's new supervisor was my principal, someone quite the opposite of a Principal Coakley. I never saw her in the halls, she didn't address students at assemblies or provide us with inspirational slogans to motivate us to give our best. In fact, I wouldn't have even known she was my principal if it wasn't for my parents. She was milquetoast – a front office statue, the lady behind the guys, which were the two vice-principals. They were the faces of the school.

In true Coakley fashion Dad stepped into his new role setting the term as if he planned on staying a hundred years. Building relationships, living in the hallways, bellowing "stay to the right," and "when that bell rings, have your face in the place, the place is the classroom." Holding tough conversations with staff, calling out disparities, holding accountability, addressing issues, inequitable practices, expanding course offerings and opportunities. Students and parents loved it, he became so popular in Gresham, he was a local celebrity. We could no longer eat at our usual restaurants in town, someone would always recognize him, interrupting our family time. Parents talked about his positive impact on GHS or their kids. Most of the community rallied around the change, loving the fact that their new principal was amongst the students, wearing GHS apparel, roaring on the sidelines at sporting events, interacting with families at grocery stores and gas stations. Others dug in their heels, in direct and indirect ways, backbiting, backstabbing, conniving and nitpicking. Circa 2000, right around the same time that I was entering the field of education as a teacher, principal Paul Coakley Sr. was going through his own personal hellish nightmare of being a Blackman in leadership in a Whiteman's world. Gresham of all places, where no one in leadership looks like you or relates to your experience. The team that recruited you buries their heads in the sand, while a jealous direct supervisor with hopes of pushing you out for outshining their five year stint as a leader in less than one year is your daily reality.

He harbored his pain deep within, looking back I'd somehow missed the sullen look in his eyes. He was worn out, beat down, weathered from the day-to-day micro and macro aggressions. Years later he opened up to me about his struggles, "she set out to make my life Hell. In her mind, I can't shine without making her look bad. It just didn't make sense" sighed Dad.

Each morning he was up and at'em, suited, smiling on his way to a job that made his blood pressure rise to unsafe heights. Thank God for Sundays, they balanced him out. He looked forward to praising, serving and worshiping at Mt. Olivet Baptist Church. Fellowshipping with like-minded people that held his best interest at heart. He called me on the Saturdays, "will I see you at church?" he'd ask. Most Sunday's I'd meet him and Mom there, briefly, things seemed right with the world. His joy came from the Lord, combined with family moments where he pushed his dread, despair and discouragement to the back of his mind.

He was a true father, constantly putting my needs before his in conversations. Probably because I was more vocal about the hellish nightmare I was going through as a Blackman in PPS. Combatting racism, ageism, colorism, cynicism and a good ol' boy system, only elevating a sparse spattering of leaders that looked like me. I became hip to the politics, people hid the keys to doors that unlocked opportunities. Just because you've earned something doesn't mean, you'll get what you deserve.

In mid-July the media picked up Dad's story, "Test scores are up, graduation rates increased, student attendance is at an all-time high… so why's Gresham High School Principal Paul Coakley fighting for his job? This story and more tonight at 7." Something similar ran on every news station. The district waited until the school year was over, students and staff were in the midst of enjoying their summer vacations when my father was called into a district meeting informing him that they planned to non-renew his contract, take away his livelihood. A chess move that they hoped would end his career. After hearing the news, he quickly called his older brother, who I called, Uncle James, known for his cool, funny and sarcastic demeanor. Through my handful of interactions with him, I knew he was smart, hilarious, witty, full of vigor and over the top, like a working class Richard Pryor in his heyday. But this was no laughing matter, he gave dad a phone number, "call this cat, this dude don't play, we got your back on this" he replied.

Dad called Uncle James's connection, a local lawyer who came directly to my parents' house and sat in the living room. "It's going to be ok, we're not going to let them do this to you Paul" he said. He was a tall Jewish man wearing a crisp classic gray suit and tie, thin wire rimmed glasses and a large smile. The kind of smile that was genuine, like he'd known us for years. "Are these your sons?" he asked, shaking our hands firmly, "nice to meet you Brian and PJ, I'm Nick Fish," he said with a grin.

Nick quickly put our family at ease with every word he spoke, I wondered how my Detroit Uncle, known for having one of the flyest suit collections of anyone I knew, always cracking jokes, who bragged about checking himself into a hospital to get away from the demanding women he dated in his early twenties had a connection to a top notch attorney who lived in Portland. Uncle James - the same guy who harangued us in the fourth quarter, four out of five games when the Blazers battled the Pistons for the championship just 10 years prior. "Clyde didn't glide nowhere tonight!" he'd say in reference to Drexler's performance. One thing about my Uncle James, he always protected his younger brother, Paul. He also knew something we didn't, Nick was a professional Pitbull waiting to be let off the leash. A graduate of Harvard Law School. Nick immediately connected with Brian who was attending as an undergraduate at the time. He also connected with me and Mom, "I have a deep affinity for teachers and the important work they do for children…my wife is an educator" said Nick… "This is underhanded, they're trying to do this when everyone is on summer vacation. We'll pack the boardroom with families, student and community support, they need to answer to the people" Nick said.

So that's exactly what we did.

The Board chair vigorously wrapped her gavel on the table to call the meeting to order. The Chair scanned the room, looking over the sea of people packing the commons area to a capacity that would make a Fire Marshall cringe. There were students, parents, Gresham Rotarians, local leaders, leaders from the Black, Latino and Asian communities, as well as a large representation of business owners, educators, pastors, church members and longtime friends. Nick stood energetically in his navy suit, white shirt and tie, reviewing his list of orchestrated speakers, it strongly represented dad's diverse spectrum of supporters. I sat on the back right corner, Mom sat to my right, Brian to my left. B was ready to take care of business, closing as the last speaker. I took on the greeter role, shaking people's hands as they arrived, thanking them for coming. Nick asked if I'd be willing to speak, but I hadn't found my public voice yet. Nor was I in the right mindset, my speech would've probably been a barrage of four letter words, spewing out angry expletives that would have tainted our families name and misrepresented my Father.

The people who shared their testimony represented him well. Students and parents expressed their frustration and disappointment in the district trying to dismiss him when student outcomes were strong. The lack of transparency was concerning to them, some even stated that it was an act of racism. The district only had a handful of educators of color, all of them showed up in support along with their White counterparts standing in solidarity of Dad during the roughest time in his career. As a principal he'd dealt with gang issues, lack of staff motivation, district division, teacher turnover, poor student attendance, increasing mental health issues, racist community members, race and poverty's impact on achievement, labor relations disagreements, even extreme behavior disorders. However, nothing was more taxing or draining than taking on systematic racism, Gresham-Barlow's lack of diversity spoke to it well. The district had created a system where the traditional power structures were embedded so deeply, a person of color can't survive in the system unless they fit into a specific box the district deemed "non-threatening." They wanted a figure head, not a leader that could evoke feelings, passions or bring about real change.

I watched closely, board members and district leaders who came to put a nail in Dad's coffin sat frozen, dumbfounded at the outpouring of community support for a Black leader in a predominantly White community. Nick orchestrated a symphony of support that started out slow and steady, then gradually got louder, ending with Brian, GHS alumni and valedictorian. The young Black Harvard undergrad shined a spotlight that illuminated the racist practices not only he faced as a student, but that Dad faced since leaving Roosevelt High School in north Portland to work under his predecessor, who never met the mark as a "good principal" in anyone's eye's – students, staff, or parents. Creating a structure built on jealousy, resentment, and racist practices that showed up in the form of a midsummer recommendation for non-renewal.

The board listened to over an hour of public testimony before dismissing the recommendation of non-renewal. Dad's contract was extended, with plans to return to GHS in the Fall.

While the community celebrated at the retention of their fearless leader, the district gloated at the retention of their systematically oppressive power structure, a dynamic that remained unchanged. "I still have the same supervisor" Dad said "and she's just as racist as she ever was. I gotta get out of Gresham" Dad said with a look of disappointment.

I knew what he was going through, I had the same feelings about PPS. I sat in the large semi -circle of the drab district office, surrounded by participants of the Aspiring Administrator cohort. It was 6pm, everyone was tired and discontent, we'd all put in a full day. There was a hot seat were colleagues were called to answer an interview question. Participants delivered the best responses they could muster at the time. After answering, each took on a berating from the Director that shattered confidence, shredded hopes, shaking their self-worth, as they ingested the brash criticism, hunched in uncomfortable humiliation before slinking back into their vacant chair in shame. One lady bolted from the meeting in tears.

Cohort members watched perturbed, puzzled, squirming in their seats. Then, on to the next victim. People began avoiding eye contact, hoping not to be called on. The Director's face held silent jubilation overjoyed by breaking a "weak" participant.

"Paul, you're next" she said. "I'm good," I said. She looked at me bewildered, "excuse me? You mean you're not going to participate?" "Nope, this isn't helpful" I said. "I suppose you know everything about interviewing? This is preparation" she spouted. "All your feedback is negative. I thought this program was supposed to build us up, not tear us down?" I snapped. I had to speak my truth, even if it was in direct opposed of the leaders that could grant me the opportunity I was seeking.

Still, my participation in the program allowed me to poke my head above the tumultuous waters of drowning applicants, stuck at the bottom of the HR pool. Guaranteed to be interviewed by principals, and district staff for vacant assistant principal positions. We sat around circular tables in small rooms held at the Blanchard Educational Service Center (BESC) located at 501 N Dixon Street. Sometimes I'd interview with principals that I knew quite well, they'd say things like "you'd be a great fit in my building" when I saw them in passing. However, when it came time to make a job offer nothing ever panned out. So I began following up with a few of those principals, asking questions like "I hear you made a different choice…can you give me some feedback on my interview?" or "I thought I gave a strong interview…do you have any suggestions on what I can do better next time?" One of the principals looked around nervously, seeing that the coast was clear he whispered, "You were my first choice. You've been selected as the number one choice by several principals, but HR told all of us to pick someone else, you're not a viable option." "Why?" I asked. "They're pissed at your Dad for leaving, so they're taking it out on you. But hey, you didn't hear that from me" he said.

As Dad and I griped about our jobs, I glanced at him with a look of frustration and said "I gotta get out of PPS." That became my mission, a continuous search for a job as an Assistant Principal, I applied to a few gigs in East County, even went to district offices dressed to the nines holding conversations with Human Resource Directors, about future possibilities in their district. These districts were much smaller than the behemoth known as PPS, rarely did they have administrator openings, most AP jobs were filled internally. King just didn't feel the same anymore. I'd earned my admin license and wanted to put it to good use. Rory popped into my classroom one morning before the students arrived "I did it man, at the end of the school year me and my wife are outta here! She got accepted to the University of Illinois doctoral program, and I landed an elementary AP job in Champaign, right there near the college, man! Booker T. Washington Elementary, the demographics are like King. It's a good district, they have a few more AP jobs open right now…, they also have a Black Superintendent, Dr. Culver. I'm telling you man, you should check it out!"

I reviewed their website, as usual Rory was spot on, they had elementary AP jobs, and Black district leaders, including the superintendent and assistant superintendent. I freshened up my resume and cover letter before submitted my application. What did I have to lose? My current situation was leaving me with no options for advancement. The school year was quickly coming to a close, with no hope for a change in position.

A week later I got a call from Mrs. Burley, the principal of one of the schools in Champaign. We had an informal conversation about her school, the interview process, as well as my educational experience. The district would be holding formal interviews for two positions in a few weeks. She offered me an interview, plus reimbursement for my hotel and flight to Champaign. "It's a panel interview with two school staffs, you may get two job offers. If that's the case, you can choose which school you want to work for" said Mrs. Burley. I was ecstatic and began looking at flight options.

I solidified my itinerary for the trip. Dad took it as an opportunity for a guy's getaway, he needed a break from the hubbub going on in Gresham. He was also always up for a father-son trip, this marked the first of its kind. We flew into Indianapolis International Airport (IND) and drove our Chevy Malibu rent-a-car one-hundred and seven miles to Champaign, Illinois. It's about the same distance from Chicago O'Hare, or Midway airport but IND was a straight shot with a lot less traffic. Champaign is approximately 2.5 hours from every surrounding airport any way you slice it. We made a pit stop at White Castle before arriving at our hotel, munching on cheesy sliders with tiny grilled onions. That night I experienced my first thunderstorm, Dad asked me interview questions late into the evening. Down pouring rain and strong gusts of wind crashed against the windows rattling light fixtures, bending tree branches to oblivion, leaving debris, moss, and leaves all over the streets. The storms bellowed on for ten to fifteen minutes, before mellowing out, exposing the humidity of the summer, then picking back up again. "Yeah, you don't know about these thunderstorms!" Dad said laughing.

The next day we drove the area, getting a feel for the lay of the land, checking out the schools, district office, grocery stores and apartment buildings. The small city was vintage, with art deco buildings, red brick schools, a downtown area much larger than Gresham, but nowhere near the size of Portland. The high rise buildings were cut in half, six stories at best. It was also segregated to some degree, not physically divided by a train track like Gallatin, but there was definitely a Black side and a White side of the city, divided by the downtown area, the more predominantly White side housed the college campus as well as city libraries and more modernized schools. Dr. Howard Elementary student body was 97 percent Black. It was surrounded by local barbershops, fast food restaurants, and corner stores. Illinois has some of the best barbeque spots in the country, a few were just a hop, skip and a jump from the school. I called Mrs. Burley to let her know I made it in and was traveling with my father. She and her husband Ecomet invited us to join them for dinner. I was excited to meet both of them, possibly my new principal and Champaign's Assistant Superintendent, Mr. Burley. For someone who hadn't interviewed yet, it was a good sign. The Burley's were fun, down to earth, they made me feel right at home, like visiting relatives. We talked about everything from education to sports. Of course, they immediately hit it off with Dad, trading war stories about school leadership. Before dinner concluded Mrs. Burley said "I mentioned this briefly, but tomorrow you'll be interviewing for two schools, Dr. Howard and

Robeson. I suspect you'll get both offers, if so, you can choose which school you want to work at."

Mrs. Burley was right, I interviewed with confidence, passion and excitement. Like a man with his back against the wall, surrounded by an angry mob and the only way out is to give it everything you've got. Shortly after the interview I received a call from HR, offering me both positions. "I know you are here until tomorrow, do you want to visit both schools and make a decision?" asked the Director. "I went to both schools yesterday, I want to work at Dr. Howard" I said. "Oh," said the Director, "may I ask why?" "From what I can tell the staff and student body are much more diverse, plus it's a Title 1 school, I think it's a good fit. I've always served at Title 1 schools, it's my passion" I replied. "Ok, I will notify the principals. I'll send you an email with your contract details, we can finalize everything in the next couple of days, welcome aboard!" Dad and I spent the rest of the time searching for apartments. Before we made the drive to IND, I'd secured a new two-bedroom apartment, with a balcony, washer and dryer and small kitchen with marble countertops. I was the first to live in the space. Excited for the new opportunity, dreading the tasks ahead, like selling my house, packing, moving across the country and downsizing raced through my mind as we began our expedition home. During the layover in Dallas, I got a voicemail from the principal of Robeson, I returned her call. She expressed her disappointment in my selection, then asked if I knew of anyone from Portland that I could refer to the position. I gave her LV's contact information, a few weeks later all three Black PTP graduates were leaving PPS to take new opportunities in Champaign, Illinois. The story made headlines in the Gazette, Champaign-Urbana's local newspaper "Three headed east for opportunities in Champaign" our futures looked bright, of course there would also be thunderstorms.

Dr. Howard Elementary school, constructed in 1910 was the oldest school in the Champaign Unit 4 School District. It felt similar to King Elementary in Portland, a square red brick building full of character, the windows were covered with dark sheer blinds, protruding portable AC units randomly stood out of certain classrooms. The large school was three stories with an annex across from the main entrance near the playgrounds football field, which was the kindergarten wing. During the year, certain hallways and rooms would get much hotter than others, or colder than most depending on the season. While the three story layout brought a unique and rare quality to the building itself, I found the program layout for delivering instruction and tracking achievement shined a spotlight on the disparity of our system. Not just a school's systems, or a district's system, but the overarching inequities, institutionally embedded racism that persist within our K-12 systems across America. A system that has been in place since 1779, when Thomas Jefferson proposed a two-track education system, that in his words he referred to as "for the laboring and the learned." At Dr. Howard, the floors represented levels of success for students, even for the staff to some degree. Walking through the school's main entrance took you to the main floor, which housed the main office and a hallway full of classrooms for grades 1 - 5, these were General Ed classrooms, full of students and staff of color. Desks were traditionally set up in rows, the teacher's weapons of choice to educate students was the textbook, and whiteboard.

Across from the main entrance was a flight of stairs leading up and a flight of stairs leading down. The upstairs housed the "Gifted" program, full of TAG students, there was much less diversity on the top floor, the students and staff were mostly White, making the school feel segregated. The gifted program was held in a large adjoined classroom of approximately 45 kids. The program had co-teachers that complemented each other's teaching style quite well. Participating in the program was based on a combination of grades, standardized tests, and teacher recommendations. The teachers weapon of choice for education students was, problem based learning, using complex real world concepts as a vehicle for teaching. The classroom had tables instead of desks, students sat in groups of five researching topics, having debates that challenged their critical thinking skills, and enhanced their communication skills.

The bottom floor held two classrooms in a hallway across from the cafeteria, called the "B.D" rooms. "What does B.D. stand for" I asked the office secretaries my first week on the job. "behavior disorder, you'll probably spend the majority of your time responding to those rooms, there's some naughty kids down there" she said shaking her head.

My office was at the top floor right next to the "Gifted" program. It was large with a grand window overlooking the playground. It had a desk, computer and small circular table with chairs. As the person in charge of discipline, I kept a walkie-talkie and was called throughout the day to respond to issues. Issues that rarely took place on the third floor. As I got to know the students and staff, the calls became underwhelming predictable. I was usually called to the main floor, Mrs. Watkins fifth grade classroom to have a talk with Malik, a tall heavy set kid who I build a relationship with through a series of conversations, mostly about his likes and dislikes. Mrs. Watkins was a jet Black, stoic teacher in her mid-fifties. She wanted her classroom orderly and quiet. She made students sit in silence completing worksheets or writing in journals at their desks. After being summoned by walkie-talkie, I'd make a b-line to her room. She'd usually give me a look before pointing to Malik. I'd motion for him to come out in the hall, he'd grab his materials slowly slogging into the hallway. Most days our conversation was brief, "What's up man?" I'd ask. "It's boring in there, she trippin,' I didn't even do nothin', just laughed" he'd giggle.

Usually a two minute conversation was enough to get him back on track. Occasionally, his behavior was an excuse, diversion, or detour to be sent out, supported one-to-one on his assignments. His exit from class usually happened during the math block. I quickly realized he wanted to do the work. His class-clownish persona made him embarrassed to ask questions or express any interest. He'd follow me to my office, explain where he was stuck, ask questions and work through his assignment. Upon his return to class he'd remain there for the rest of the day. Principal Burley and I talked about finding an incentive that would motivate Mailk to improve his attitude towards school, his behavior and overall grades. Mailk was usually on the football field, playing two hand touch, a game that I refereed regularly during recess. "Hey Mailk, what's your favorite restaurant?" I asked heading back in the building. "Culvers" he said with a smile. "Never heard of it, what kind of food is it?" I asked.

Mailk laughed, tapping his friend Sean, "Mr. Coakley don't know what Culvers is." he giggled. "They got the best burgers, shakes and fries around, it's right down the street," he said.

I checked the place out, returning to school the next day ready to make a deal. Principal Burley and I called Mailk to the office. "What's up?" I asked when he appeared at the door. "Am I in trouble?" he asked. "Have a seat…Mr. Coakley tells me that you like Culvers" said Principal Burley, "he also tells me that you're a good student with a lot of potential." He looked at me and smiled, while I sat silently. "So here's the deal, if you have two weeks of good behavior, no removals from class, disruptions or missing assignments Mr. Coakley will take you to Culvers during the lunch block, you can get whatever you want," said Mrs. Burley. "For real, bet!" said Mailk quickly. "Two weeks, you can check-in with me before school, during lunch or after school, just not during class" I said. "What about Mrs. Watkins?" asked Mailk. "She knows all about it, she's on board" said Mrs. Burley.

Mailk found me every morning before school to make small talk, nothing significant. Before he headed to class I'd always say "have a good day." We'd catch each other on the football field during recess, or at the end of the day. The day's end was nothing more than "the nod" or fist bump, a quick acknowledgement that meant I see you, before he headed home. For Mailk, the check-in and short-term incentive worked for the most part. I'd treat him to lunch at Culver at least once a month. He was in his element, cracking jokes, enjoyed his deluxe burger basket and strawberry shake, the Mailk special. As the year progressed Malik's discipline referral diminished and walkie-talkie calls to Mrs. Watkins' class were greatly reduced.

The majority of my time was spent downstairs, checking in on kids in the "B.D." rooms. Which has to be one of the worst terms a school can use to describe a class of children. "Those kids have behavior disorders," a girl whispered to a friend, skipping quickly passed the doors to lunch, peering in swiftly as though the room contained Hannibal Lecter. The way I saw it, the rooms weren't filled with "naughty kids" as the office secretaries described, but kids dealing with a lot of scary issues.

Students living in circumstances indescribable, enduring unspeakable things, things they pushed down deep in their subconscious and harbored below the surface. Issues seeded so deep that an educator would only know and possibly intervene with by building a trusting relationship with the student over time. The two classrooms were created to house the elementary kids of Champaign who had seen the most trauma, poverty, mental, physical and verbal abuse.

As I worked through situations and conversations with the students in our downstairs classrooms, I got to know them as individuals. They were kids who depended on the school's breakfast and lunch to survive, reliant on medications to function. They often showed up with bruises, bite marks, cuts, and burns. But most of all, they were kids. They enjoyed books, movies, sports, drawing, playing and listening to music. They smiled at positive affirmations from their parents, teachers and administrators. They knew about their "B.D." placement, and longed to go back upstairs.

The downstairs classrooms had a spattering of traumatic events. One day I had to snatch a pair of eight inch scissors away from a student that was threatening to harm his teacher. In responding to the call, I sprinted to the classroom, his classmates were all cowering in a corner behind their teacher. The teacher held her hands out in front of her pleading with the student to put down the scissors. It was a student I knew quite well, and checked-in with regularly - Trevor. "Hey, I know you're upset, but I need you to put down the scissors or I'll have to take them from you" I said in a calm voice. Trevor yelled… "I'd like to see you tr.." but before he could finish, I lunged to the side, quickly yanking the scissors from his hand by grabbing his shoulder with my left palm, then pulling the shears away with my right. He screamed, which was followed by a barrage of cussing, throwing, spitting and lunging. I restrained Trevor while his peers and teacher evacuated the classroom. Although trained to do so, the worst part of my job was retaining students, but those situations were few and far between.

My day began with greeting students as they came off the bus, looking for the high flyers, kids who were often referred to me for behavior, making sure they had breakfast. If they hadn't eaten, we'd head to the cafeteria so they could eat. The majority of those same students also took prescription medication, Ritalin, Adderall or Concerta - medications used to treat attention deficit hyperactivity disorder, known as ADHD. Ritalin takes effect in one's system rather quickly, research shows it may have harsh side effects like stomach pain, lack of appetite and insomnia. Adderall and Concerta take more time to take effect, but they stay in the system longer, with even harsher side effects, nausea, vomiting, dizziness, headache, diarrhea, fever, dry mouth, weight loss and trouble sleeping. As an educator from Oregon, I was unfamiliar with serving a population of students on meds, a duty held by our School Nurses. In Champaign it was the norm, School Nurses weren't provided to elementary schools. The percentage of students taking medications to control behavior seems rampant. I was frustrated with educator's over identifying students for special education, and medical professionals freely wielding their ability to prescribe what they believed to be the answer, parents helplessly searching for a quick fix, the dreadful combination of all of these factors. The plan was for students to take their meds at home before school. However, that wasn't always the case, so our office had backups of each child's prescription in case they forgot to administer it at home.

On morning duty, I observed students exiting the buses, kids like Matt, Izzy and Josiah would sprint to me, some days their eyes were wilder than other days. "I need my medication" or "my mom forgot to give me my meds." It was like they were subconsciously crying out, "I want to have a good day at school, but I can't do it without this drug." They'd follow me to the main office. After taking their meds they ate breakfast in the cafeteria. Sometimes I quickly saw a shift, the wildness left Matt and Izzy's eyes before they headed to class. Josiah's medication took more time to take effect. The days he took meds at school were days he ended up hanging in my office until the end of the day.

Principal Burley and I led reading groups during the school's uninterrupted 90-minute literacy block. Every student in the building received 30 minutes of core instruction (on grade level), and an hour of reading intervention (at their actual reading level). My passion for teaching reading continued, this was one of the highpoints of my day. I taught a group of third graders, slightly below grade level. The kids were positive and seemed to look forward to participating in my group. I'd gained the reputation of being nice but also able to switch, snatch scissors, or restrain the toughest kids at Dr. Howard, it made teaching a breeze. On days when I was called by walkie-talkie to respond to an issue during the literacy block, my group was covered by Mr. Johnson, a hilarious Educational Assistant (EA) who took a liking to me being the only Black male in an administrator role that he'd ever worked with directly. My first week on the job he stopped by my office. "Hezekiah Johnson" he said with a smile, then continued "you from Portland? How do you know the Burleys? What made you want to move here?" He had bulbous eyes that protruded at the end of each sentence he spoke. After the friendly interrogation, we were fast friends. "Hey Mr. Coakley, you're needed downstairs, don't worry. I got your reading group covered" he said with a silly grin. "Thanks" I said as I headed for the stairs.

One day I was stuck in my office interviewing students who rarely ever had a problem, but that particular day, they got into a scuffle. They sat separated in my office while I tried getting to the bottom of the issue. Mr. Johnson half knocked on the door before entering, "Mr. Coakley, I think I got something you're gonna enjoy" he said with a laugh. "Since you stuck up in here with these knuckleheads I brought you some lunch from the chicken shack! Gizzards with the fries and hot sauce." "Good looking out, how much I owe you?" I asked. "Don't worry 'bout it" he said, excitedly exiting the office. I'd never eaten gizzard before, or tasted many that I liked after that, but that day they hit the spot. "You just gonna eat that right in front of us? That's cold" one student mumbled. "It's my office" I quipped, "you're lucky he brought me some lunch, I get grouchy when I don't eat. While I eat, you two read, grab a book, you had lunch" I replied.

Each day from 10:45am to 1:15pm, I hovered around the cafeteria and playground supervising interactions while talking with students. Dr. Howard's master schedule was a tightly run operation, three lunches and recess breaks happened during this whirlwind window of time. Lunch began with kindergarten, first and second graders in the cafeteria, while grades three and four were outside on the playground. Every EA was on duty, stationed inside or out, while teachers had their 30 minute duty free lunch. I crafted a duty schedule that rotated by month, each EA worked at every station throughout the year to make things fair. I was a floater, not assigned to a station. I was the person called to respond to issues while Principal Burley supervised the cafeteria. Principal Burley kept the lunch line swift and orderly, keeping noise to a dull roar before dismissing anyone to the playground. "These tables should be spick and span for the next group of students" she'd announce. The downstairs "B.D." classrooms went through the lunch line right before the K-2 kids rotated outside. Our downstairs kiddos ate in their classrooms and took a recess break on a different side of the school during the 3 - 4 lunch. The playground they used was fenced in with two tetherball stations and space to play wall ball. They stayed with the EAs assigned to their classrooms. The first two lunches always ran pretty smoothly, conflicts were rare, even the most reserved student enjoyed being outside play-ing freeze tag, shooting baskets, talking to staff or just walking around bundled in the cold brisk Illinois air.

The fourth and fifth graders required a higher level of supervision, their time was scheduled without other grades overlapping. There was twice the amount of staff during lunch supervision. Principal Burley and I hovered over the cafeteria tables like hawks, talking with students, expe-diting the pace of the lunch line while the EA's were stationed in specified locations of the cafeteria assisting with students that had specific needs. The lunch procedures were tight, consistent and orderly. The students understood the routine and got the hang of following it quickly. They supported one another in cleaning tables, exhibiting the behaviors that got them excused from the cafeteria and out to the playground early. Mrs. Burley was a stellar example of active supervision and a model for holding high expectations. She spent her time engaging with students while monitoring the playground and cafeteria as she paced though high traffic areas, using her proximity to kids as a natural de-escalation tool. She also spent time building relationships with some of our toughest girls by joining them for double-dutch. They were surprised at her ability to jump rope even in a business suit and flat heeled dress shoes. The girls would laugh, smile, enjoying their time getting to know her. She carried herself as a role model, it was evident that she was a leader our students looked up to.

I spent the recess time weaving in and out of the football field refereeing the game, intervening in arguments, supervising all areas of the playground in proximity to the field. That's where our toughest boys burned off steam every lunch period. Some of them would say "Mr. Coakley are you reffing today? If not, I'm not playing, too much cheating." The game usually began with me picking two team captains. Usually it was two of the most talented players to ensure they weren't on the same team, but every now and then I'd switch it up, to allow everyone the opportunity to be captain. Teams were created from there. One day, Mattie, a goofy kid from "the gifted" program who was one of the only African-American students on the third floor, rushed on the field with the worst idea I had ever heard. "Instead of picking teams let's play gifted vs. non-gifted" he blurted, touching his chest as he emphasized the word "gifted." "Hey, we're not doing that! Besides, those words are reversed out here on the field, you kids from upstairs would get completely blown out" I snapped with a serious look of annoyance. Everyone in earshot cracked up at the comment. "I will allow Mattie and Quayshaun to be today's team captains, now let's even up these teams" watching to ensure the lineups were not created solely on the segregation of our school's physical structure.

Besides our usual Friday evening get together at Lil Porky's BBQ, (which only served beef ribs on Fridays) or the occasional happy hour, Rory, LV and I were buried deep in finding our way as school administrators. There wasn't much do in Champaign, it was one of those cities that kind of closed up shop around 8pm.

This led to road tripping to Indianapolis to visit my boy, Dante. He was a young principal who I met a few years prior at the National Alliance of Black School Educators (NABSE) conference when it was held in Atlanta. We stayed in contact over the years, so when I moved to

Champaign, he helped me escape the boredom of the weekends. Every now and then LV would join me on the excursion. In November the NABSE conference was being held in Detroit, I couldn't wait. I drove down to Indianapolis to crash on Dante's couch the night before. The next morning, I hit the road with Dante's crew. "Check this out" he said, putting our destination in the newly released Global Positioning System, aka (GPS). "This thing talks to you!" Dante said ecstatic.

"In less than 200 feet, make a sharp right turn on MLK boulevard" said the robotic female voice. "Yo, this thing's fire!" Dante exclaimed, throwing his hands in the air. I had to admit, it was amazing, revolutionary, like nothing we'd ever seen before. "That's crazy" I muttered, monitoring the estimated arrival time.

The conference was not only a learning experience, it provided a broader snapshot of Black Educators from all walks of life. There were teachers, counselors, principals, superintendents, authors, professors and researchers in the education space from every state and district you could imagine. The keynote speaker that year was Asa Hilliard, a college professor and educational researcher who compiled the _African-American Baseline Essays_, a series of educational materials adopted by Portland Public Schools in 1987 with the hope of providing content that could be taught in school on the history, culture and contributions of African-Americans. "Dr. Hilliard, I want to say hello, I think you know my father, Paul Coakley" I said after his presentation. "Man, you look just like your Daddy, that's my boy!" he laughed. Then we chatted for a few minutes, "make sure to tell your Dad I said hello" he said headed to the next workshop.

When attending a conference in a state with relatives, visiting them is an automatic expectation. In addition, they usually don't come to your location, you're expected to come to them, which limits the possibility of actually seeing them. I was glad that wasn't the case for my Uncle James. Through the time in our lifespan that overlapped, we didn't have many face-to-face interactions, maybe 5 or 6 that I can recall. We stayed in contact through phone conversations, stories told by family members, holiday photos and greeting cards. So, when I got a missed call on my cell and heard "Hey PJ, this is your Uncle James, give me a call, let me know what hotel you're at and I'll come by and pick you up" I called back immediately. Breaking free from the conference to hang out with the Uncle I hadn't seen since a family reunion my parents hosted in Portland my freshman year in college. He pulled up in front of the downtown Marriott at the Renaissance Center in a black Lincoln town car. Detroit is known as the Motor City, home of Ford and General Motors. Several of my relatives work for Ford, or at some point worked for Ford, my uncle's always been a loyal consumer of American made cars. He joked that my parents became traitors when they purchased their Honda Accords. Detroit was also known as the murder capital of the world, the newly renovated downtown had art exhibits, upscale restaurants and swanky hotels. It also has streets, markets and city dwellers one should avoid at all cost, places were lives are lost over side glances, mumbled words, and miniscule amounts of money.

"Hey nephew, check you out" he said giving me a hug under the Marriott awning "hop in" he motioned as he slunk his long torso into the car. Uncle James Nibblet was my only uncle with some height, he stood about 6'2", he and my father had different dads so the hope of me gleaning any of his height as a kid was immediately dashed. While my Uncle was known for staying fresh in his collection of suits, today he wore black dress shoes, black slacks, a tan mock neck sweater encased by a warm looking blackish gray wool car coat. "Tuck that Milky Way under the seat, diabetes…it's a real bitch" he chuckled. I stashed the candy bar laying on the passenger seat underneath without question. "Let's head on over to the MGM, you haven't eaten yet have you?"

We pulled into the large parking garage of the MGM Grand Detroit Casino, stepping out of the car Uncle James was quickly greeted with "Whacha' say Nibblet?" from the parking attendant. He waved and pointed at him, "They know me up in here" he mumbled to me … "excuse the place, this remodel makes it look like a crapper, but they have a decent buffet" Uncle James said as he looked around the parking lot. "A lot of shoot-outs happen in this parking lot, they scope you out, and soon as you hit for some real money, they follow you out here and rob your ass. That's one of the reasons I keep a concealed burner on me" he said calmly. "Really? What's the other reason?" I was intrigued. "My job," he replied.

We made our way past the craps tables and loud one armed bandits chiming, ringing and bonking before we grabbed a table in the buffet area that overlooked the casino floor. "The other good thing about this place is that it's the last place on earth that a guy can smoke a square. You mind?" he asked me while tapping his box of Newport cigarettes on the table. I shook my head no, as he pulled a menthol from the pack, reached across the table for the ashtray and fired up the stick. He took a long serious drag that shriveled his cig to fifty percent, then exhaled hard, blowing a hefty cloud over the perimeter of our table. "My job" ...he said, picking up where he left off, "Teamsters union, they call me in to negotiate the large government contracts, I represent the people" he said proudly blowing another cloud into the atmosphere... "sometimes the conversations get so heated we lay our guns out on the table!" I chuckled, "yeah right." "No joke, once I left'em with a contract so bad them dudes followed me out to the car! I backed out of the building grippin' the steel in my jacket - like this" he said reenacting the story through hand movements, "never took my eyes off 'em, I thought I heard shots. When I got home I found two bullet holes. One in my bumper, the other had shot out my tail light." "Damn, that's crazy" I said while reflecting on the story. "Yeah man...I left them with what card players call, a *bad beat.* Listen nephew, you're new to administration so you probably haven't got into much contract negotiations, but when you do, stand firm for the group you represent, go in knowing your non-negotiable, what's the baseline expectation for everyone to do a good job. Like I said, I represent the people, the everyday workers. Now, you," he said with a serious stare... "you represent the children... sure, you care about your staff and want things to be a win-win as much as possible, but you always operate in the best interest of the kids, anything less than that just won't cut it! You keep that in mind and you'll be ok" he said with a smile, then he gave me a fist bump from across the table.

We finished our meals chatting about sports, cars, relationships, and of course relatives, some who were heading off to college, a few heading to prison, but through conversation I recognized our bond, an innate close connection, no matter how much time had passed since we'd last spoke. Before driving me back to the conference he gave me a historic tour of Detroit, "there's my office" he pointed out, "this area we are about to go through is the city's historic district. This street here was the hub, your grandfather had a barbershop in the bottom of that building to your left. We lived in that tiny space above it" he said pointing out the building, as he went on, "he was a tough little ol' dude, your grandfather, didn't care much about nobody but Paul, was hard on the rest of us, but we weren't his kids."

I looked around at the abandoned buildings, ruined by dilapidation, crumbled brick, busted windows, overgrown laws and mossy stairwells. I tried to overlook the zombie-like figures that scurried in and out of the shadows glancing swiftly at slow driving cars in search of their next fix. I briefly pictured a time when the area was full of thriving Black owned business, pride, clean, crisp, while sharply dressed men and women walked around shopping in the hustle and bustle, Paul's barbershop full of joy and laughter, smiles and hairstyles. "This place ain't nothing now…I call it crack alley" said Uncle James, bringing me back to reality. "But Detroit is making a comeback, renovations are happening in the downtown area as you see, same thing on the south side, in Royal Oak and Southfield, eventually everything will be rejuvenated, of course many Black families will lose their homes to gentrification, not me. Never give up your land Nephew, unless you're strategically doing so to gain more property."

That was the last time I saw my Uncle James in the flesh, of course we still stayed in contact through phone conversations, updates by family members, as well as greeting cards and the occasional holiday photos before he passed a few years later. Although I can count my personal interactions with my father's older brother on one hand, he somehow left a lasting impact on my ability to navigate spaces both personally and professionally. He was an original, classic, one of a kind, a Black man comfortable in his own skin, able to navigate any space regardless of race, economic status or social class. I never knew of a time that he wasn't himself – flowers to the one and only James Nibblet, made in Detroit.

In Champaign, the winter months were extremely cold. While I've always been one that enjoys the possibility of December and January turning the landscape into a winter wonderland, after selling my house which proved to be quite a stressful task from out of state, I quickly purchased two plane tickets. I was going back home to visit my parents for both Thanksgiving and Christmas break. In my experience, the west coast's lightest smattering of snow on the ground almost always results in school closures. Oregonians aren't use to driving in the snow, even though it usually snows once a year, the city is unprepared to deal with clearing icy roads, fathers unfamiliar with chaining up tires, school districts tend to close their doors allowing their students to enjoy a day of snowball fights, making snow angels by flapping their arms and feet vertically and horizontally, some siblings even have the fortitude to build the occasional snowman and spend the next few days watching it melt away.

In early December after a relaxing and enjoyable Thanksgiving visit to Portland, I awoke to Illinois frosty winter wonderland. Pulled a knit beanie down over my ears, tossed on my heather gray champion hoodie and fuzzy slippers, then stepped outside my balcony overlooking downtown Urbana. Nothing but snow as far and the eye could see. I took a deep breath, exhaled, watching the fleeting midst of my breath form in the extremely cold air. Quickly stepping back inside my apartment, I closed the sliding door. It was 6:15 am, I called LV… "What's up Bro, are we closed today? There's like 12 inches of snow outside?" "Hell nah', they don't do that out here, the main roads are already plowed, they've been clearing them all morning. I'm just going to take my time getting to work" he replied. "That's crazy, well then I better get movin', later LV."

The apartment parking lot didn't have a carport, so I spent 15 minutes scraping my window, while warming up the Lexus GS 300. It cost me a thousand bucks flat to have it shipped to Illinois, the jet black beauty was still in pristine condition and was an attention getter in the streets of Champaign-Urbana. Its tires trudged through the parking lot snow, the main roads seemed clear, but side streets and parking lots held heavy accumulation. I followed the tire tracks of previous vehicles to navigate my way out of my lot and made a left on University Avenue. I clenched the steering wheel, picking up speed as Das EFX album Straight Up Sewaside played softly through the speakers. Cars traveled at approximately 40 miles per hour. About ten miles per hour slower than usual on the freshly plowed highway. I felt the Lexus lose traction, sliding straight forward, braking and steering were quickly out of my control. I tried turning the wheel and pumping the foot pedals. Glancing to the left in slow motion, I honked my horn to alert other drivers. I was sliding from the far right lane to the left at high speed. Just missing a collision with two vehicles in lane position, the GS continued to slide all the way across the highway, over the median and into oncoming traffic. Finally halted by a high curb that bent my tire into oblivion, angling me into oncoming traffic, I was facing a large truck moving at full speed about thirty feet away. I pounded the steering wheel, blasting the horn, until I felt the truck's hood pummel into the front of my Lexus. I recall the deafening crash, the sounds of screeching metal simultaneously paired with broken glass, my ears rang as my body slammed into a deployed airbag, then things went dark.

I woke stiff, sore and bruised, bandaged around the left knee and right hand. Blinking hard to gain focus, glancing around the room using the left handrail to scoot up, awkwardly positioning on the rolling bed. Carle Hospital, the room was small, cold and dry with eggshell white and cyan hues, light blue divider curtains that encased beeping monitors, screens, tubes and machines. In the visitor's chair sat the Assistant Superintendent, Ecomet Burley. He glanced at me quietly with tears in his eyes, "I'm sorry man, we should have closed school, you Portland fellas don't know how to drive" he said softly. I giggled a bit but was stopped short by the pain.

"You're lucky to be alive" said the doctor as he entered the room. "Where's my car?" I asked. He answered frankly, "Gone, totaled. They had to use the jaws of life to pry you out of there. A police officer is here, he'll give you information about where your vehicle was towed. When you're feeling up to it, you can go out there and get your personal items." I gave a nod of understanding.

Shortly after, a police officer came to my bedside, "No need to sit up, glad you're doing better. How did you end up on the other side of the median?" he asked. "Black ice" I replied. "Yeah, well it sucks for me to do this, but Illinois uses an *at fault* system for handling car accidents which means I am giving you a ticket for reckless driving. You'll have to dispute it in court. The judge can reverse or lessen the charge. Also, the address on this business card is where you'll find your car" he placed both documents on my chest and left the room. I laid in silence feeling defeated, no car, no nearby relatives, reeling from the shock of the accident, I clinched the ticket in my fist, "typical" I thought.

CHAPTER 6
Shifting Priorities

It's interesting how life works. One moment we're heading in a specific direction, the next, a life altering experience can shift our priorities. Through reflection we sometimes realize that our current situation is blocking us from the things in life that we value the most.

The collision left me in a state of steady contemplation, hyper focus on the fact that I had a system of support and life-long connections in Oregon. If the car accident would've ended me, the impact would reverberate in Oregon, across a few pockets of Michigan and Tennessee, but in Illinois it would've been nothing more than a local news blurb. A day where Dr. Howard students and staff could visit a counselor, sharing a memory of a time I helped them complete an assignment or work through an issue. The brutal reality was that I needed to go home. The doctor was right, I was lucky to be alive. Evidenced by my visit to the scrap yard to gather possessions out of the mangled metal mess that once was referred to as the Lex Bubble. Inside, foam and paneling hung in the balance as the front of the car was pushed so far in, that engine parts and dashboard knobs were touching the front seats, making it impossible to do anything but reach in through the destroyed driver side door. I managed to retrieve a wave brush, a black compact disk holder containing twelve CDs. The music I was listening to at the time was trapped in the pinned shut trunk of the vehicle's six disc changer, along with my NY Yankee's hat and leather briefcase. After yanking on the trunk and trying to get the items by prying open the back seats to no avail, they were surrendered to the scrap yard. The used eggshell white Jeep Cherokee that I purchased with the cash from the insurance company left much to be desired.

In February, Dad called at 5am, "hey dude, I'm downstairs, your Mom's upstairs asleep." Of course she was, it was 3am in Portland, which was even early for Dad, who was an avid 5am riser. "Hey Dad, why you up so early?" I asked. "I went to the doctor a few days ago, because of chest pain. I was getting winded going up the stairs, so I got it checked out. He called me yesterday evening and told me I have a blockage, I need open heart surgery."

"What, when!" I asked "why did they send you home?"

"It's going to be ok" he said quietly "I talked to B, they have to schedule it… they told me to just take it easy - eat light. You know, this is your brother's specialty, he knows the best heart surgeons here and in New York. I have options. I can do the surgery at OHSU, or fly to NY and do it with B's team…he's going to make sure it's a bypass surgery, not a stent, he says there's not much research on stents, they eventually collapse causing issues in the long run. A bypass surgery is like getting a rebuilt engine. Once it's over with, it could add years to my life. I plan on being around for a while. Live to see some grandkids" he chuckled. My dad - the only man I know who can find the positive, while staring death in the face - in the form of open heart surgery.

Open heart surgery or stent? A stent is a scaffold used to open the blocked blood vessels that are limiting the amount of oxygen flowing to the heart. Research says the surgery is less time consuming, plus the patient is less likely to trigger a stroke during the procedure. However, over a span of time after surgery patients with stents have a larger probability of having a heart attack.

Bypass surgery takes a healthy blood vessel somewhere in the body, grafting it above and below the blockage which allows blood to flow through the newly grafted pathway to the heart. In most cases the surgery requires a large incision in the chest which temporarily stops the heart. The doctor cuts the patient's chest breast bone (sternum) in half spreading it apart. Bypass machines are used to pump blood to the heart while the heart is stopped.

From a less researched perspective, word on the street, especially amongst my relatives, was that a stent will take you out! We'd lost relatives, friends, colleagues, church members, neighbors and acquaintances. I'd heard plenty horror stories of Black folks passing far too young after implanting a stent. While opening one's chest seems unnerving, based on B's recommendation and believing his own eyes, Dad's mind was made up. Dad did his quote-unquote "research"... "hey P, they can crack my chest wide open! Let's do this thing right, I want the bypass, fuse me together. I don't want no stent...you remember Carlos, he was fifty something' - got a stent...that thang didn't last no time, he was gone like that" he said snapping his fingers, I could hear the loud snap echo in the phone's receiver. "That's also how we lost my dear brother James, God rest his soul, his stent just snapped, if I'm gonna do this thing I'm gonna do it right" he said emphatically.

Text messages and calls set our phones a blaze, a triad of messages between Mom, B and I trying to keep up-to-date on Dad's condition and the scheduling of his surgery. Check-ins became more frequent, "How's my favorite Vice-Principal in the whole wide world?" he'd ask when I answered the phone. "I'm good, how are you? Did you decide if you're flying to New York for surgery?" I asked. "I decided to stay here and get it done at OHSU. I don't want to do all that traveling, that's too stressful. Brian has a copy of my medical records, he spoke to my doctor several times, he says I'm in good hands. He's even trying to come here during the surgery, I'm good with that. I can relax here at home the night before and prepare. They gave me a list of instructions to follow the night before, I plan to do everything exactly as instructed."

Dad's surgery was scheduled for the second week of March, which overlapped with my Spring break. I requested a few additional days off to make it work. Mrs. Burley was in support, approving my request to be with Dad in his time of need. She and her husband called him, sent flowers and a card of encouragement to our family.

Mom, B and I sat quietly in the waiting room's olive, turquoise and orange chairs sipping on Starbucks in quiet reflection. Occasionally, I wandered to the large fish tank, peered through the glass for a change of scenery. I caught myself pacing back and forth a few times, nervously biting my nails to the nubs, my mind ran wild with worry. Brian sat reading, giving us the occasional update, calming us in a doctor type of way. Brian knew OHSU's doctors, they gave him frequent updates on Dad. After a lot of doctor speak, B eventually relieved our worries by letting us know the surgery was successful. Three to five days was the expected hospital recovery time before Dad could go home, followed by eight weeks of home recovery to allow his chest to fully heal.

For five days Brian and I alternated nights staying in the recovery room, sleeping in a small window seat cushioned bed, about half the width of a single bed. Mom stayed by Dad's bedside every waking moment in an uncomfortable looking chair with reclining legs. The farthest that Mom would travel was down to the hospital's cafeteria, which became our dining option for the week. It was tough watching Dad lay there hooked to monitors, IVs and contraptions protruding underneath his freshly bandaged chest, which had been joined back together with hooks slightly below the skin. He could hold light conversations, he'd sit up to watch TV. Visitors poured into the hospital in droves with cards, and colorful bouquets, wishing him a speedy recovery. So many neighbors, friends and colleagues, I felt like a bouncer working security at a nightclub, standing in the visiting room lobby. No more than four guests were allowed in the tiny room at a time. I'd escort one group out and usher another in. Brian became frustrated by all of the commotion, "I'll be glad when visiting hours are over, let Dad get some rest" he protested.

I arrived to the hospital early on day three to relieve Brian from the hospital cot, when I entered through the double metal doors of the intensive care unit, I spotted Dad walking slowly down the long hallway with his right hand on a mobile monitor on wheels, using some assistance from the Physical Therapist on his left. "Hey P" he said in a scratchy voice "I either move it or lose it" he said seriously. I smiled "ok, just don't push yourself too fast" I replied. Over the next 72 hours he'd make significant progress. His appetite increased a bit, he was able to get himself out of the bed to move around the room. He even managed to walk down the hallway and back at a respectable pace. On day six he was released back to his domain, his normal surroundings, a successful surgery was behind him. He was determined to cut out junk foods and maintain a healthy lifestyle. "God gave me a wake-up call," he said. He was in good hands, we knew Mom would make him drink water, take his medication, and eat the food his doctor suggested. B gave his additional instructions before getting back to the patients of Mt. Sinai. It was also time for me to return to the students of Dr. Howard. Leaving Dad in his weakened condition was difficult, but I made a commitment and had to see it through, at least for the remainder of the school year.

In a short period of time, strong relationships were built at Dr. Howard, it was my home away from home. I returned to smiles, cards, notes from students saying "I hope your father gets well", and "we miss you." Upon returning, I planned on giving my best to the school community, 100% of myself every day. I fell back in the groove, Principal Burley and I were in sync, running reading groups, supervising on opposite sides of the playground, rotating by keeping an eye on each other's movements. I responded to walkie-talkie calls, swiftly moving between all three floors of the tall brick building, it was my domain, supervising arrival, dismissal and cafeteria duties. We ran the day-to-day operations like a well-oiled machine. Disseminating meds to students, prescribed to take them at school upon arrival. Taking Josiah to grab breakfast "even if you ate at home, it's a long time until lunch so let's see what they got" I said. He began eating breakfast on a regular basis in combination with taking his meds. Mailk also found his groove, he seemed happier, rarely called out of class. He'd find me every day before school and during his lunch/recess to crack jokes. "Mr. Coakley, my grades are on point, you probably own me about 20 burgers by now" he smiled. That Friday I took him back to Culvers, he had grown in maturity and height. He was a big kid, about 5'10" and 250lbs. "You'll be heading to middle school soon, then high school, which one will you go to? I asked. "Central" he responded. "Nice I'll connect you with the new Vice Principal, he's a friend of mine. "Tight," Mailk said smiling. LV had made the move from elementary to high school mid-year, the opportunity presented itself, "why not gain some secondary experience" LV said. Rory switched districts, taking a job as a Middle School Assistant Principal in Rantoul, a neighboring district near Champaign after making some community connections. He made the transition while keeping positive relationships with the leaders in Champaign.

I kept a close eye on job postings in Oregon, hoping to land a job with a July 1 start date. I planned to move back home at the end of the school year. Just a year prior, I was elated to leave Portland, but the car accident, Dad's recovery and a long distance relationship was collectively calling me home. Not only is Beaverton, Oregon the world headquarters for Nike, it was also the third largest school district in Oregon, serving approximately 40 thousand students. My old stomping ground, where I'd burn the midnight oil. Beaverton opened a vice-principal "pool" posted on their website, with a plan to hire several administrators. While I was skeptical about the "pool" scenario, I submitted my materials by email and hoped for the best. I talked with Principal Burley about my plan, she was supportive, "it's been a tough year with the car accident and your father's surgery, you're doing such a good job, but I understand." Her and her husband were from Texas, all their family still lived there, they'd moved to Champaign because Ecomet landed the Assistant Superintendent position. "We aren't going to be here forever either, eventually we'll go back to Texas, I'll write you a letter of reference" she said with a sigh.

The weather in April shifted from the extremely cold temperatures, to the mid-seventies. On the west coast the mid-seventies is quite peaceful, but in Illinois it felt like the mid-eighties due to the humidity. It hangs heavily in the balance, leaning on your shoulder until beads of sweat begin to accumulate on your forehead. Especially if you worked at the top floor of a three story brick building constructed in 1910, making multiple trips up and down the stairs. Nonetheless I'd given my word to Principal Burley that I would conduct the full teacher evaluation process on five probationary educators all in their first three years of teaching. I actually looked forward to providing fellow educators with helpful feedback, supportive suggestions to strengthen their practices, ultimately benefiting student learning. While from a research standpoint I had taken the Supervision & Evaluation courses for administrators, was well versed in the current literature, such as City's Instructional Rounds in Education, Danielson's Framework for Teaching and Evaluating - a multi-tiered rubric that breaks down teaching and evaluation into four key domains: *Planning and Preparation, The Classroom Environment, Instruction and Professional Responsibilities.* Danielson's rubric was adopted as the tool used in PPS, and Champaign. As a classroom teacher, I used it to reflect on my own lesson plans and teaching practices. I'd also coached colleagues on how to use the rubric to guide their instruction.

However, actually entering a classroom as one's supervisor, having a pre-conversation about their plans, observing their lesson, then facilitating a coaching conversation about its effectiveness was new territory for me. Not for lack of interest, fear or initiative, it was a door that was closed, locked and forbidden for a leader who looked like me to open. Experience observing teachers was something the HR Department in PPS in particular held onto with a tight grip. They dangled it over their aspiring leaders like a doggy treat before throwing it way out of reach. "You need to gain some experience evaluation teachers" was uttered over and over again by HR administrators with no suggestions, opportunities or scaffolding to gain that experience they spoke of without holding an administrator position. It was a tactic used to weed out candidates for leadership positions. Candidates they thought were too young, too old, candidates of color, candidates that fell outside what was deemed normal, candidates they felt should remain in the classroom for whatever reason, Black male candidates like me, LV and Rory.

Shortly after Principal Burley hired me, she handed me "the key." It came in the form of a piece of paper containing the staff roster. She had scrawled "Coakley" at the top, fluorescent orange highlighter indicated the teachers I was responsible for evaluating. "Your five teachers are highlighted here, this takes a huge weight off of me. Last year I evaluated the entire staff by myself," she said. "Thank you, I can do more if you want" I beamed. "No, those probationary teachers require several formal and informal class visits, so this is great" with that, she smiled, disappearing down the narrow hallway. That paper represented the opening of a door that was barred shut. A stumbling block removed, crushing excuses that hovered over me like invisible hands pinning down my shoulders. My goals in plain sight, but unable to reach because my arms had been stuck. Principal Burley released my arms through a one minute conversation, empowering a young Black man with an administrator's license so new that the ink printed on my certificate was hardly dry. Invisible shackles - removed, I was free.

I outlined my plan for success, met with each teacher one-on-one early, completed goals conferences, we met regularly, building trusting relationship having real conversations about teaching, learning and classroom management. By April, they were used to me being in their classrooms, it was the norm. Four mini observations were required - when an administrator randomly visits for about 15 minutes or less, looking for specifics highlighted in the rubric, then they document the unscheduled observation. Written feedback can be overwhelming, I find it's best to focus on the teacher's effectiveness of applying one specific skill.

Sometimes it is helpful to focus your attention on the planning of the lesson, the educator's confidence, skills and knowledge of the content or subject matter. Depending on the teacher's level of experience, many times the engagement of the lesson is the focus area. It's helpful to observe the students' then provide the teacher with information on the class's participation after instruction. You can also assess student work, whether or not they were able to apply the skill that was taught. The observer may drop in at an awkward moment - the teacher eating a snack while students are working independently, or a moment where younger kids are transitioning from their desk to the carpet, or the class is listening to a read-aloud. It's also likely that the teacher is dealing with a specific student's behavior. It's important to understand that these are not wasted moments, they're beneficial opportunities to observe the culture of the classroom, gather information about the learning environment, assess the norms that have or have not yet been established. How does the classroom feel? What is displayed on the walls? What are students doing? How does the teacher multitask while responding to their learners?

When observing I start with the positives, documenting what's working well. As a teacher, I found it important to know what worked so I could continue to build on that specific practice. Teachers are the most influential in improving student outcomes and ensuring that kids have a positive school experience, they work with directly with students. Administrators are tasked with providing supportive environments that allows teachers to thrive, so every student has a high-quality experience. Also an important role, but much more indirect in correlation to the student's daily experience. I view myself as a coach, there to listen, support, share strategies, techniques and tools that enhance the culture of their classrooms. It's also important to share an area of growth, a specific strategy that can be improved upon.

All five teachers I was evaluating needed to be "formally" observed three time throughout the year. Formal observations are scheduled, teachers provide lesson plans in advance at a pre-conference where a conversation is held about the lesson and the intended outcome. I decided to observe a teaching technique called "gradual release" for each teacher. Gradual release begins with the teacher modeling a skill, then working through that skill as a whole group until the group has a strong understanding of how it works. Lastly, the students work to apply the skill on their own. Gradual release can be assessed by reviewing students' independent work for accuracy.

I opened the door quietly, then sat in a tall wooden chair near the back of the classroom. Mrs. Riggs, a second-year teacher with a nervous demeanor, took her place at the front of the classroom, she began explaining a method for solving story problems. The students listened attentively, "please pay close attention because you guys will have to complete these on your own soon." She spoke enthusiastically, clear and concise. Her pace was perfect for explaining the problem step-by-step. Once the problem was solved she said "let's work through a few more together." I sat quietly jotting down notes while students raised their hands excitedly sharing the next step in solving the equation. Mrs. Riggs used open ended questions allowing her students to explain the next step to the class. "What comes next?" she asked, holding out a marker before handing it to a student. The student completed the next step at the whiteboard. The class completed three problems as a group, she checked for understanding. "If you now understand know to solve these types of problems quietly hold up your pencil." Glancing around the room, pencils pointed to the sky with the exception of one student sitting in the front. "Okay, open your math workbooks to page sixty one, complete the first five story problems." Papers rustled, pencils etched, some counted on their fingers, while Mrs. Riggs sat near the struggling student supporting him individually. I moved from my seat and checked in with two students, "how'd you do?" I whispered they showed me their story problems, accurately completed. With that I said "Mrs. Riggs," getting her attention, she looked up I smiled, gave her a thumbs up, then swiftly exited the classroom. She had come a long way this year.

A few days after applying, I received a phone call from Beaverton School District, I was ecstatic. They set up a phone interview for the following week. I made it through that hurdle and got a call to participate in an interview for an AP position at one of their comprehensive high schools. I found it was strange that the pool led me to a high school position. My experience was mostly K-8 focused, nonetheless I was excited for the opportunity, confident that I could do the job. The quick turnaround time yielded a hefty amount for a plane ticket. My excitement took a small dip after hearing "we aren't able to do that" when I asked about flight reimbursement. "No problem, I'll make it work" I swiftly respond.

Suited and booted, I stared at the large modern layout of the comprehensive high school, from the window of my father's new silver Chrysler M300. Dad had picked it up slightly before the heart surgery, although I'd rode in it back then, I barely paid it any attention. This time, I noticed every detail of the pristine vehicle. The new car smell, the light gray leather interior, the wood grain gear shift and steering wheel. The circular clock and speedometers gave the powerfully sleek looking ride a vintage touch of class. Dad had gone all out on the upgrades, opting for the Bentley like grill, 20 inch chrome wheels, and heavily tinted windows. That morning he handed me the keys, "take my new car, it's washed and waxed" he said. "You roll up in there, tell the competition to step off… you're in a 300!" he said in his best Martin Lawrence impersonation.

I sat in the vehicle silently taking in the surroundings. I could feel the affluence of the area, a collegiate aura, an industrial type vibe very similar to Nike's World Headquarters. I arrived about ten minutes ahead of schedule and was greeted at the front doors by the energetic young principal. He shook my hand firmly, smiling widely, "nice to meet you Paul, we have a full day ahead." I followed him through the large hallways, he greeted students as we walked through the building to the main office. I took a seat while he disappeared, he quickly came back with two other AP candidates, a young White male and female, both possibly in their early thirties. The principal was excited to embark on the interview process he crafted with Beaverton's HR staff. "Most districts hold traditional interviews. I became an administrator by just sitting at a table talking with a bunch of people. Not today, we really have a thoughtful process that'll help us get to know each of you." I found the interview process fun and engaging, it began as "breakfast with staff." I sat at a table with a combination of teachers and classified staff answering questions, while taking small bites and tiny sips infrequently before touring the building. There were conversations with student council, board members, then large and small group interviews. The process culminated with a school assembly, each candidate grabbed the microphone, introducing ourselves to the student body. On the way home I tested the sound system in the 300 listening to SiriusXM, hip hop throwback station. I gave Dad his props on his car selection before giving him the lowdown on the interview process. I felt pleased with my overall performance in the process.

In early May I could see light at the end of the tunnel. The 25th was the last day of school before summer. I was used to working until late June before summer break arrived. In the Midwest, school begins in mid-August, the west coast usually begins after Labor Day. I planned to move back home right after the close of the school year, more time to land a job. It was a productive school year, my evaluations were complete, student behaviors were minimal, lunch and recess supervision was on autopilot, attendance was solid, math and literacy scores were trending upward. Principal Burley and I were like Kobe and Shaq in the early 2000s complementing one another's abilities through dynamic court play. All seemed right with the world, until I was walkie talkie to report immediately to Mrs. Watkins 8th grade classroom. I arrived to find Mrs. Watkins and another teacher standing in the hall in front of Malik, slouching with his back against the lockers. The hallway was crowded as students entered the building, opening lockers and entered classrooms to start the day. "What's going on?" I asked tensely. "I was monitoring the hall when I saw this fall out of his backpack" she walked closer to me, handing me a black handgun wrapped in a paper towel. I took the weapon conspicuously, holding it low with two hands concealed in the tissue paper. In uneasy silence I quietly said "let's wait for the bell to ring."

The halls cleared, Principal Burley heels clacked swiftly, cutting the silence as she approached. I lifted my hands slightly opening them, revealing what was inside the paper towel. "I'll take that, you get him" she said sternly. I handed her the pistol then walked over to Mailk who was hanging his head in shame, placing my right arm around his shoulders, we walked toward the office as he cried. Once we settled in the office my anger and frustration put me in a calm but intense state of mind, "talk to me, what's the problem, you trying to shoot up the school?" I asked. "No" he blubbered as tears rolled down his cheeks. "Then, why!?" I snapped. "I have it for protection" he mumbled. "Speak up, Malik, don't give me that protection crap, from who? You're the biggest kid in school" I responded, staring him in the face as he hunched in the seat. "It ain't for here, it's for home, cause my older brothers, I work with them…slangin'…my whole family slang. You know, sellin' dope. This weekend I was on the corner, I forgot the gun was in my backpack" he said, reaching for the tissue box. I pushed the box towards him, he wiped his face. "You got dope in there too?" I asked, he shook his head no, "You sure, you know they're gonna check it." "There ain't none in there" then he pulled his pockets inside out showing that they were empty. I leaned back in my chair, we sat quietly "thanks for telling the truth" I said. We looked through the glass window of the office door, a school resource officer from the high school stood in the main office talking to Principal Burley. "They called the cop Mr. Coakley, what's going to happen?" Malik asked. "I don't know, probably expulsion…it's a gun on school grounds, expulsion is what's stated in the student handbook. I'll tell them you didn't plan to harm anyone... it had to do with life outside of school, but to be real with you, it's out of my control."

Soon I was called in to speak with the officer, "He wasn't planning to harm anyone, the kid's got a rough home life, he said it's for protection over the weekend...forgot it was still in the bag" I said after being questioned. "Well, his family members are known gangsters, they're into everything, I'll take it from here" said the officer.

That was the last time I saw or heard from Malik, regardless of his much-improved behavior, academic growth, and personal growth. No improved data, certificate of achievement, or well-deserved lunch off of school grounds would stop him from being expelled for a year. He wouldn't finish the year with his peers, nor would he attend middle with his friends next fall. The incident changed the course of his K-12 journey. He attended Novak Alternative School after serving his expulsion.

I slowly exited the main office, sitting in silence in the black swivel chair in my office, reflecting. Echoing thoughts...what will Malik be in 5 to 10 years? A prisoner? A statistic? A success story? A dropout? A college student? Where will he be? In a cell? In a casket? In an office? In a classroom? Will he ever live down this mistake? What are his chances? Under what circumstances? Will he push through this obstacle and eventually graduate? I wish I knew how his life turned out, but I don't.

The school to prison pipeline is a vicious cycle that starts with referrals in primary grades, out-of-school suspensions and expulsions in upper grades. Exclusions based on behaviors, mistakes, life-altering choices, district policies and practices. As we dig into the data, school's behavior referrals, suspensions and expulsions records, we find an overrepresentation of Black and Brown children. On the other side of the coin, Black and Brown students are merely a blip on the radar in advanced placement courses, college preparatory classes, talented and gifted programs. A large percentage of students with multiple suspensions never cross a stage to be handed a high school diploma, reducing their chances even further of getting a living wage job. A 2022 report from the Federal Bureau of Prisons identified 38% of US prison inmates are Black and 30% are categorized as Hispanic, another 4% was accounted for by combining the Asian and Native American population. A whopping 72% of inmates in the United States are people of color. The mass incarceration of BIPOC faces being locked behind bars working for pennies on the dollar. The Oregon State Constitution, Article 1, Section 34 clearly stated:

> *There shall be neither slavery, nor involuntary servitude in the State,* **otherwise than as punishment for crime,** *whereof the party shall have been duly convicted.*

This slavery language was not removed from Oregon law until 2022. A similar excerpt exists in the Thirteenth Amendment of the United States Constitution, providing exceptions to the slavery that happens behind the prison walls, merely crossing the minds of those navigating their busy lives outside of those walls.

Could I have done more for Malik? Did I fail him? Was there anything in my scope of influence that could have stopped this situation from happening? After years of reflection I finally came to a resounding "no." As educators, we can positively impact the iceberg, fixing portions of it by providing kids with educational environments that allows them the opportunity to learn, grow, connect, be seen and be heard. Educators worth their salt can get below the surface, through trusting conversations that allow us a deeper glimpse into the lives of the students we serve. Deep conversations reveal the trauma that students face outside school walls. In reality, much of what happens beyond school hours is out of our scope of influence.

Often I think of the iceberg metaphor when exposed to hidden trauma. Picture an iceberg with its peak cresting above the surface of the water. Underneath the surface there is so much more than meets the eye, a huge portion of a glacier's enormous circumference in weight, width, length and mass. Each day students enter school buildings with invisible ordeals. Most days a smile, decent school clothes, or haircuts leave the naked eye no red flags of the turmoil a child may be dealing with. Be that as it may, many kids deal with pain below the surface, the stress and anguish of not knowing where your next meal will come from, or dealing with the shock and torment of living in an abusive environment, the stress of extreme poverty, homelessness, mourning the loss of a loved one, forms of bullying, early exposure to drug use, criminal minded role models, gang culture and unlimited access to television content warping the mind with sexual images, negative influences, stereotypes and violence. Endless issues impact kids in overt and covert ways, as we work to create safe retreats from reality for about eight of the twenty-four hours a day asking children to shed those hurts and engage in learning. I assume that to some extent, Malik was exposed to almost every trauma imaginable - damaged by the cards dealt by life. In the short time I had with him throughout the school year, I had just begun to scratch the surface, exposing a small portion of what made him the hefty, closed off, semi-tough, stereotypically Black eighth grader who looked for me each day, as the staff member more relatable than others he came in contact with. My hope is that I gave him something to think about, something to reflect on, maybe planted a seed of encouragement, confidence or positive motivation. He was an iceberg, engulfed in the vast rapidly paced ocean water. As an educational leader I had no buoy, no life raft, no magic antidote to save him from the mass of issues below the surface. My efforts were more along the lines of a small chisel, gradually chipping away at the water's edge where the glacier met the waterline just before it began to spread in circumference disappearing into the deep.

It was the last day of school at Dr. Howard. My apartment was boxed, office depersonalized and mind full of uncertainties. I entered the cafeteria to engage in my first round of cafeteria duty. Kids ran up to staff asking for hugs, giving out thank you cards while talking about their plans for the summer. We hoped for an uneventful last day with students, the staff knew I was moving back to Portland, but the students were unaware. I talked with as many students as possible, trying to encourage them to read over the summer. A few asked me if I would be working at the July summer school. "Nah, I'll be spending time with family," I replied.

While I'd participated in two rigorous AP interviews in Beaverton, neither of them panned out. I later received a call from their HR department asking why I hadn't applied for a specific elementary principalship that was posted on their website. "It seems like it may be a good fit," said their HR Director. I had looked at the posting over a dozen times and determined it was Beaverton's "Black elementary school." There was an African-American principal who was leaving the position. Despite the "good fit" the money I had spent on travel, combined with the fact they had vetted me twice already, left me feeling tainted toward jumping through any more hoops to possibly become an administrator in Beaverton. While I've never been an advocate for burning bridges, I've also always been known to speak my truth. Even way before it was popular to do so. "I saw the posting but decided not to apply. Some districts like having people of color in the finals of their process, but they never actually hire them. Besides, if I wasn't a "good fit" for your AP jobs, then I assume that a principalship is out of the question" I replied extra snarky. "I'm sorry you feel that way" was the Director's response on the other end of the phone.

I was heading back to Portland with a brushed up resume and cover letter, a year of admin experience under my belt and absolutely no leads on where my career was headed. While I was not looking forward to temporarily moving back into my parents basement, I was glad to be leaving the rough Illinois winter behind. Moreover, the ability to check on my Dad's recovery from the quadruple bypass surgery that left a ruler size scar down the middle of his chest brought me a sense of relief.

I watched the last school bus drive down the road, waving to students, they smiled, waving back from their windows. The hallways were quiet, drab and sullen, staff escorted me into the library for coffee and a corner piece of sheet cake that read "We will miss you Mr. Coakley." It was a nice social event, although a bit sappy. I enjoyed the small talk, we joked about some of the more memorable points of the year. I knew Principal Burley and I would stay in contact, we'd bonded like relatives. There were so many others I enjoyed working with, this moment was the end of the road. Mr. Johnson walked up smiling, "Next year just won't be the same without you. Put down that piece of cake, I got you something I know you're gonna enjoy - from the,...drumroll, chicken shack!" he blurted before handing me a gizzard basket with fries. "I told them to put the extra hot sauce on there, yeah, you like it spicy" he laughed.

CHAPTER 7

My Time at the Beach

Just three and a half weeks until Labor Day, followed by the first day of school for most Oregon districts, my job prospects were null and void. District's surrounding Portland had made me a finalist for their administrator jobs more times than I could count. Portland Public's AP pool had tied an anchor to my application tossing it in the deep end where it lay at the bottom. At this point, Oregon's systematic hierarchy of gatekeeping, surreptitious racism and glass ceilings literally locked me outside its doors. I didn't need to bust the doors down, nor did I expect to be handed a key. I just need someone to look back and prop a door open so I could sneak back in undetected. This slight shift in mindset helped me realize that I may have to temporarily take a step back. Oregon's culture was much different from Illinois, more covertly closed to diversity, built on good ol boy handshakes and old guard conversations. The liberal philosophies, themes of political equality, large scale support for free speech and push for culturally shifting the educator workforce was big talk, little action. Diversifying the workforce is heavily visible in statute and policy with no real intent or accountability for implementation.

My job uncertainty combined with the looming first day of school made me queasy. I called the doctor, not one who diagnoses ailments or prescribes medication. I called Dr. Harriet Adair, not only was she my Dad's buddy, she was an exemplar of Black educational leadership in Oregon. Dr. Adair held every position in PPS's organization from teacher to principal to district office administrator before eventually becoming

120

Assistant Superintendent of Early Learners, Schools and Student Supports. She was given nothing, but accomplished everything, faced every challenge, persevering through racial and institutional barriers put in place to ensure people who look like me don't hold positions of leadership. A system built, where Black and Brown kids rarely see educators that look like them, creating the narrative that we don't belong in these spaces. In reaching the upper echelon of leadership she was boots on the ground, actively fighting against closed door politics. She wasn't scared to prop doors or even push them wide open, finding cracks in the racist infrastructure and exposing those cracks for people of color. Dr. Adair's wit was unmatched, she received her undergraduate degree from my alma mater Portland State, two master's degrees from the University of Oregon, and received her doctorate from Brigham Young. She was the premier Black female leader that people wanted to listen to, hold space with and learn about. To me, she was the lady with the cool house, the loud funny cackling laugh, a close family friend. When I was in elementary school she'd say "PJ show me that new dance the kids are doing" then have me perform in front of my parents' colleagues while they commented on my agility.

So when I rang her line, she picked up, giving me the inside scoop. She informed me of a K-8 school in north Portland that needed a Student Management Specialist, a person to handle discipline and support the principal. While it wasn't an administrator position, it was a way to get me foot back in the door. The process for hiring was more principal dependent than district dependent. I thanked the doctor and told her I was interested, she said "go to Beach School tomorrow and meet the principal, her name is Ms. Fox, I'll let her know you're coming."

Shortly after the call I received a text from the principal, we agreed to meet at 10am. I parked on Humboldt street across from the school, which was constructed of the same classic red brick as most of Portland's schools. The Beach neighborhood was familiar to me because it was not far from Ockley Green. Soon, a car pulled up in the handicapped space closest to the front entrance, a young lady with bright blond hair got out of her car with crutches and a cast on her right foot. She propped herself up by leaning heavily on the side of the car, adjusting the crutches under her arms to hobble into the building. Allowing enough time for her to settle in before I entered the building, I met the secretary. Principal Fox invited me into her office for a conversation. She was young, energetic, easy to talk to, through small talk, I found out she had broken her foot on a ski trip in Colorado, "my boyfriend's a professional skier, me - not so much" she giggled. She asked about my educational background, and my most recent job in Champaign. Principal Fox was bilingual, Beach was a dual immersion school, many students schedules had English taught classes in the morning and Spanish in the afternoon. I'd taken Spanish in high school, hung with several Latinos, but my language retention was nada. However, Ms. Fox let me know that wasn't an issue. "You don't need to know Spanish to do the job, our staff will support you in conversations."

After chatting awhile, I felt good about the possibility of Beach being my new home so to speak. "So, this is amazing, next I'll submit your name to HR, they'll call you with the job offer, also...you have an Oregon administrators license...this year we have about 470ish kiddos, when we reach 500 the district will fund an Assistant Principal position. I'll move you into that position" she said with confidence as she shook my hand. That news filled me with hope, motivation and excitement. "Thank you, please let me know if you run into any issues with HR, they don't like me very much" I replied. "They will call you, it's not up to them, this is my hire" she said.

A week came and went, sitting by the phone on pins and needles, I hadn't heard a peep. Finally, I received a call from Principal Fox. "Have you heard anything yet?...I can't believe they're dragging their feet, school is about to start" she vented. "I also left a message for Harriet letting her know that HR is holding up my hire, let's go people!" she said in a frustrated voice. "Thanks, do you need anything on my end?" I asked, feeling defeated. "No, just sit tight."

48 hours later I received a call from HR and a job offer which I quickly accepted. I spent the next three days at Beach setting up my office, meeting the staff, becoming familiar with the building. The li-

brary, gym and auditorium were located near the office off of the main hallway. The school had K through eighth grade classrooms, middle school students were on the upper floor of the three-story building. Outside of the main building encasing the playground was a large one story annex, with approximately a dozen classrooms, the dual immersion program was located there. My office was on the lower level of the main building, adjacent to the cafeteria, their lunch schedule ran similar to Dr. Howard which worked well for me. I was comfortable supervising recess and lunch back-to-back, and managing those transitions. My office window I had a clear view of the playground, also the annex doors. I was near the stairwell giving me quick access to the main floor and upper hallway. My office resembled an overgrown storage closet recently emptied, I could care less. I didn't plan to spend much time in the office, my goal was to live in the halls and classroom spaces.

Once kids were inhabiting the space, the job was a natural fit. I was as comfortable there as King, Ockley or Dr. Howard. I quickly learned kids names, made connections, especially with the "high flyers," kids who took meds (which was only one or two), regularly checking in with staff to support their needs. Beach was diverse, over twenty different home languages were spoken in the school, the majority of the staff was White. At times I felt like I was filling a stereotype as the "Black discipline guy." "Do you want me to call Mr. Coakley?" a teacher would threaten. Then, here comes the only Black guy on staff ready to scare you straight. I noticed a theme during the district's monthly discipline meetings, more Black male faces, all hired in discipline roles, working in schools with similar demographics as Beach, but this was no time to knit pick, at least I had a job! On Monday mornings five of us met before school as a leadership team. Principal Fox, me, the school counselor, and two of our strongest teachers. I loved our meeting structure, we discussed what was working well and what wasn't, reviewed assessment data, discipline data and planned professional development. We discussed families in need, struggling students, safety concerns, I incorporated several ideas from my time in Champaign into our work, refining and improving protocols and procedures.

We started quarterly middle school dances as an incentive for positive behavior. We hired a local DJ, provided food - usually pizza and soda, plus party favors. Most importantly, we created the hype with our students forming a line outside the gym - to create the anticipation of getting in. "To get in you have to be on the list" I barked. If a student had two or more behavior referrals they couldn't get in. I situated myself like a bouncer, pretending as though I was granting access to a club. The music blared, the line stretched down the hall, wrapping around the corner. Teachers and Educational Assistants stationed in specific areas supervising, all enhancing the anticipation and excitement of our students. You'd think they were entering a Vegas nightclub, or concert. While slightly corny, it worked.

I held daily and weekly check-ins with kids, some of which our staff associated with Latino gang culture, students that Principal Fox quickly connected to me with. Instead of me finding them in the mornings, they found me, followed me around making small talk until the bell rang for school to begin. After a few of them were not admitted to the first dance, they were on their best behavior. They were mostly 7th and 8th grade boys who were girl crazy, similar to me in 8th grade. They saw the dances as their prime opportunity to connect with girls. Juan was a seventh grader with a few younger siblings in our dual immersion program. He was introduced to me by staff my first week on the job as sort of the "Malik" of Beach. I was told his family was "gang related," he received a referral early in the school year for "tagging" spray painting "18 street" on the red brick wall on the front of the school. Instead of the traditional suspension, PPS behavior management system was focused on reducing out-of-school suspensions, increasing ways to provide students with restorative alternatives that allowed them to learn and grow from their mistakes when possible. Juan served his consequence in-school by making amends with the custodial staff and assisting a staff member in reorganizing the copy room during his lunch recess. He stopped by my office after lunch to let me know the task was completed.

Most mornings, he and his siblings were on school grounds early, opening the door for me as I entered the building. "What's up Mr.

Coakley, I'm doing good huh, can I still go to the dance?" he'd ask. "Yeah, so far, you're good, just stay out of trouble and have a good day. If you need anything, just let me know" I replied. "Well, these little guys didn't get breakfast" he'd say motioning to his siblings. "No problem" then they'd follow me to the cafeteria to grab breakfast.

Over the course of two years, I got to know Juan pretty well. I found that most of what I heard about him and his family were false stereotypes. He didn't come from a "gang related" family. His parents owned a food truck that was located near the school. One day after working late I stopped there on the way home, surprised to see Juan and his siblings playing in the parking lot near the truck. "This is my parents' place," he said with a smile. "This is my principal," said Juan to his family. "I'm more like a vice-principal" I said. "It's on the house," said his father, refusing to take any money, he handed me a compostable clamshell container filled with some of the best street tacos I'd ever tasted.

We soon ditched the pizza company, hiring Juan's family to cater our school dances. They parked their food truck on the backside of the gym providing our middle schoolers with a fresh, authentic, flavorful experience. The kids and staff loved it, the gym was full of positive energy, music, and laughter. The girls were huddled together on one side of the gymnasium, boys stood on the other side. Both groups were too shy to mingle. Juan leaned up against the back wall of the gym trying to look cool, I walked over to mess with him. "Hey man, you told me your family was 18 street gangsters, what's up with that?" I asked. "Not the whole family…my cousin, also I got an uncle in prison" he said softly. "Makes sense… I'm just saying that's not your only option, you're a smart dude. You can do whatever you want in life" I said. He smiled, "I'm a lover not a fighter" he chuckled. "Well if that's the case why don't you ask one of these girls to dance? When I was in eighth grade I wasn't just playing the wall, I always had girls" I grinned. With that, he crossed the invisible barrier of the gym and spoke to one of the girls. They walked to the middle of the gym and began dancing. A few moments later some of the guys standing around did the same. Juan glanced in my direction and smiled, I gave him the nod before I walked on the other side of the gym changing my line of supervision.

I got married the summer before my second year at Beach. Through marriage, I not only gain a wife, but also a daughter, Azaria. She quickly became a Coakley, immediately forging a father/daughter relationship. She was my roll dawg. I gave her a series of nicknames: Zari, Z, Z-blizz, Blizzard, and Blizzrow, using them interchangeably depending on the mood. The success of my career was no longer just about me, there was an important little girl that looked up to me and depended on me. I'd pick her up from the Boys and Girls Club, and ask about her day, we joked about how excited we were to finish the school year. She was smart, a good kid, really respectful. "You got any homework?" I asked. "A little, is it okay if I finish it after dinner?" she asked. "Sounds like a good plan" I replied.

Things were going quite well at the Beach. Principal Fox and I had a great rapport, she trusted me enough to put me in charge of the building when she was sick, attending conferences, workshops or traveling to visit friends and family. Since she was in a long distance relationship she traveled often, which was fine with me, I enjoyed gaining principal experience. On the tail end of spring break Principal Fox let me know that she'd be gone for a week to visit her fiancé. "Cool, I got you covered," I said. The week was uneventful, however that Thursday, two administrators from the district office came to visit the school. They came to conduct a drop-in observation on Principal Fox. Our secretary informed them that she was out, "Mr. Coakley is covering the building, he could give you a tour" she said. I was called to the office, met them with a smile and a handshake, I told them I was the Student Management Specialist. They followed me through the halls while I spoke to students, conducted check-ins and talked to staff members during passing time. Their visit culminated in the cafeteria as students entered for the first lunch block. "So, you are running the building...HR wasn't aware of that, we usually have a retired principal substitute cover the building when the principal's away" said one of the district office people. "There's really no need, I have an admin license, I like doing it, plus the kids know me" I said. My comments were met with silence. "Please let your principal know that we came by...looks like things are going well. There's no need to see us out..." the other stated. With that, they left the building.

When Principal Fox returned, I briefed her on HR's visit. Things were moving like clockwork, the school culture felt positive, our student population had grown just above 500. "When you become AP, you can help me hire someone in your role" Fox said confidently. After a few visits to the district office, her confidence had waned. "They said since we reached 500 during the school year the funds to add the AP aren't in this year's budget, but as long as our enrollment holds steady we'll get the funds next school year." While the news was a bit disappointing, I never really got my hopes up, it was a gatekeeping strategy used broadly across Oregon's K-12 system - overpromise and under deliver. Year after year people of color clung to underpaying jobs, gaining "experience" for decades, motivated by the glimmers of hope of an overpromise. I'd seen it time and time again, Black males with administrative licenses stuck in discipline roles, paid on teaching contracts, holding on to broken promises mumbled in one-off conversations with HR representatives. They gave them hope that one day they'd allow them to dust off the old admin license and put it to good use. This new clarity on Beach's enrollment led me back to the drawing board, filling out job applications, updating my resume and cover letter. I even used MapQuest to gauge whether or not the unknown district that I was applying to was commutable. As long as the drive was less than an hour, I applied. The furthest job that I applied for was an hour and fifteen minutes each way, that's how much I wanted out of PPS.

The following week, Beach received another unexpected visit from two administrators from HR, but they weren't coming to see Principal Fox, they came to see me. I found myself sitting at the round table in my office with HR, being questioned like a suspect in an episode of the *"The First 48."* "What kind of educator would do such a thing?" asked HR 1. "There is no way this reference letter is real," said HR 2. I was being accused of a crime I didn't commit – forgery. An offense that would be grounds for termination, possibly even a suspension of licensure by the Teacher Standard and Practice Commission. Even the possibility of being put on leave and investigated to later be proven innocent could cause irreparable harm to my career in K-12 education and beyond. They placed a piece of paper on the table in front of me, exhibit A. It was a letter of recommendation, written by the one and only Dr. Harriet Adair. She wrote me a glowing letter soon after attending my administrative practicum presentation. Sure, the Assistant Superintendent of a district with over 45 thousand students, and 7 thousand employees isn't going to make most people practicum presentations, but she came to mine, she arrived early, beaming with pride. "I wouldn't miss it for the world PJ, this I got to see" she said jokingly as I uploaded my PowerPoint presentation on the projector. Before I returned from Illinois, Dr. Adair updated my letter and sent me several signed copies, in hopes that I would land a job.

The letter lay crisp on official PPS Office of the Superintendent letterhead, strong, powerful descriptions of my leadership style, strengths and potential as a school leader. The bottom of the letter displayed Dr. Adair's signature in black ink. HR 2 touched the paper with her open hand, "how did you get this letter?" she said coldly. "I got it from Dr. Adair" I replied. "There is no way Harriet wrote this letter for you" HR 1 snapped. "Do you understand that you could be terminated for forging a letter?" said HR 2, staring into my eyes with contempt.

While I've always taken pride in being independent in my approach and leadership ability, I also knew my contact so I replied "I won't answer any more questions until I have my union representative present." Those words halted the conversation, I left my office and made a b-line to Principal Fox's desk. I let her know what was going on, then I made two quick calls, I called LV, he gave me the number. Then I dial Dee. Sure, every school has a building representative, if a teacher is being questioned or disciplined the representative will sit in on the meeting, listen and take notes. That was not what Dee was known for, she worked at the union's headquarters, known by district leadership as a force to be reckoned with, a strong Black woman that wouldn't stand for the poor treatment of teachers, she fought the discrimination and racist practices that happen behind the scenes. She called issues to the carpet while others swept them under the rug. I just pray that she picks up… "hello…I'm on my way, you just stay out of your office and don't say a word til' I get there!" I sat huddled in anger with my fists clenched. "This is bullshit!" exclaimed Principal Fox, "you're going to be ok" she declared pacing back and forth.

Dee walked through the front door less than fifteen minutes later. "Where they at?" she said, stomping through the halls with a jet black raincoat and tall black leather boots. She looked at me "you work on getting Harriet on the phone, I'll deal with HR." We walked back into my office where HR 1 and HR 2 commandeered my circular table. "Oh no!" Dee said loudly, "this is not going down, you think you can question my members without representation!?" While Dee gave them a dressing down, I sent up a Hail Mary call to Dr. Adair, who was out of town, attending a conference. I nervously dialed as beads of sweat ran down my forehead. An unanswered call could inevitable ruin my career. I held my breath while the phone rang, exhaling in relief when she answered on the third ring. "PJ, what can I do for you baby?" "Thank God" I muttered…my strange tone uttered something along the lines of "HR's in my office, they think I forged your letter, they are going to put me on leave…Dee's here." The room fell silent, Dee grinned widely. "Yes ma'am" I said, handing the phone to HR 1. While I couldn't clearly make out what the doctor was saying, I heard a rapid fire verbal assault that left shrapnel in the ear of the listener as HR 1 began holding the phone at a further distance. Dee and I stood at attention, although the phone was not on speaker I clearly heard "get up, and get out of his office, right now!!!" HR 1 handed me my phone and nervously, she began to collect her things, "Mr. Coakley, there's been a terrible mistake, Dr. Adair says she's known you since childhood, I had no idea…" I stood in silence holding my phone near my pants pocket, shell-shocked from the day's events. After they left, Dee looked at me intensely, "you got a discrimination lawsuit on your hands, get your documentation together."

I stood in a daze during dismissal frozen in the moment, a living statue, hollow-eyed, gazing steadily in the distance as kids, parents, colleagues, buses, trees and the school itself rotated 180 degrees around me. I could see mouths moving, feet stomping, dogs barking, car engines revving, bus doors opening, babies crying - but all I heard was silence - like a mouse walking on cotton. A newlywed, still figuring out the meaning of the words husband and father. I could feel HR's grasp pulling me towards the imminent demise of my career.

Later that evening, the clouds lifted through a call from Rainier School District, extending the opportunity to interview for the Elementary Principal position. Rainier was the farthest of any district that I had applied for, an hour and 15 minute drive from home no matter how you slice it. The interview was scheduled for the following Thursday, it required me to take a full day off work. The secretary explained "the interview process starts at the elementary school at 11:00am and ends with a community forum in the boardroom which begins at 6:00pm, lunch and dinner were included in the process." I quickly accepted the interview and let Principal Fox know that I'd be taking that day off. "I hope you get it, after what happened I don't blame you. I used to think that your suspicions about HR blocking your opportunities was in your head, but now I get it. I've never seen something like this happen to anyone else" she said humbly.

On the other hand, Dad was fired up, "they got their nerve accusing somebody of forgery, they don't know who they're messing with! I never thought that me leaving Portland would have such a negative impact on you. Now you are up for a principalship…I got a feeling you're gonna get this job! We need to do a dry run you know…drive out there this weekend and get a feel for the place so you know exactly where to go. You don't want to get lost or arrive late, a dry run will prepare you for the unknown." Dad loved a road trip, plus it made sense, no need of taking a risk getting lost, or stressed out the day of the interview… so that weekend we hit the road to Rainier. There are two ways to get to Rainier from Portland, you either take I-5 North, which is ninety percent freeway and usually clear of traffic once you get out of Portland, or you can take Highway 30. Highway 30's a more difficult route, it curves through small towns, the cities of Scappoose, Warren, St. Helens and Deer Island, a treacherous one lane stretch of road full of 18 wheelers and police speed traps. Not knowing any better, Dad and I took Highway 30. I nervously drove past big rigs on the opposite side carefully watching the speed limit. Dad sat in the passenger seat pointing out police cars and restaurants. Much of the commute is filled with nothingness, just tall trees towering over long stretches of road as you curve uphill for miles. "Make sure you have a full tank and watch your speed, the last thing you want is to get pulled over out here in the middle of nowhere" Dad remarked.

Twenty minutes outside of St. Helens, we entered Rainier, Oregon. The small city was built on the Columbia River which stretched along the right side of the highway. Shotgun houses, buildings and local businesses lay bunched around three square blocks of its downtown area. To the left was mountainous terrain that sprawled for miles, the homes above seemed to be larger and more pronounced than the houses below. We continued north, to a place where the highway curves straight up into the sky, intersecting with cars quickly entering Oregon from Washington's portion of the Lewis and Clark bridge. A section of highway so steep that you really have to put the pedal to the medal to keep up with the flow of traffic. Eventually, on the left was a sign that said "Rainier School District." We hooked left, curving past a cemetery, and a barn-like building that prominently displays the words "Rainier Gun Club" before reaching the school district which I later learned sits on what used to be a golf course. The District Office, boardroom and alternative school consisted of three connected double wide trailers. Up a tiny hill adjacent to the rear of the trailers was Rainier Jr./Sr. High School, which served grades 7 - 12. The building looked like a bomb shelter made of gray concrete slabs with forest green trim, on the backside of the building was a long row of concrete steps that led down to the elementary school, Hudson Park, home of the Cougars. The elementary school was made of the same concrete construction as the high school but had red trim instead of green. Rainier School District served 1,500 students, 550 of those attended Hudson Park. Dad and I rounded the elementary parking lot in his Chrysler 300, "this is where the interview process begins" I said smiling. "Make sure you get here early, this is quite a trek" exclaimed Dad. We took the I-5 freeway home and realized it was a much easier drive. I clenched the steering wheel steadily on the Longview bridge, finally relaxing once the bridge was in my rearview. We stopped at the Panda Inn restaurant on Washington Way for lunch before heading home. The "dry run" put me at ease, so the next few days I focused on answering interview questions.

On the big day I left my house at 8:00am, I took the long easy drive up the I-5 freeway, a straight shot through the Washington cities of Vancouver, Ridgefield, LaCenter, Woodland and Kalama before exiting at Longview. The further I got outside of Vancouver the scenery became nothing but hillsides full of fir trees. I drove in silence thinking of interview questions, answering them out loud, assessing the strength of each answer, redoing my responses, refining, then reassessing. As I reached Kalama above a clearing in the trees was a large billboard that read "Jesus Christ" in big bold blue letters, underneath in lighter blue it said "crucified - risen - returning." I took it as a sign that God was with me, exhaled deeply, then began praying as I took the exit toward Longview making a hard left - curving above the overpass and cruising beyond dozens of car lots, dive bars and mini marts before making a left onto Washington Way. It was 9:05am when I pulled into Starbucks near the bridge, grabbed a coffee and breakfast sandwich, and sat at a corner table reading "Winning the Interview Game." At 10:30am I clenched the wheel of my rickety Jeep as it climbed the cantilever Lewis and Clark bridge spanning high above the Columbia River before placing me in Rainier, Oregon. I entered the doors of Hudson Park Elementary at 10:40 in an all-black suit, black dress shoes, white dress shirt and red tie.

My morning began with a 1:1 conversation with the outgoing principal. A heavy set White guy in his mid-fifties with a buzz cut who stood outside his office door drinking a cup of coffee. We shook hands, "come in" he said with a smile. The office had a large window that overlooked the playground, there was also a separate structure for the elementary gym located in plain sight. The principal explained the process to me, "today you will take a tour with our student representatives, have lunch in the cafeteria with staff, participate in a formal interview in the boardroom, then complete a writing prompt at the district office. Lastly, if all goes well there's dinner with board members at 5pm followed by a community forum. But first you have time with me…what would you like to know?"

We hit it off quickly…he told me that he just landed a job as a Superintendent in Washington, he was leaving Rainier on high note and planned to stay in contact, his new gig began July 1st. I asked him a lot of questions about the logistics of the school, the master schedule, reading and math blocks, discipline referrals, and strengths and challenges of the staff. "The union president is a teacher here in the building, it's no issue, just build a relationship with her, keep her in the loop and you'll do fine." He also talked about overcrowding, "kindergarteners and sixth graders are in portables. Enrollment is up to 550, space is an issue." Then it was off to the races, I enjoyed touring the school with student leaders. The library is on the main floor, it was the focal point of school, grade 1st - 5th are separated by pods - three classrooms behind double doors - the students took me into the first grade and third grade pods "the classrooms are open, there are three third grade teachers, all the classroom in the building look like this" said a student. "My desk is right there" a student said pointing. Off the library a large carpeted ramp lead to the second floor, the fifth grade POD was there, as well as an exterior door that led to the shared cafeteria. The school counselor stood at the top of the ramp, "thank you so much kids, I'll take it from here." I introduced myself to the counselor, she gave me a quick tour of the outside portables and gym before I joined a mix of staff for lunch in the large cafeteria. A split level space with an upper and lower level separated by grades. With all of my experience running an orderly cafeteria I thought this is the ideal space. Holding grade level competition between the upper and lower level, this place could be amazing. There was a small room off the cafeteria with pizza and salad for staff, specifically for the day's events. "Fancy, this is not the norm," said the counselor. We each grabbed a slice, I took bites between conversations with staff.

Wandering on the backside of the cafeteria, I walked past the large concrete steps that lead up to the Jr./Sr. High School, checking into the doublewide trailer labeled District Office. The secretary smiled "I'll come get you in about ten minutes, just make yourself comfortable." I sat up straight in an uncomfortable blue stationary chair with wooden arms. In came a notably tall man in a royal blue suit and two-tone oxford dress shoes, he had to be at least 6'5" with elongated hands, face and smile. "You guys are running behind schedule," said the secretary. "Geez, last time I checked I used to run this place" he said jokingly. He ducked towards the back of the trailer for a few minutes before headed back out the door.

Soon I was called into the connecting trailer labeled, boardroom. I took the hot seat in front of an interview panel of six, the district's administrative team. The business manager, the technology director, the special education director, the high school principal, a school board member, and the tall guy with the royal blue suit sporting two-tone oxford wingtips was the superintendent, Michael Carter. The interview questions were straightforward, my answers while solid, met with serious faces and notetaking. Afterwards, I went back to the district office trailer to complete the writing prompt, creating a principal's newsletter to the community introducing myself as the new principal, listing my hopes and expectations for the school year. I spend about thirty minutes on this task before spell checking my letter, proofreading it and handing it to the secretary. She stacked my newsletter neatly on her desk and said "they're narrowing the process down to three candidates, are you able to come back for dinner with the board at 5pm to participate in the community forum?"

"Yes, great, I'll be there," I replied. "Ok, dinner will take place in the commons area, the same place that you had lunch today" she said. It was around 2pm, I headed to my car and drove down the hill into the downtown area before parking on west B street near City Hall, a Doric-columned historic building resembling a miniature version of the White House. I made calls from my jeep, reflected on my answers to questions, reread portions of the interview book, I even tried power napping to kill the time.

At 4:40pm I was refreshed and back in the commons chatting with board members. Throughout the day I hadn't seen or interacted with another person of color, there weren't any as far as I could tell. The staff, administrative team, board members and 98% of the student body were White. As I reflected on the conversations I had throughout the day, I could tell people were intrigued. A Black school leader in rural Oregon wasn't the norm, right across the bridge Longview, Washington had more diversity and was 3% Black, but I had crossed the barrier into territory where a Black male had never held a position of leadership. While faces can be hard to read, it was evident that the thought was exciting to some, their smiles were welcoming, they actively listened, they nodded in agreement as I spoke. For others it raised anxiety, they were standoffish, quiet, biting their nails or avoiding any eye contact with me. The structure of the dinner gave me the opportunity to see the other two candidates, a White male and female, both a little bit older than me. We all sat at a table that had a few administrators and a few board members. The cafeteria staff catered and served the meal, grilled chicken, mashed potatoes, steamed vegetables and French bread. The food looked good but my stomach was too nervous to actually eat. I took small bites to keep up appearances while answering questions and listening to board members tell war stories from the past.

The process culminated with the community forum, a packed boardroom full of parents, staff and Rainier citizens. I sat in the middle seat with a finalists on my right and left sides. Board members sat in the front row of the audience asking questions, allowing each participant an opportunity to respond while everyone listened. With each question my confidence rose, I had ascended to a familiar space, my "proving people wrong place." A place deep within, that shows up when opportunities to break stereotypes, eliminate barriers and create opportunities arise.

After the Board's questions the mic was passed to members of the audience for a brief Q&A. A community member in a camouflage hunting jacket who'd obviously drowned his sorrows at a local bar before the forum directed his question at me. "I got one for Coakley" he said stammering and steading himself on the podium... "you're from the big city" he explained holding up his index finger... "why do you wanna come out here to our community and work with a bunch of kids that you don't represent?" he stammered. "Good question"...I quickly responded, I made eye contact with the man in the camouflage jacket... "as a school leader, I'm here to serve all kids, regardless of their race, gender, ethnicity or their zip code. I believe I can work in any school or community and make it better" I said calmly. The packed room was silent, the other two finalists held their heads down low, I sat up straight, facing forward, with a serious face waiting for a response. The man turned away from the mic and blurted "don't get caught in town when the lights go out!"

With that threat, Michael the superintendent, who had already made his way near the man when he asked his question, stepped toward him and escorted him out of the boardroom, towards the school resource officer standing directly out front. The community forum concluded swiftly after the man's comment. The other two candidates hightailed it to their cars, I lingered a moment, speaking to board members and thanking the board secretary for all of her help before heading to my car. Michael rushed to my car and shook my hand, "Nice job today, don't let that get to you, that guys are a jerk, he doesn't represent the feeling of the community" he said. "I'm good," I said, "thanks for the opportunity." "We'll follow-up on this process soon," said Michael.

I turned down Lupe Fiasco to a whisper in my car speakers as I gripped the wheel, clenching my teeth over the Lewis & Clark Bridge. As I exited the bridge into Washington it felt as though I was landing an aircraft. When the bridge was in my rearview mirror I turned my music back up.

CHAPTER 8

You're in the Big Leagues Now

My cell phone vibrated in my pocket as I stood outside of Beach, supervising the playground during dismissal. Most days I wouldn't even notice the vibration which would result in a missed call, but these last couple of days I was hyper vigilant about answering my phone. With the number of applications I had pushed out to surrounding districts every missed call was potentially a lost opportunity. I glanced at the phone and could tell by the 556 prefix that the call was from Rainier, "Hello" I quickly answered. It was Superintendent Michael Carter, whom I grew to call M.C. He was quick and to the point, "This Paul? Hey, I'm calling you first, you gave a strong interview and I am really impressed with the way you handled yourself during the community forum. Most people would've lost their cool, but you...you stayed professional and student-centered, that's real leadership! So, I feel real comfortable with you and I'm calling to offer you the Hudson Park principalship."

I was stunned, sitting speechless on the other end of the call. "Hello, what do you think?" said M.C. "Wow, that's great!" I slowly responded... "can I have a day to think about it and call you tomorrow?" "Well, what do you want to think about? Maybe I can answer your questions" M.C. replied. "Well, I'm newly married, so I guess I should talk it over..." M.C. quickly chimed in "the job posting offers a broad salary range, I'll give you top of the pay scale if you give me a yes." "Yes, I accept," I responded.

We exchanged information and scheduled a time for me to come to Rainier to take care of paperwork. After the call I stood looking over Beach's playground floating on cloud nine, taking it all in. That call was the game changer that I needed, shifting my trajectory, shattering the glass ceiling, completely annihilating barriers. Who knew that I would need to commute over an hour to a rural all White community to do so. I called my brother B, "Congratulations, man. That's great news!" he declared. Then, I disclosed my hesitancy in accepting the position. It wasn't the long commute, or the threat from a community member, nor was it the lack of diversity, or the need to talk it over with my spouse. It definitely wasn't fear of taking on a much broader scope of leadership. "Yeah...I am excited, I almost didn't accept it because of the bridge. Every time I drive over the Lewis & Clark Bridge I'm so freaked out that I begin to question whether or not it's worth it." B sat quietly for a moment before expressing his utter frustration "PJ, that's the most ghetto reason I've ever heard for turning down a good job in my life!" I laughed... "yeah, well...I'm just keeping it real. I'm putting my life on the line, daily, you know I'm scared of heights" I asserted. "You'll get used to the drive and the bridge, congratulations man" B said calmly.

M.C. was the king of Rainier, his house was at the top of the hill with large floor to ceiling glass windows and a view that overlooked the city. We met at the district office and finalized the paperwork. "Let's celebrate! Le'me take you out to lunch" M.C. exclaimed. We hopped in his classic Mercedes drop top R107, the soft top roof was tucked away under the deck lid as M.C. whipped through the back hills of the city pointing out areas were students lived: distinct neighborhoods, specific trailer parks, and local businesses before winding down the hill into the downtown area and parking at El Tapatio Mexican Restaurant. It was a sunny Saturday in May, we sat on the back patio facing the Columbia River, glancing at the menu while crunching on chips and salsa. "You're in the big leagues now, you're the boss, the teachers and students will follow your lead. I won't let you fail, I heard a lot of good things about you and your father, plus your references were impressive, solid stuff. You've got a lot of people counting on you and I'm in your corner to take you to your next level of success" said M.C. confidently.

The more I listened, the more relieved I became. We talked for hours, he was a man of stories, transparent in his sharing, his wide range of life experiences somehow led him to the path of Superintendent. MC played in the NBA for a year as a walk-on for the LA Lakers, was friends with Mychal Thompson, Kurt Rambis, and A.C. Green, he also coached college ball, before becoming a teacher, principal and superintendent. Through our conversations I began to understand that for M.C., it wasn't a stretch to take a chance on a young Black principal even if it was out of the norm for most districts in Oregon at the time. He was an ally, before the word "ally" was an overused term spoken in affinity spaces, conferences and coffee shops by locals who deem themselves politically "woke" or consciously "with it." I wasn't advanced through the interview as a finalist to fill a diversity quota or to keep up appearances, ensuring the interview process expanded the applicant pool beyond its normal scope. I was hired based on my interview performance, display of leadership qualities, coachability, potential and the affirmation of references.

"Speaking of setting you up for success, the school has been in need of a covered playground for quite some time. I have a contractor scheduled to put one in this summer. I will have you oversee the project and make sure they complete it before school starts…that'll give you a quick win with the staff and community" he said. M.C. had thought out his plan for setting the new principal up for success. "Sounds good, thanks" I said with a smile. "You bet" he said giving me a fist bump before switching gears, "we need to get you registered for COSA Seaside; we attend the conference every summer as an Admin. Team, we annually host the social for the vendors. It's a great opportunity to meet everyone, it's important to stay engaged in professional development. These jobs are about lifelong learning, becoming an expert in all areas so you can lead others."

COSA is the Coalition of Oregon School Administrators, the statewide association that provides professional learning opportunities, support and guidance to all Oregon's principals, superintendents and central office administrators. Each state has a similar organization all of which are directly linked to the American Association of School Administrators (AASA). Oregon's summer conference is held in Seaside, Oregon, a small city known as a local tourist attraction nestled on the coast. Celebrated for its beach access, crowds of people walk the main drag - Broadway street, visiting tiny boutiques, seafood restaurants, hotels, arcades, ice-cream parlors and dive bars. There's also a large convention center where the conference holds the majority of its sessions, in conjunction with other nearby hotel's conference rooms all within walking distance. COSA Seaside is always three days long and overlaps with my birthday, June 23rd. I rode up with M.C., the rest of our team took their own cars, but M.C. asked if I wanted to carpool. While I am usually not a carpool guy, I had never been invited to hang out with my Superintendent, so I left my car in Rainier and we hit the road to the coast. "It's about an hour and fifteen minutes dive, but I can make it in sixty minutes flat," he chuckled. We stopped at a Costco in Warrenton just twenty minutes outside of Seaside, "time to stock up for the party." A quick dash and soon we were stocking M.C.'s trunk full of booze, half gallons of rum, vodka, bourbon, beers, wines, champagne, scotch, tequila and bags and bags of ice. "That's a lot of booze" I said laughing. "I told you, we host the vendors' reception, we take care of them, make sure they feel appreciated, our kitchen staff brings the food, they're on their way up, you'll see. Me and you, we're bartending…you ever tended bar before? No sweat, there's nothing to it."

Soon we were pouring drinks in a room full of conference vendors and school administrators, networking through a series of introductions and small talk. All of the key COSA leaders and big wigs from the Department of Education stopped by to grab a drink and M.C. introduced me to all of them. "This is my new principal, Paul Coakley, we got lucky snagging this guy from Portland, he'll take care of you…what are you drinking?" he asked. The vendor's reception coupled with Michael's big personality put me on the radar making me known to state level leaders that would have never recognized me in a million years working in a larger district. That, plus the fact that I was usually the only Black male in the room. This became the summer ritual, attending COSA Seaside, hosting the vendors reception and celebrating my birthday at the coast. Any learning opportunity I attended in the state I was greeted by the state's heavy hitters with, "Hey Paul, how's Rainer treating you?" or "I hear a lot of good things" the occasional "Are you keeping Michael in line?" and in the summer a lot of "happy birthdays."

Working through a process has never bothered me in the slightest. My ability to de-escalate situations is one of my biggest strengths, not just on the job, but in life in general, especially when I have the opportunity to talk through the issues. When contractual issues arise, don't look for the quick fix. When it comes to processes "take the time to go through them, things will be better on the other end." Anytime I didn't follow that advice, I regretted it one way or another. So, when I received an email the first week of school from a fifth-grade teacher, who was also the president of the teacher's union urgently requesting to meet with me to discuss a possible grievance, I responded with "please stop by my office after dismissal. I look forward to talking with you." I actively engaged in supervision during dismissal, trying to learn as many students' names as possible, greeting parents, talking to bus drivers and observing staff to figure out the strengths and weaknesses of our dismissal procedures. When the last bus was out of sight, I headed to my office to work on emails. Shortly thereafter, Mrs. Bea - a small quirky spitfire in her mid-sixties poked her head in my office door, "is this a good time?" she asked bluntly. "Yes, come in and have a seat." She had a hand full of papers and was lugging a heavy tote bag full of books, binders and loose-leaf handouts. She plopped down in one of the drab looking office seats directly across from my desk. She sat her tote on the floor, adjusted her glasses and held up a print out of the Master Schedule that I had created. "Your new schedule doesn't provide transition time for teachers" she said flustered. "What do you mean?" I asked. "Like here" she said pointing... "I can't be expected to pick up my kids from music at 1:10pm and begin my science lesson at 1:10pm, it takes me time to walk them from the music room back to the classroom!" "Right, that is why I extended the time by an additional five minutes. The old schedule had built in five minutes of transition time, correct?" "Yes!" she said confused. "Okay, now take a look at this key here below, it indicates seven minutes of passing time for transition between every class...you would actually pick up your kids from Music at 1:00pm and begin Science at 1:10pm. This is also true of teachers prep times and lunch blocks…when I taught second grade I remember rushing back with my kiddos after specials, trying to stay on pace, so with the new 90 minute reading block and 60 minute math block, I figured our staff would appreciate the additional transition time. We are really focused on boosting our core instructional time so we should be able to give a bit of time back to get prepared for the next subject."

She smiled widely baring her teeth, stood quickly and shook my hand firmly "you just saved yourself a grievance. This new master schedule looks so different from what we had last year, and you know people don't like change. But… now that I understand it, I think it will be well received." she giggled. "Sure, I'll take some time at tomorrow's staff meeting to explain how it works," I replied. Before she left the office, I added … "Mrs. Bea… before we open any formal inquiry processes, let's see if we can talk through concerns that are brought to you and resolve them informally. I have an open-door policy and I like to be proactive." "That sounds great, we'll discuss any possible grievance before filing" she said formally. "Grievance sounds so punitive, I like to think of it as opening an inquiry process" I said plainly. I knew she disagreed with that statement, but I felt the need to put it out there. That was the first of many proactive, productive, collaborative conversations which led to more effective ways to serve students, while retaining staff and working within contractual guidelines. After we established trust, our conversations became brief informal check-ins when we saw each other in the hall, library, cafeteria or playground duty. Contractual issues were few and far between.

While I worked to uphold and respect contracts for staff, as M.C. soon pointed out, I failed to read the benefits listed in mine closely. One morning, he brought me coffee while I watched students shoot baskets, play tetherball, and hula hoop under the newly constructed covered playground before the bell rang to start the day. "What's up man, did you read your contract?" he asked inquisitively. "Yeah, I'm up to speed on both the teachers and classified agreements, why is there an issue?" I asked. "Not those, yours. Most principals skim the thing, they don't even understand the benefits and opportunities available to them." I laughed, "I skimmed it," I said with a chuckle. "I'll dig into it soon." "It's a good contract, we pay your membership for COSA every year, you get a cell phone stipend, mileage when you need to travel beyond a 30-mile radius to a required meeting or workshop. We even pay for your courses if you get accepted in a doctoral program, but no one ever takes advantage of that…read it and let me know if you have any questions" he said straightforwardly. "I will, and I might take you up on the doctoral degree as well" I said with a smile. He gave me a fist bump and disappeared.

Hudson Park Elementary school (HPE) was a K-6 school with approximately three teachers per grade level. HPE had Music, PE and Library, a School Counselor, a Literacy Specialist, Special Education teachers and about a dozen classified staff members. As the sole building administrator, I was responsible for evaluating all of them. All probationary teachers, those with less than three years' experience, required three formal observations a year. Contracted teachers with more than three years of experience required one formal observation and a fifteen-minute drop-in observation, an unscheduled visit to the classroom that was documented with written feedback. I drafted out an evaluation schedule that met the observation requirements for the year. My secretary held the time on my electronic calendar along with every other meeting requirement… administrative meetings, staff meetings, COSA principal's academy workshops, school board meetings, and Hudson Park events. My e-calendar was the compass for staying above water, but I didn't just want to stay afloat, I wanted to get into the comfort of sailing. Michael had put me in the game, I was ready to prove the haters wrong, close the mouths of the naysayers, converting my nonbelievers into believers. I began devouring educational leadership books, even listening to audiobooks on my commute to and from work for a good six months. Filling my mind with ways to use assessment as a roadmap to rigor, walking the walk as a school leader, creating systems that ensure success, scheduling observations and providing effective feedback, using tools to hold high accountability and coaching educators toward greatness.

The first half of the school year I attended a two-day workshop sponsored by COSA called the Breakthrough Coach, a training focused on managing your time, creating work-life balance and working smarter not harder. On the second day of the training school leaders are joined by their secretary or administrative professional to help each leader implement the strategies that were taught on day one. The gist of the training is about adopting a CEO mindset. An attitude that teaches one to delegate non-leadership tasks to those responsible for the work, so the leader isn't dogged down by busy work. On the first day school leaders left the workshop invigorated, rushing back to their workspaces motivated to "clean their office of clutter" eliminating binders and paperwork, personal family photos and office trinkets, turning their offices into sleek, empty spaces with minimal furnishings, void of office supplies and personal effects. "You're the leader of a school, why spend time in your office? Raise your hand if you have scissors in your drawer and a stapler on your desk?" bellowed the speaker, looking around the room at the sea of hands in the air. "Why?! Get rid of it! " he continued, "what are you going to do with it?...give the stapler to your secretary and the papers that you planned to organize, that's their job. Yours is to get into classrooms to provide feedback that positively impacts teaching and learning."

Day two was about trusting, appreciating and empowering the secretaries with the ability to do their jobs without school leaders getting in the way. Principals arrived at the workshop with boxes full of loose papers, after being tasked with bringing all the paperwork that was on their desk to the workshop. Each leader was accompanied by their secretary. The principals and district administrators in attendance left empty handed while their school secretaries left overwhelmed, holding boxes of loose papers, with stacks of "task sheets" provided by the workshop indicating the assignment that needed to be completed and the deadline for completion.

The following week I was ready to implement step 1, clearing your office of clutter. I've always worked to keep my office clean and organized, but I did have a small cardboard box so I could pack any office supplies that stopped me from achieving a leadership mindset. In it were scissors, unread outdated binders, paperclips and the dreaded stapler. As I "CEO'd" my office M.C. walked in giggling and looking around. "What the hell are you doing? Breakthrough Coach? What did you think?" "It was a good two days, I wish I would have taken that workshop in the summer. These office supplies can be a real time suck" I replied. "Well," said M.C., "the biggest take away is to delegate, use your secretary so you can focus on visibility in the building. Some of the other concepts they're teaching are pretty out there" he said, moving his right hand around the top of his head and then pushing it towards the sky like he was doing an imitation of Kramer from *Seinfeld*. "Professional development…none of this stuff is exactly right, no one has all the answers, just find the key takeaways, apply them and move on" he said.

M.C. was right, the main takeaway for me was don't be afraid to delegate, let people do their jobs. At the end of my day my office was more organized, spick and span. I met with my two secretaries and told them that I plan to delegate more and really communicate my needs on a regular basis, so I can spend as much time in classrooms as possible. "I won't be adopting this full process" I said, holding up a stack of task sheets and tossing them into the large blue recycling bin. "Oh thank God!" said my head secretary with a smile. However, my secretaries got really efficient, they focused on the right work, customer service, completing paperwork, and allowing me to spend the majority of my time in classrooms. In doing so, I quickly became familiar with the strengths and weaknesses of my teachers. There were those in need of support, and those who were so outstanding they could help others increase their skills and enhance their performance.

A young teacher in her third year of teaching stood out as one of my strongest teachers in the building. She was high energy, her reading outcomes were off the charts, students listened to her and she was able to connect with the toughest kids. She was super organized and also was just as strong at teaching other subjects. The teacher was Megan Keplinger, small, energetic, detail oriented, and driven. Somehow after a few observations, I knew she was a future school leader that could help me move our school's outcomes upward on a path to success. We began having conversations about school improvement, and she agreed to begin coaching several of her peers. She was humble so it took some coaxing, but in a short amount of time, my frequent visits to the classroom became more interesting. I began observing higher levels of student engagement, exceptional listening skills and teachers explaining concepts in multiple ways based on the students preferred learning style. Our educators were allowing students more time to ask questions, absorb information and apply the skill they were learning on their own.

We recruited a handful of staff made up of teachers and classified, meeting once a week before school as a leadership team.

Our team loosely modeled Beach's team, but focused more on improving teaching and learning than managing behaviors. Our goal was increasing student outcomes, using multiple sources of data to drive decisions. We planned ongoing professional learning opportunities for staff, before rolling out grade level Professional Learning Communities (PLCs). Like the school leadership team, the PLCs focused on improving student outcomes, they used multiple sources of data to meet their students' needs.

During this cultural shift, I read books on school culture, principal leadership, best practices and successful classrooms. Three books that really stood out to me were: *The Principal's Role In Shaping School Culture*, by Deal & Peterson, *Leverage Leadership: A Practical Guide to Building Exceptional Schools*, by Paul Bambrick-Santoyo and *Transforming School Culture: How to Overcome Staff Division*, by Anthony Muhammad.

Dr. Muhammad's work gives school leaders a plan of action, he categorizes a staff into four distinct terms: the *Believers*, the *Tweeners*, the *Survivors* and the *Fundamentalist*. My handpicked leadership team was made up of Believers, intrinsically motivated people driven to make a difference. They took no excuses, confronted negativity, removing barriers that impeded student success. Whenever I had the opportunity to hire new staff, my goal was to enlist more Believers. The Tweeners were those educators who remained in their comfort zone, they enjoy what they do, are enthusiastic about teaching, but haven't quite reached the tipping point to going the extra mile of ensuring struggling students get what they need to make gains. Through coaching conversations, support, encouragement, collaboration and trust, our leadership team helped many of our Tweeners become Believers. HPE had a handful of Survivors, educators negatively affected by change, they may have started as Tweeners, but overtime they became burnt out, moody, holding low expectations for students, letting negative student behaviors control their classroom environment. I honed in on these educators, closely monitoring them through plans of improvement, letters of expectations and coaching conversations that often led to resignations, or seeking jobs elsewhere.

However, the most entrenched and damaging to a school's culture is the Fundamentalist. Those who looked at their leader as an individual who are hired to throw their world in upheaval. A Fundamentalist will fight their principal tooth and nail every step of the way. Their attitude is "I was here before you came and I'll be here after you leave, this too shall pass." The Fundamentalist loathes change, hoping that the change agent will fail and ultimately go away. They'll disrupt initiatives, defame Believers, and distract professional learning. It took me a while to identify them, but once I did, I declared war. Early retirements, resignations and moves across the bridge were at an all-time high. I heard one informing their colleagues "I am leaving, I got a job in Longview!" My theory: Fundamentalist can't endure working in a healthy school environment full of Believers.

With a few solid years under my belt as principal, HPE felt calm, peaceful. As a staff we had gained momentum, moving together like a well-oiled machine. Our reading program was assessing students, monitoring progress every six weeks. Our students changed reading groups moving to new teachers based on their growth or level of support. Our hallways, playgrounds and cafeteria were orderly, respectful places where behaviors were minimal. We knew our students by name, our "highflyers" had a staff member they checked-in with on a regular basis, even multiple times a day, providing them breaks and one-to-one assistance. The school leadership team was a group of problem solvers, monitoring achievement, strategizing, gathering input and refining plans. They presented information during staff meetings, planned events to engage families in the good things that were happening: family literacy nights, science fairs and musical performances. They held school-wide competitions, the walls were covered in student work, brimming with pride, art and creativity. As Principal, I'd helped create a healthy culture, giving me the ability to spend more time with students and staff, coaching, motivating and empowering them to give their best each and every day.

Confident in my ability to lead HPE to the next level of success, I applied for Portland State University's doctoral program in educational leadership. A program designed to balance concept acquisition, social justice, research and reflection with an educational leadership framework that participants apply while working in their jobs as practitioners. After a series of interviews at the college I was accepted into the program. During my time in Rainier, I was one of the lowest paid principals in the state, but the lived experience I was getting along with fully funded doctoral tuition made it all worthwhile. The program was made up of a small cohort of leaders from around the state. Year one centered on mastering academic writing and conducting research. Our cohort took classes together, met quarterly as a group, usually at a local restaurant to get to know each other and ask questions of our cohort leader, Dr. Tom Chenoweth. Tom was a retired principal, published author, college professor and an ethnographer, his work captured successful practices of educational leaders, explaining them in a way that could be replicated, scalable by schools, districts and programs. There were about ten in our cohort, a few transferred to Portland State after a long pause on their doctoral work conducted elsewhere. PSU advertised it's doctorate as a three-year program, for most participants it took much longer, many dropped out completely, other restarted, some in year three saw no light at the end of the tunnel. A guy who'd transferred from California had been working towards completion for ten years. I was determined to finish in three years, strike while the iron is hot, push myself to the finish.

The ten of us became close colleagues, supporters of one another, there were three people of color. My go to accountability partner was Peter, a student studying abroad from Tanzania. He was a reverend in the Catholic church, and a mental health counselor, motivated to earn his doctorate to improve academic outcomes in Tanzania by offering training and professional development for principals. He'd often share stories about the lack of training for school leaders in his country, the void of opportunities for leaders to collaborate around best practices and research based strategies.

Despite our vastly different backgrounds we gravitate towards each other through an unspoken Blackness, like long lost cousins, I'd become used to being "the only" Black face in professional and academic settings. Suddenly shocked, drawn to the idea of holding conversations, supporting and encouraging accountability of someone who brought a familiarity I'd been missing since post undergrad. Peter greeted me before class with a formal "hello Paul" which I responded to with "what's up my brotha" extending a handshake. We meet regularly in the tech lab digging into course concepts, critiquing each other's writing, making suggestions, holding each other accountable for deadlines. "There aren't many people who actually finish this program in three years, some have been working on graduating for the past seven years, that's crazy" I remarked. "Yeah, I don't have that kind of time," said Peter. "Who does, look man we're gonna complete this thing in three. Our entire cohort should finish together. We've got what it takes to walk across that stage, but I can already tell some aren't going to make it. I got your back…I'll hold you accountable, you do the same for me…hold me accountable" I said with a serious face. "I got you Paul" he said calmly. Then he said something that really resonated with me, "my country has put their trust, funds and hopes into me completing this degree. I promised them I would come back to do what I was sent to do, I won't let them down. What about you Paul?... What motivates you to finish?" I sat for a moment in quiet reflection, then it hit me, "my school district is paying for my courses, so that is definitely a driver, but actually my motivation is that we're expecting, it's a boy. I'm going to dedicate my dissertation to him as something he can look back on, letting him know that he can accomplish anything he puts his mind to!" Full of joy, pride and hope, my son hadn't even arrived yet, but already I was driven to be an improved version of myself, for his benefit. Peter smiled, "there you are my brother. When you don't feel like writing or putting time in this work, think about your son, the one who motivates you. You have to do this now, get it out of the way, so you can spend time with him, you won't fail him."

Choosing a dissertation topic can be tricky, it needs to be something you're passionate about studying for a long period of time. The topic needs a broad field of research, something relevant to the work you are doing that benefits others in your profession. At the helm of HPE's transformation, I knew I wanted to help school leaders create a healthy school culture. Intrigued by Dr. Muhammad's work, I researched his background, he'd served as a teacher, assistant principal, and principal before becoming a well-known educational speaker. He was the CEO of his own consulting firm. As luck would have it, he had an upcoming speaking engagement in Oregon at the Spirit Mountain Casino, an easy drive halfway towards the Oregon coast. I registered, excited to hear him speak.

During my usual drop in on my parents, I told them about the conference. "Why don't you just email him? Let him know where you work and what you are doing? Then see if he wants to grab lunch" said Dad. This was an idea that seemed unorthodox to me, this guy was a national speaker and author, in my mind he was damn near a celebrity. "Yeah, right," I retorted. "Look man, you know of him because you're a doctoral student researching his topic of expertise. He's no celebrity, he was a middle school principal, just like me! Send him an email, he'll probably appreciate your support" said Dad emphatically. Of course Dad was right, Dr. Muhammad quickly replied to my email with a positive message of encouragement, appreciation for reaching out, and a plan to grab a bite in the hotel casino's main restaurant after he was done speaking.

I listened intently as he spoke to the large group of educators in attendance. He confidently connected educational concepts with stories, real-life examples and his own personal experiences. I took notes not only on information that he shared through PowerPoint slides, but also on his presentation style in general. Dr. Muhammad was about my stature, if I had to guess, he was maybe about five years my senior. He wore a dark gray suit with a burgundy tie with gray highlights, his hair was freshly faded with a half inch of curls on top. His demeanor was positive and affable. His large smile reminded me of my Uncle Bobby. His keynote feature was a solid forty-five minutes, hitting on key points from his book, he closed by saying, "Later today I will be doing a book signing that can be found in your program, I'll hang around awhile for those of you who have questions." Then he walked down from the podium, standing ground level in front of the audience. He was greeted with handshakes, thank yous and messages of appreciation. I stood in the circle of participants until there were only a few people left. "Hi Dr. Muhammad, I'm Paul" I said with a handshake. "I thought that was you, being that you were the only Brotha. let's grab some lunch" he chuckled as we headed to the restaurant. "Dr. Muhammad, I really appreciate you doing this," I said. "No problem, call me Anthony, a few years ago I was in the same place that you are, a principal working on my dissertation." We talked over sandwiches and side salads, I asked lots of questions. We touched on everything, the principalship, leadership teams, dissertations, PLCs, speaking engagements, and publishing. I soaked up as much information as possible, what stood out the most was the advice he gave me on choosing a dissertation topic. He said something along the lines of "for your dissertation topic, don't try to save the world. Center it on a process. Your job's to lead the process from point A to B. Gather information, research and literature on what you learned. Your topic should provide information to other school leaders about how to successfully navigate that process." He went on to explain that so many people start off with these giant topics that are so broad they will never be able to complete them. "Hold off on saving the world for your book, once you have your doctorate."

"I got it, I said "that is super helpful" I affirmed. "You got it, you're good?" he asked, "before I go, I got something for you" he reached into his messenger bag and pulled out a copy of his latest publishing, *The Collaborative Administrator*, "do you have this yet?... ok this is for you"

DR. PAUL E. COAKLEY

he said quickly jotting in black pen inside the jacket cover. "It was nice meeting you, best of luck on your dissertation, you got this!" The book was a compilation of educational researchers under the Solution-Tree umbrella, each responsible for a chapter where they share their insight on working together as a professional learning community. The book provided some great insight that was directly related to our work at HPE. Anthony's chapter was called *"Teaching Matters: Leadership that Improved Professional Practice."* I purchased a copy of the book for everyone on my leadership team, in my copy etched in black inside the jacket cover it says "Paul, thanks for all you do for kids!" - Anthony S. Muhammad.

CHAPTER 9

Good Morning Dr. King

On June 22, 2009 at 11:56pm my son Paul Eli Coakley was born. He was 8 pounds, 10 ounces, the fourth Paul to carry the Coakley name. Our birthdays were just four minutes apart. Directly after midnight I sat perched on a tiny loveseat in the birthing suite with him nestled in my arms while his mother rested, thanking God for the best birthday present I'd ever receive. It was the first time I missed COSA Seaside in seven years. For once, work was furthest from my mind. I studied the miniature me. No matter what, I'd be there for him, through good times and bad. I'd be to him, what my Dad was to me, an earthly protector, provider, encourager, and support system. He lay peacefully curled in the crook of my right arm, yawing silently before closing his eyes.

The next morning the delivery room was packed with relatives, all hoping for a moment with our beautiful newborn Paul. The hospital planned on exiting us within 24 hours. I spent 12 of those hours prepping the house for his arrival. Vacuuming, dusting, swiffering, even scrubbing the baseboards. The Ridgefield crib gleamed, the cherry wood floors sparkled like never before. On Thursday, June 25, 2009 we had until 1pm to check out of the hospital. My champagne colored Mercedes E-class slid through the car wash tunnel. Daydreaming, I reminisced while long soapy textile strips applied pressure to the car's exterior, rainbow colored foam rapidly sprayed across the windshield, bubbles covered the egg shaped headlights, scrubbers danced back and forth. The Benz glistened as we pulled away from the hospital, followed by grandparents, siblings, neighbors. Azaria had just completed eighth grade, all week she was in big sister mode, running errands, and interference on relatives and friends who continued dropping by.

Once we got home the news rang out about Michael Jackson's tragic death. He passed at 2:26pm that day - gone at the young age of 50. The king of pop, who's iconic performances and collection of number 1 hits were the theme songs of a generation. He was the soundtrack to my childhood, as well as a half a billion others. Countries, nations, cultures and religions in all parts of the globe moonwalking in mirrors, imitating hand movements with sequined gloves, spinning on linoleum in penny loafers while singing the words to their favorite MJ songs. I wore a red "beat it" jacket with silver shoulder accents, with multiple zipper pockets in elementary. Flashbacks of the MJ themed birthday party my parents threw me at Chuck E Cheese, where an almost believable impersonator took pictures with me and my guest. Kids kept asking "Is he the real Michael Jackson?" I never gave them an answer. The party was great, though deep down I knew that something was amiss with the dude's nose and Jheri curl. Joy, sadness, hope, grief, excitement and loss filled my living room. I sat near the basinet eyeing the bundle of joy securely wrapped tightly, gripping his teddy bear. We listened to the murky details of MJ's death which involved a deadly cocktail of sedatives and an anesthetic, propofol, administered by his physician. In disbelief, I trying catching my breath, the week moved at breakneck speed.

Paul the fourth's nursery was filled with balloons and gifts, showered by family and friends. Hudson Park staff threw a baby shower on the last day of the school. I left work with a car filled with presents, an abundance of clothes, blankets, baby shoes, toys, books and a large cake made up of diapers. I sat in the grand rocking chair in his bedroom, one corner purposely set up like a classroom reading space, he slept. Staring at his little nose, tiny hands, and teeny eyelids tightly shut, peacefully napping. Maybe he'll be president someday, or the next king of pop. He was born in the social media era, the rise of technology, NBA half court shots, giant flat screen tv's, and the first Black President. His parents worked demanding full-time jobs, which yielding plenty of time with his grandfather. Dad's early retirement allowed him the opportunity to fulfill a new assignment, one he was elated about. He was up at the crack of dawn, by 6am he was quietly wrapping on my door with a giant smile on his face. "Where's my grandson?" he'd say as I opened the door. "Asleep, good morning" I quietly replied. Dad joked "I'm not here to make small talk, where's Little Paul?" he laughed. Dad had lost weight after the surgery, he was looking good, feeling good, strong, energetic, his grandson gave him a new lease on life. "You've lost some weight," I commented. "Yeah, and I'm keeping it off, with all these grandkids I'd better stick around a while" he chuckled.

Dad arrived at the same time each day, "where's my grandson?" he asked, as we rushed out the door. From what I could tell, their days consisted of napping, eating, reading books, watching sports and resting. After work I'd find my son nestled in grandpa's arms on the couch, both dozing off between commercials. It was a special time for the two of them, building block to an unbreakable bond between Paulie and Papa – the nicknames that finally stuck after testing out several variations that didn't make the cut.

While academic outcomes, teaching and learning, growth, graduation and preparing students for life beyond high school is the foundational work of educators, our first priority became more than clear, quickly rising to the forefront in an era of mass shootings - safety. Safety is no easy feat in public schools. Every news station provides the gory details of school shootings in nearby states, cities and towns. Success stories of graduates, students giving back to their community, or helping those in need are nonexistent. The media highlighted the copycat killers, cowardly, suicidal, unstable, evil individuals who take the lives of innocent people. Horrific acts flood our television screens, our minds, and hearts, creating fear, shifting focus, leaving us analyzing plans for the future. The stress, anxiety, loss and feelings of helplessness compiled with repeat tragedies in schools, malls, concerts and gatherings lead many educators burnt out on the job. A national study on staff retention indicated the number of teachers leaving the profession increased from 10% in 2000 to 28% in 2009. For educators of color the rate was approximately 35%. Districts began experiencing a mass exodus of teachers, classified staff and administrators leaving the profession. Substitute teachers became scarce, job postings more difficult to fill. Teacher and principal preparation programs didn't prepare unarmed civilians to deal with the threat of a gunman setting foot on school property with deadly intentions.

The gun toting residents of Rainier drove trucks displaying shotguns in their rear windows, board members wore camouflage to meetings, and hunting season destroyed student attendance. I became attentive, vigilant "not on my watch" was my mindset. I was responsible for the safety of everyone on our campus. Our administrators felt the same, we became hyper proactive, preparing, frequently conducting lockdown drills, debriefing situations, discussing tragedies on television, training for the worst. We reassured staff whose minds were in a perpetual state of dismay and trepidation. We installed cameras, automatic locking doors, upgraded window locks. The era shifted focusing on student achievement to increasing safety and security. Academic outcomes became our second priority, first was survival.

Living in Ridgefield had pros and cons, but the advantages outweigh the downside by a landslide. An even commute, forty minutes south to Portland and forty minutes north to Longview, then a quick jaunt over the bridge. Ridgefield, Washington was full of luxury subdivisions, 3,000 square foot homes, four bedrooms, two and a half bathrooms and three car garages. We landed in a subdivision called Cassini View renting a large three-story home from the builder. The rent was significantly less than our mortgage in Gresham where we owned a two story 1,500 square foot duplex. My wife took one look at the place, heard the price of the rent and said "we'll take it." The ninety-minute commute to Rainier was taking a toll on me, especially on nights when I attended events or board meetings. The quiet and somewhat affluent Ridgefield neighborhood gave me a sense of pride. It had an office, a den, a dining room and a loft overlooking the formal living room. The front of the house had a large balcony, early mornings I'd sit out there in a white Polo robe reading the paper while sipping coffee, taking in the beauty of the neighborhood. I never cared to learn about my neighbors, and they could care less to learn about me. The navy McCain - Palin yards signs surrounding my house spoke volumes. I was surrounded by haters. They made their assumptions of me based on skin color, stereotypes and the Obama - Biden yard sign placed predominantly in my front yard.

The balcony was my space to gloat. Our 56th President Barack Obama had achieved the unattainable, the unimaginable, something Black grandmothers, grandfathers and elders thought would never happen in their lifetime. They had difficulty understanding or believing what they had witnessed. They were direct descendants of slaves, experienced Jim Crow laws, treated like they had no value. Even the generations of Black folks after them, the Boomers lived through desegregation, the civil rights movement, fighting for equal rights. In 2008 they casted their prayers, hopes and dreams into ballots boxes. Many of my peers were never taught an uplifting story about Black history in our K-12 classrooms. We grew up thinking in the grand scheme of politics, our voices didn't matter. History taught that our heroes, leaders and shining stars were killed for elevating their voices. This election presented an option that hadn't been there before, it was time for change. People of color showed up to the polls, encouraged by celebrities of all races, backgrounds and ethnicities.

The results reverberated, the butterfly effect caused ripples, impacted everyone across the globe, directly broadened my shoulders as a Black male leader. For a brief sliver in time I felt what it must be like to operate without barriers, or glass ceilings. Fearless, unstoppable, living in the moment, worry free. For a brief period, I moved with a false sense of joy and freedom. Elation that disappears the moment your car is followed by police for fitting a description, or some other micro-aggression, bringing you back to reality. Even this election won't change the world we live in. There was a constant barrage of negative media, controlling the masses, pumping fear, promoting stereotypes, keeping us all on high alert. Albeit, my hopes drowned the current reality, joy squelched temporary sorrows, I was fueled by the election of the first Black president. The narrative changed the landscape, shifted mindsets, a transition took place, and Black leaders began emerging in my corner of the world, where they weren't represented before.

As an educator in an elementary setting I'd become accustomed to getting sick at least twice a year. I worried about catching a nasty cold then spreading it to my family. Soon after Paulie was born a deadly virus was gaining traction across the globe, the death toll was rising, cases increasing state by state. The name alone was enough to send chills up my spine - Swine Flu or H1N1. There were 1,833 confirmed cases in Oregon, some were in Rainier. A few students were absent for long periods of time, the families made us aware they'd contracted Swine flu, they were quarantined until they recovered. Brian always called with medical advice, "go to a drug store, like Rite Aid and purchase a surgical mask, your school nurse may have one. Forget how it looks, just wear it, wash your hands frequently, especially after being in close contact with people. That's the best way to protect yourself." I began wearing a mask, distanced myself during meetings.

Influenza A, the vaccine for Swine Flu, was developed in the seventies, had been through phases of testing, it was released about three months after we began seeing cases in our district. We collaborated with health professionals, closed school for two days, turning our commons area into a shot clinic open to the public to receive vaccines. Our administrators, school nurses and counselors were the first group to receive shots. Minor side effects of the vaccine were possible headaches, nausea and short-lived fevers. Luckily, M.C. and I had no side effects, we spent the next 48 hours running the shot clinic. Cafeteria tables were nurses' stations, counselors were stationed at the door deploying masks and getting people checked-in. The lower half of the cafeteria, was a waiting area, nurses called recipients one-by-one. After receiving the shot, folks waited at least ten minutes to gain composure. We worked nonstop until the entire city of Rainier made their way through our doors. Our staff was thanked by elementary parents, students, and residence, leaving with a stronger connection. A trauma bond, the past few months we'd all been coping with the same sense of trepidation, we'd gone through the fire, making it out together.

Launching a clinic in conjunction with health professionals led to stronger partnerships, collaborative conversations, regular meetings about community needs. The partnership forged the opening of the first school-based health center in the county, the Rainier Health Center. The center's mission was "supporting community health and wellness." Staffed with a certified nurse and assistant, it was located in a new portable trailer, installed right next to the district office. I served on the implementation team, charged with hiring staff, determining location and identifying the hours of operation. Open four days a week, 8am - 4:30pm to address chronic medical problems, provide annual preventive check-ups, laboratory services, immunization, sports physicals, well care checks, referrals for specialists, and counseling. As the need expanded, staffing increased to include mental health services.

Rainier's Health Center was gratifying, a dream I helped make a reality start to finish. A grassroots effort, that began with an idea, becoming a solution that addressed the needs of our community. The health center thrived, frequented by parents, students, staff and residents on the daily. Its success motivated me to take on larger, more daunting issue's, like our declining enrollment. At the inception of my principalship at HPE, Rainier school district's enrollment hovered around 1,500 students. Our small campus was almost at capacity, we got creative with space, added portable classrooms, repurposing libraries and office spaces to teach small groups. Our graduation rate was flat, but HPE's reading and math scores had increased, our staff retention and morale was solid. The past few Septembers indicated a steady decline in enrollment. In just four years district enrollment dropped about 300 students. Declining enrollment equates to budget cuts - staff reductions, slashing programs, trimming offerings and opportunities for students.

Through doctoral courses, I befriended Dan, a six-foot something Director of a virtual charter school. Since the beginning of our program, I was curious about his virtual school, their enrollment, curriculum, theories, and framework for serving students. I found the ability to provide education, support and credit in the comfort of one's home intriguing. "What about students who don't do the work? Or are struggling…how do you support them?" I asked. Dan's response was thorough, "we have drop-in spaces at onsite locations, students can either connect with a teacher in-person, or by phone. Our program monitors whether a student is working through the curriculum or just guessing, skipping through, playing around or not progressing. Teachers have student caseloads, they monitor progress and keep a contact log, interacting frequently with students and parents through emails, calls, or scheduled in-person meetings, it's a good system."

In an era of mass shootings, K-12 districts across the nation experienced an extreme decline in enrollment, losing students to homeschooling, and virtual programs. In Rainier, every student we lost had an impact, a gut punched, the traditional brick and mortar school system wasn't best for every learner. How could we keep our students, while meeting the needs of those who wanted to learn online? Dan shared key resources, state-level handbooks and guidance for online programs with me, plus he was always available to answer my questions.

Public school enrollment requires students to live in the district of the school they attend. If a student moves out of district, they must attend school in the district where they reside, unless they apply and qualify for a hardship transfer. A hardship transfer only applies under specific circumstances. It's a mechanism that supports the student's best interest in extreme cases: homelessness, foster care, military deployment of a parent, or documented medical conditions. Yet, virtual schools can serve any student in the state regardless of their residence, no boundaries or parameters. Oregon had very few virtual schools, their enrollments increased rapidly. They were serving students all over the state. Dan was an expert in the field, a colleague and trusted advisor. We'd hang at COSA events, he'd get snarls and side eyes from superintendents. He was the Steve Jobs of Oregon's education space, the guy changing the game, successfully offering a new option that everyone wanted.

"I think I can solve our enrollment problems," I uttered to M.C., we sat in his small office in the wee hours of the morning sipping coffee. "I'm all ears, what you got?" he replied between sips. "Add a virtual option to our alternative high school" I grinned. Our alternative high school was just two portable classrooms, two teachers and twenty-five students. Trailers adjacent to the district office with a sign: North Columbia Academy, (NCA). NCA had a tighter wrap-around model than the traditional high school model. The smaller setting provided more 1:1 supports. A handful of students were placed at NCA as an alternative measure before expulsion. A last-ditch effort through round table conversations with the student, parents and staff. M.C. knew every kid by name, he was in those classrooms regularly, talking with students, learning their interests, finding out what made them tick. M.C. was the principal, responding to discipline and attendance issues, he also evaluated, coached and supported its teachers.

"How? What are the benefits?" M.C. asked. "We'll probably retain kids who are hoping for online learning, if we advertise and have a good program. Online programs can serve any kid in the state. Our county's online options are limited, nothing within driving distance. A struggling learner has to drive an hour for an in-person check-in. If we're open, they'll probably choose us. We hold a space for scheduled in-person meetings for students needing help" I replied. "I like it, how long will it take? Let's see if we can pull it off" M.C. said, rubbing his chin.

Soon, I was in the weeds…lengthy calls, long email threads with the State department, digging through documents, webpages, and resources about online learning. Eating burrito bowls with Dan at PSU to outline next steps. M.C. and I sat through sales pitches from curriculum vendors, haggling over contracts terms of service. When Thanksgiving neared, we had a solid plan, a framework for offering a fully accredited online program. We chose a platform, trained staff, creating a schedule that split time supporting students both in-person and online. Our marketing strategy created enrollment buzz, sparking interest statewide. Our little district, fighting against behemoths, Connections Academy and Strive K-12's national online platform. Hell, they weren't even districts, they're corporations, raking in the big bucks, running commercials, poaching kids, driving district enrollment into the dirt, leaving us to face deep budget reductions. We were a means to an end, at least we were local. Little Rainier, providing option for students across Oregon, ensuring access to real teachers, administrators, supports and services.

Our online students could participate in sports, attend prom, field trips and all NCA events.

On the flipside, my doctoral work was at a stalemate. Coursework completed, two chapters written, the problem statement was clear and concise, my literature review yielded a solid body of evidence. I took Dr. Muhammad's advice, focusing on a process. My dissertation focused on providing school leaders with a playbook for taking staff through a large scale change - successful shifting their school's deliver of Title I service. Moving from supporting small groups of learners to supporting every student at their specific level. My message to staff "We'll meet every student where they are, meeting their individual needs to learn and grow." It was a yearlong process, a series of meetings with the district improvement team, consisting of teachers, specialists, classified staff, parents and administrators. The required steps for this process were clearly outlined by the state. As long as we followed the process, we'd make it to the finish line. A technical change with adaptive components, I created at tool that provided leaders with guidance on navigating the transition while maintaining a healthy school culture. Principals could adapt the process, it should be student centered, elevate voices, engage communities, promote real conversations, so when it's completed, the staff believes in the work, puts the plan in action - strengthening their delivery model. I led the process while running HPE's day-to-day operations, in addition to scale up our online program. I just needed time to capture this work on paper. To complete a dissertation, you actually have to write, explain the nuances, document the research, analyze the outcomes, record the findings, then identify the steps to success – but I hadn't found the hours to do so.

Working in a small district has several benefits, one being the close connection with staff. The ability to bring your team together, hold conversations, and shared experiences that boost morale. One of M.C.'s greatest strengths was creating a fun environment. When I joined Rainer, I quickly noticed that rituals, events and traditions tied us together. Opportunity to enhance relationships were baked into our calendar. The vendors' reception at COSA kicked off the summer. Then, our Welcome

Back Staff Barbeque, we'd take a group photo, distribute new ID badges, and chat during lunch. Our small leadership team ran the grill, while staff socialized. We held an End of Summer Appreciation Lunch for our maintenance and custodial crew. Fultano's pizza buffet, just fifteen minutes up the road was our crew's preferred hideaway. They slogged their guts out every summer, repairing, rebuilding, restoring spaces in dog day conditions, it was the least we could do. They laughed and joked about our suits, dress shoes and matching ties while piling hard plastic plates high with slices, completely skipping the salad bar. Every fall M.C. even played intramural basketball on a team made up of our staff. They battled locals in the Hudson Park Gym. Rumor has it he'd dunk every now and then on just the right fast break. Our yearly events brought us together, create connections, build trust, foster comradery, and strengthen relationships. It was magic, these were the settings where real conversations took place. The year was an assortment of celebrations, ceremonies and occasions that promoted partnership, participation, and positivity, influencing how we treat each other, ultimately impacting how we showed up for students.

Hands down the most revered event was the District Holiday Party. A festive dinner held in downtown Rainier's City Hall just before winter break. Our cafeteria staff was known for catering, the food wasn't run of the mill lunchroom grade. They took pride in putting out a restaurant quality spread, equip with traditional holiday fixings. The hall was decorated with lights, shiny garland, ornaments, candles, wreaths and the standard Christmas tree. M.C. worked the bar, fully stocked with booze he provided from his own personal stash. He wore a Santa hat making him appear close to seven feet tall, smiling and asking "what can I get ya'?" Sinatra's rendition of Jingle Bells blared in the background. Each December the event was packed, staff, kiddos, spouses, significant others, school board members, volunteers, substitutes and retirees attended. However, this particular year, attendance was sparse. We were in the throes of bargaining with both unions, classified and teachers, on a shoestring budget. The inadequate State School Fund projection commandeered the headlines of every Oregon newspaper choreographing looming budget cuts. We knew the level of funding wouldn't allow us to maintain our district's current level of service, let alone increases in salaries and insurance. Four years of developing a healthy district culture wither away in thirty days' time, plummeting positivity, corrupting comradery, tanking trust, sinking solidarity. We'd hoped to band together, elevate our voices, stand firm for our community and advocate for adequate State School funding but negotiation years cause upheaval.

So instead of solidarity, December exposed a divide, our unions boycotted the holiday party. A swift gut punch to our superintendent, a right cross to the chin of administrators, we had a long bargain ahead. I stood between the high school principal and M.C., looking up at the two giants before scanning the sparse group of attendees. A couple classified staff, aspiring administrators, the maintenance crew, us, some board members sprinkled here or there. Paulie was two, he danced around the hardwood floor to Christmas jingles, my wife snapped pictures on her phone while Azaria perused the appetizers. M.C. steamed, "they're boycotting over a damn COLA, what the hell?" He picking up Paulie, holding him in the air so they could see each other eye-to-eye. With all seriousness, M.C. divulged his deepest thoughts, "whatever you do, don't join the union kid," then he drained a glass of eggnog. "This winter just disconnect," he said, "don't come in, and don't respond to email. I'll cover December, you cover January as superintendent, we're getting out of dodge man. I'm taking the wife to Europe. Can you handle that?" asked MC. "I got you, no question," I replied. He gave me a fist bump nodding in agreement.

Each day I woke at 5am, my phone's vibrating alarm buzzing on my chest, careful not to disturb the house, I'd tiptoe to the home office. The goal was getting as much dissertation writing completed as possible. I'd done the footwork, held meetings, focus groups, interviews, had colleagues test out processes and share their feedback. It was time to put the collage of research and sticky notes on paper. It was a cold December, frosty driveways, scarf, knit hat and glove weather. Our house was full of holiday cheer, a twelve-foot Christmas tree in the living room full of ornaments dazzling through red and green twinkle lights. I nestled in my comfy zip-up hoodie and red flannel pajama pants with the white snowflakes all over them. Why not stay in the holiday spirit while typing away, proofreading, revising and restructuring paragraphs. Sipping black coffee under the soft glow of the classic Christmas Story "leg lamp" I got as a gift just two years prior due to the nostalgic fondness I had for the movie. I delved deep in the depths of dissertation. Capturing the study chapter-by-chapter, page-by-page, paragraph-by-paragraph, one sentence at a time. Somedays, I conquered three or four hours of writing before the family was up and moving. Other days I was lucky to get 30 minutes, those days I typically barricaded myself in the office after dinner scrambling to acquire some additional writing time. By oneself, you wrestle with interpersonal thoughts, distractions can deter you from accomplishing your goal. I found evening writing sessions extremely difficult. My attention span - brief, lethargic after eating, inattentive and easily side tracked. Focus, it's going to take grit, consistency and determination to reach the finish line. Morning was my time, I was steadfast, alert, focused, attentive, keying away vigorously into my Apple PowerBook until it was time to refill my mug with dark roast java.

Christmas came and went, the New Year rang in with text messages, phone calls, Time Square's ball drop counting down on the large flat screen mounted above the den's fireplace, flashing Happy 2013! Roman candles booming in the distance as well as shotgun blasts from moron neighbors firing off hunting rifles in the sky. Surprisingly I felt rested, balanced, accomplished, ready to take on my role, covering as Superintendent, while M.C. took a well-deserved European vacation. I handed my freshly written chapters to my advisor, Tom, for feedback guidance and revision. "You've got some reading to do, I've been writing all winter" I said proudly, handing him a hard copy of a hundred or so pages clasped tightly together with a large metal binder clip. "Wow, alright, you're motivated! I need you to talk to the others in your cohort about your writing process, many people are stuck. They'll listen to you, you're a leader" he replied. "Sure thing, I want to graduate this June, I've gotta' get this done" I smiled.

M.C. had hipped me on running the daily operations, I felt ready. Megan was HPE's acting principal in my absence, she was also working towards administrator licensure, and needed practicum hours. She was confident, capable of covering me at HPE. We welcomed kids back from break the first week of January, "just walkie me if you need anything, I'm going to start the day at the high school, then spend time at the District Office making calls to online students that aren't making progress" I heading up the concrete stairs towards the high school. "Sounds good" Megan replied, speed walking down toward HPE.

That first week the classrooms were chilly. Students and staff wore coats in classrooms, complaining when they saw me in the halls. "Are you going to close school?" students asked. "It'll warm up soon, we'll be alright" I quickly replied. Monday's at 4am our maintenance crew fired up our old temperamental boilers, they took their time heating up, by 10am classrooms were warm. With temperatures below freezing, any precipitation would turn to snow. During recess we got a light dusting. Kids cheered hoping to catch a snowflake on their tongue. Megan walkie-talkie me to discussed the weather report, Portland was projected to get three to four inches overnight. "If Portland gets that much, we'll get ten to twelve inches here," she stated. Every January Rainier schools closed due to inclement weather. When Portland flakes were barely sticking, Rainier accumulated enough to close school. I'd become accustomed to the additional days off, paying little attention to M.C. process for closing the district. He'd master it, shifting with ease, to him it was as natural as opening the building.

I knew sending students home early was a nightmare. Working parents, unmet kids locked out of their homes on unexpected early release day, parent complaints, angry phone calls and upset board members. I gathered the transportation director, maintenance lead, high school administrators, technology director and interim principal Keplinger. The snow was swift but wasn't sticking, nervous teachers, students anxiously hoping for early release. As superintendent, decisions falls squarely on your shoulders. "Early release is a bad call, we can make a full day in just a few hours, probably close tomorrow. Thoughts?" I asked the group.

They nodded in agreement. "let's hold a unified message, stay positive, we're monitoring the situation and planning for our regular dismissal time" I said confidently.

Watching the snowfall outside M.C.'s window, I noticed a red Jeep Wrangler quickly approaching. It was Chet, board member and HPE parent, known for telling it like it is. He hopped out in bewilderment "Coakley, what the hell are you doing!? I live up there" he said, pointing to the hills. "Many of us do, why didn't we close? It's bad up there" he belted. "I met with transportation, we'll be ok, they're confident they can make the routes, worst case, we'll run snow routes." I replied. Chet fired back, "the transportation director's an idiot, next time call me, I'll give you the real deal, good luck!" with that he hopped in his Wrangler and disappeared.

Our head of transportation was a rookie hired in the summer, a delivery driver from Texas. He was nervous, jumpy and annoying. He'd frustrated me to know end, ringing my office phone in sheer panic three days in a row in September. Before I could say "hello" he'd launch into "we got a lost kid," then he'd call back five minutes later, with "all is well, he wasn't sitting in his assigned seat." By day three I snapped "look, your systems' broken, fix it. Don't call me before the driver takes roll, kids change seats. I've been here six years, I've never got a call about a lost kid until you got here!" Needless to say, he fixed the system.

An inch accumulated by dismissal, around 3:10pm the last bus pulled out of the lot. Staff scurried to their cars, rushing to get home before it got worse. A steady snow, the temperature dropping by the hour. "Don't stay too long, you won't make it home" said my secretary. At 4:30pm transportation notified me that every bus route was successfully completed. I quickly locked up, defrosting the window's and warming the engine of my wife's 2001 X-Type Jaguar. It had four-wheel drive so I used it in winter months after finding my Benz would lose traction in the slightest bit of accumulation. Before reaching the bridge, the snow picked up speed. Large flakes streamed, blurring visibility, I cranked the wipers to full speed. White streets, freeway markings were nonexistent, cars moved at a snail's pace as inches amassed making the roads a skating rink. The right side of the freeway became a parking lot, cars in ditches, some stuck in banks, others pulled over to put on chains. The X Type trudged along like a tank, over the snow packed highway, scooting past fender benders and collisions. The heater worked overtime pumping all it could muster through the circular vents. I alternated my hands, one on the vent, the other on the steering wheel.

Hours passed, loved ones called to check on me. I pulled to the side of the road to remove blocks of ice off from the windshield wipers. Every forty minutes or so they turned into encased popsicles. Overjoyed by the mini box of Junior mints I found in the glove compartment, I scarfed them like a starving prisoner. The radio was spotty, the six-disc changer played through repeatedly. It took seven hours before the trusty jag pulled into my dark snow-covered driveway in Ridgefield. I closed the district for the remainder of the week, checking in with staff and key board members living in higher elevations. They texted me photos of their neighborhoods the night before. I'd debrief with the transportation director before making the final decision.

M.C. returned in week 3, the day of our board meeting. He was rested, refreshed and ready to tackle the issues that were fast approaching. Full of ideas and energy, he was back in the office, ready to talk. I met him outside of the boardroom. "How we doing? You're looking sharp, man" his voice boomed. "Thanks, you too." I wore a dark navy suit, he had on a gray four button pinstripe. He pointed out his new oxfords, "check these out, got'em in France, it's amazing there, gotta show you some pictures" he smiled. He was holding a paper bag from Starbucks, "I got us some breakfast sandwiches, there's coffees in the boardroom, you got time?"

"Sure, thanks" I said walking into the boardroom. "Great job covering me, much appreciated" M.C. said smiling. "I don't know, that first day of inclement weather was rough, Chet was fired up that I didn't call an early release." M.C. giggled, "what the hell's he know, everyone thinks they can do this job, but they can't. Everyone made it home safely, you kept calm, that's a win in my book. If a board member wants the job, first get the licensure, then get in line, am I right?" he said, extending his fist. I gave it a pound, chuckling, "exactly." He quickly shifted gears, "how's your doctoral work coming?" I told him I wrote all winter break to play catch-up. "You're nuts, you're gonna' piss of your wife!" he joked. "What's the plan? Where do you go from here? Not trying to push you out, you're hard to replace. I'm surprised you stayed this long… six years. You're a big fish in a small pond, don't stay forever" he said directly. "Not sure, I'm still dedicated to it" I hadn't given it much thought, M.C. ended with, "at tonight's board meeting I'm going to move some things around. We're in budget cuts, uncertain times, what do you think about being Assistant Superintendent?" "Right, we're cutting staff, but adding District Office, that'll go over real well" I said confused. "I got some ideas, whatever happens tonight, we stick together, deal?" We shook hands, "what's going to happen?" I asked. "Not sure, still trying to figure it out, I'll direct the cuts. You need to cut an FTE at HPE. We'll figure out what that looks like in a few weeks." "Alright, yikes!" I replied.

In preparation for Black History Month teachers were reading stories to students tied to writing projects about historical Black figures. The walls were filled with drawing and student's reports, the third-grade wing of the building had a display of Martin Luther King Jr. and Rosa Parks. I spent time perusing students' writing. "Good morning Dr. King." said a small voice. I turned to find a new student, a little girl who just moved to Rainier after the New Year. "Very funny" I said unamused. "Well isn't that you?" she asked with a serious face pointing to the illustration on the cover of the children's book, Martin's Big Words. "No, that's not me, but I'll take it as a compliment" I smiled and gave her a fist bump before leaving the second-grade hallway.

Board nights for me were extremely long, not enough time to go home so most evenings I'd head over to Longview to grab some dinner, or order some food to go from El Tapatio in Rainier, but this evening I stayed in the building. I'd packed leftovers from home to heat up so I could take some time to respond to emails while eating. I'd become a pro at power napping, I could fall asleep in less than five minutes. I'd turn off the lights, lean back in my office chair, prop my feet up on the desk, setting me phone alarm for 20 minutes. For some reason, I was most comfortable when I would place my elbows on the arm rails, and cross my fingers with my hands over my chest. After I found my comfortable pose, I was out. Once during mid-nap, I awoke to a blood curdling scream. "I thought you were dead" my secretary wailed, "I need you to sign some papers…that looked scary" she said panic stricken. After that incident I began locking the door, that way if someone needed me they'd knock, and I'd wake up. While quickly being able to doze off seemed to be a good skill, I've always been a very light sleeper, moving right out of slumber with the slighted sound, voice, knock or thump. This particular evening, I got twenty minutes of uninterrupted sleep before the alarm sounded. I'd stretch, wash my face, freshen up, brush my teeth and hair, then walked across the campus to the triad of double wide trailers, into the middle one for the board meeting. I was greeted with smiles and handshakes from board members, our high school principal, vice principal, and the rest of our tiny admin. team. There were a few community members and parents in attendance, I said hello before grabbing a seat in the front row. Chet came over and said, "Hey sorry about the other day, sometimes I can be intense, you're doing a good job." "No worries, all's well that ends well" I replied.

At 6:25pm M.C. rushed through the door wearing a royal blue suit, white shirt and tie. He was holding his brief case together with both hands. It was bursting at the seams with papers. "Here, let me help you with that," said Mary, the board secretary, taking his bag as he sat in the middle of the board table. He seemed taller, agitated and a bit jumpy. After the usual formalities, he went into his Superintendent's report… "as you are aware, this year's state school fund is woefully inadequate. While our numbers at North Columbia Academy are up due to our online component, numbers continue to drop at the Jr./Sr. High school, even a bit at HPE. Based on these variables we're looking at a 5% cut across the board. That means, we will need to discuss what we will reduce next year. We could cut outdoor school or close the pool." Moans, groans and grumbles came from the audience and member of the Board. "We'll need to cut three teaching FTE, two at the high school and one at HPE, two classified FTE, one from each building, and one administrator position.

Our least senior high school administrator will be cut. Next year, I will serve as Superintendent/High School Principal, to ensure the support I need to keep things running smoothly Principal Coakley will serve as Assistant Superintendent/Elementary Principal."

With that statement, the high school principal was demoted to vice principal, the vice principal was cut, and I was promoted in the same moment. The board sat stone faced, they knew it was coming, M.C. had explained with reasons to all of them, they were all on the same page. From the seat behind me I heard "screw you" I glanced back to find the vice principal flipping me the bird. They had been blindsided and thought I was in on the plan. I gave him a look like, what do you want from me? After the superintendent's report, the high school administrators left the building. I stayed till the end of the meeting, saying goodbye to board members and helping Mary put things away. Once the coast was clear M.C. walked over "what do you think Chief?" he asked. "Crazy, why didn't you say something?" I asked. "Sometimes you can't show all of your cards, you'd probably try to talking me out of it, plus I didn't know if I'd get any pushed back from the Board. I got nothing" he grinned. "Drive safe, wait till' you tell your father. Congratulations, we got our work cut out for us next year" said M.C. with a sigh of relief.

The remainder of the school year our comradery with the high school administration deteriorated, the VP quit that next month, the high school principal quit soon thereafter. M.C. assumed the role of Superintendent/Principal earlier than expected. So, I began taking on more responsibilities to fill the gap. We directed the cuts to balance the budget, negotiating with both unions, we reached agreement towards the end of the school year, both with three-year contracts taking year one as flat (no salary increase). My duties were heavily HR tasks, investigating complaints, conducting processes, reviewing policies and presenting them to the board for adoption, familiarizing myself with the ends and outs of union contracts. To most educators HR is last place they'd want work, it felt technical, disconnected from students. I on the other hand loved it, the responsibility, the level of leadership, holding people accountable for performance. I never felt disconnected from students, I spent more time in classrooms, not just at HPE, also at the Jr./Sr. High, NCA, the health center and meeting with online students. As I look back, I realized I was in the zone that year, writing reports, rising at 5am to do dissertation work. I moved like a train at top speed, nothing dropped, went unnoticed or was left incomplete. M.C. had also hit his stride, we were a strange duo, performing each day as superheroes. We met every challenge, conquered it, coming out better on the other side.

That June I received my doctorate with two other cohort members, Peter and Dan. We pushed each other enough to graduate, each of our dissertations was tied to a product that assisted school leaders to improving practice. I developed a handbook entitled, Moving to A Schoolwide Title I Program: *the path principals should follow to maintain a healthy school culture.* There were two graduations, a smaller more intimate hooding ceremony hosted by the College of Education, as well as Portland State University's larger graduation ceremony, held at the Memorial Coliseum, the original home of the Portland Trail Blazers, the stadium was pack each graduate walked out through the team tunnel, on to court to take their seat, doctoral students entered first, I was the first graduate leading the graduating class of 2013 on to the floor, followed by Dan, Peter, then our advisor Professor Emeritus, Tom Chenoweth. The graduating class was approximately two thousand students, the first name called on the microphone was "Dr. Paul Coakley" I walked on stage with Tom Chenoweth who hooded me as the College President shook my hand, handing me my doctoral degree. I could hear my Dad's voice roaring over the large crowd. Tom remained on stage to hood my colleagues before we took our seats. I was on cloud nine, "now we just sit and wait" said Tom, I looked at the sea of graduates waiting in anticipation of their names to be called, "Yeah, I guess so."

That fall I officially took on the dual role, on the first day back for staff M.C. announced me as the Assistant Superintendent, then asked me to say a few words, which was met with applause. I rambled something along the lines of "it's a pleasure to serve in this role and support all aspects of the district. I'm also still serving as the principal of HPE… I hope to see everyone more because this year we will be improving our

Professional Learning Communities or PLCs for those who are new." That was met with a less applause, even some groans.

To ensure that my staff at HPE didn't feel they had been reduced to a halftime principal, visibility was really important. I knew this would be a concern because I was tipped off by Mrs. Bea, past union president. We'd built a good rapport over the years and worked through some hard situations. She approached me at the staff BBQ, "Hi Paul, or should I say Dr. Coakley? Congratulations" she smiled. "Paul of course, Dr. Coakley is for students, maybe it will motivate them...how are you Mrs. Bea?" I replied. She launched in without answering the question, "we like our principal, we're concerned that you're spreading yourself too thin, and that we won't see much of you anymore. They've reduced you to halftime" she said with a sad face. "No, that's not the case...I'm still your full-time principal, PLCs, HR tasks and policies, are things I was already working on last year, they're responsibilities that I can do in my spare time. Which now I have more of since I'm not working on my doctorate" I said. It was an answer that she wasn't satisfied with, but it was hard to dispute, "Ok" she said, giving me a side hug, "we want our HPE principal." "Understood," I said in an assuring manner.

I built a schedule that allowed me to hit all the high traffic areas, be seen by students and staff daily, morning and afternoon supervision, cafeteria duties, class visits. Megan was the Dean of Students at this point, she'd completed her administrators license and was a strong support. We rotated locations for supervision, providing staff with support, frequently checking on students especially those that would benefit from a brief 1 to 1 conversation. My classroom visits, duties and meetings were all scheduled, Google Calendar was the navigation tool I used daily to guide my success. Quarterly, I was out of the building to attend a full day of training at our Educational Service District (ESD) in St. Helens, a small group of administrators across the region would collaborate on strategies for moving achievement, discussing PLC process, sharing findings, challenges and offering suggestions.

Educational researcher Robert Dufour defines PLC as "a professional learning community where educators are committed to working collaboratively in ongoing processes in collective inquiry and action research to achieve better results for the students they serve. PLC operates under the assumption that the key to improved learning for students is continuous job-embedded learning for educators." In Rainier, we rolled out PLCs two years ago, it was an initiative that came with a lot of passive resistance. Teachers met in grade level teams, some were looking at data, following the protocol we adopted from Dufour's book, Professional Learning Communities at Work. Other team, I'd find talking about movies, browsing their computers or preparing plans for a substitute teacher, this was the case at all of our schools. We rolled it out with too much anatomy, it was difficult to monitor, there was lack of commitment, leaving us with little to no improvement in results.

My first priority was to fix the issue, revamping the way we operated PLCs. I strategized about my plan of attack, beginning with small technical changes. The first was a reboot, retraining all staff, HPE, NCA and our Jr./Sr. High School teachers together in the Commons. I presented on the key components of a PLC, leveraging the research of Dufour and Eaker, visiting and listening to the teams in deep discussion, wrestling with essential questions identified in the research. It went on like this for about three weeks, conveying the entire teaching staff across the district into the commons at circular tables, while they engaged in PLCs, principals were present, engaged in discussions, rotating to tables providing support and ensuring accountability. Discussions were focused, student-centered, they process followed the process with fidelity, teams became consistent in the approach. However, the technical shift of moving the teams to a central location during our late start Wednesdays to engage in PLCs, removed the autonomy. The Survivors and Fundamentals were slowly growing resentment for me and the process, which I was holding with a tight grasp. Finally, one of them launched a missile, hoping for a direct hit. "So, now that we understand the process and can properly follow it, how long do we have stay in PLC jail? Will we ever be able to meet in our classrooms?"

Table conversations froze, the room became silent. It was a voice that I had become accustomed to over the years, one of my teachers, strong, passionate, sometime known for being negative and resistant to change. "We've seen more progress these last few weeks than we have all last year, this is the only location where teams and coaches have access to each other. I think we need to stay the course until we get the results we want for kids" I said, which was met with some nods of agreement as well as some groans of disappointment. M.C. piped up and was less diplomatic, "these late start Wednesdays are approved by the Board for professional development, it's district directed time, the administration determines the location, this is it. We're not going back to classrooms. Last year I'd visit our PLC's and find people on their phones or doing emails, that's not what it's for. If your heart's not in it, there's the door... or we can easily make this day a regular school day, I'm sure the parents would appreciate it. Now can we get back to team conversations?" he asked loudly. After thirty seconds of pure silence the banter picked up again. I looked around the room, teams were back in full swing, the teacher who asked the question had fled the room.

After PLC time I made a beeline to her classroom, she was crying. "Hey, you ok?" I asked. "It's not just me who feels that way, I'm the only one with the guts to speak up" she said wiping her tears with a tissue. "You're a good teacher, I know you can guide your team without a central location, but not everyone can. Also, this work is not about adults getting what they want out of the time. This is about really understanding what kids are learning, meeting them where they are, then helping them overcome obstacles in their learning. In the future, I'd appreciate a one-to-one conversation instead of being blindsided in front of the group."

"Sorry, that wasn't my intent, ok, I will." she said softly. "Thanks" I said before leaving the classroom.

If I wasn't dealing with staff issues, it was parents, spanning from the overly dedicated enthusiastic chaperone, to the single dad looking for support, the parents focused on academics, the covertly racist ones that despised the idea of a Black principal, to the downright wack-a-doos that make you worry about their children, questioning the strange behaviors their kids exhibit at school, sometime engaging in conversation that warrant a report to Child Protective Services (CPS). In Columbia county,

CPS's operated with little to no confidentiality. Under code of law, every district staff member is a mandatory reporter, staff must immediately make a report anytime there is reasonable cause to suspect child abuse. Our staff held up their end of the bargain, filing reports when necessary. On multiple occasions shortly after the report was filed, I'd have an irate parent on the phone or even worse, at the school ranting about our staff filing false reports. "How do you know it was the school who called?" I'd ask. "CPS told me" was the parents' response.

So, it came as no surprise, when our Board Secretary burst into a Cabinet meeting to let us know that Sure Shot Steve, one of my most wack-a-doo parents, called pissed about a CPS report and was on his way to "shoot up the school." We sprang into action, calling a lockdown, notifying our School Resource Office, sprinting to our respective locations based on training and repetitive drills. The technology director and I ran toward the Commons crouching down low with our heads on a swivel, checking the hillside for Sure Shot Steve's raggedy truck to come racing up or down the hill. I held my key fob in my hand quickly scanning the door for fast entry into the building. It was a ghost town, not a student or staff member in sight. The tech director split in a different direction. I made my way through the commons to HPE. HPE was silent, no one in sight, all doors were locked. I peered outside at the portables, then the parking lot, finding the coast clear, I ran to the portables, yanking on door handles, thankfully they were locked, the only doors that couldn't lock automatically. I swiftly made it back in the building and positioned myself in the bookroom, located before one would reach any of the classroom, with the door cracked open. Eyeing the school's main entrance, I practiced flinging the door open and throwing a hard-right jab. I imagined myself tossing open the door and throwing a haymaker that connected with his face.

We sat in silence for what felt like an eternity, eventually getting a call that everything was all clear, we could come out of lockdown. I made the announcement, then doors began to open and noise filled the air. I checked on classrooms before making my way back to the district office. "Michael, wrestled the gun away," said Mary when I entered the trailer doors. "No way!" I said. "Seriously, he came up the steps with a shotgun, Michael opened the door and ripped it out of his hands, then our resource officer took him away. CPS is coming to get his kids." I walked into M.C.'s office, "hey you're a hero, you saved us!" I said. He was out of breath, sweating like he had just played a full court B-ball game, "you'd do the same, that crazy bastard tried to kill me" he replied.

Interestingly enough there was no news media, no accolades, little to no recognition given to our superintendent. Only the appreciation of those in the district office, the rumors of his heroic act amongst staff. "We need to call the media, this is crazy" I said. "Pipe down will you, no one gives a crap…if he shot one of us, then they'd run a story."

Research tells us that the impact on a student taught by a low performing teacher for a year, can have negative effects for three years. Even having one excellent teacher can't offset the damage done by the ineffective year's impact. In other words, your school is only as strong as your weakest link, if you have a teacher that isn't coachable, burnt out, mediocre or ineffective a good principal must intervene. Someone can be ineffective for a variety of reasons: some lack the skills to manage their classrooms, others have a weak grasp of the curriculum, or are poor at explaining concepts. Some may be too aggressive and are feared, others are too passive and not taken seriously. Then there are those who are too quirky, exhibiting odd inexplicable behaviors that disrupts learning, and leave students with a lack of confidence and a low perception of the teacher. At the elementary level parents usually notice things like: a teacher who's always absent, their student used to enjoy school but now they don't, or the teacher's strange behaviors have warranted several requests to the principal to switch classes.

In the midst of all that was happening in my dual role, in the spring I received several requests from parents to move their kids from a specific fourth grade teacher's classroom. Let's call her Mrs. X, she had always been a quirky person, awkward with interactions, and easily distracted. However, she knew the content but lacked belief in her students. I always had a concern about Mrs. X. I'd documented lack of passion and performance in her past evaluations. I had tough conversations with her in previous years about inclusion, differentiating her instruction to accommodate all students. I observed a lesson she taught where she avoided engaging a student with disabilities. She also received a letter of reprimand for providing answers to a student on a state required exam. A report was submitted to the state licensing commission, so they opened an ongoing investigation. I heard nothing on that front so based on the contract, she continued to teach, but was a nervous wreck, her attendance had become spotty, her quirkiness was at an all-time high.

During my classroom walkthroughs I intentionally made a visit to her room. Students were all over the room, sitting under desks, lying on the floor, others had their heads down on tables. Her desk was positioned far away from the students, she sat in her teacher's chair wearing a thick down parka and a fuzzy pair of earmuffs. "What are you guys doing?" I asked a girl sitting on the floor near the entryway. "S.S.R," the student whispered. S.S.R stands for *Sustained Silent Reading*. A concept built on the premise that the more time you spend doing something, the better at it you'll become. In most cases, I find this to be true, but in elementary classrooms where a teacher is checked-out, monitoring for noise level at best, S.S.R is useless. In any elementary classroom it shouldn't be used more that fifteen minutes, for Mrs. X, it shouldn't be used at all. Swiftly scanning the room I saw several variations of S.S.R. I observed *Sustained Silent Resting, Sustained Silent Relaxing, Sustained Silent Recess*, for some it was *Sustained Silent Romper Room*. I even have a few kids enjoying their personal favorite, gathered together for S.S.R, a *Super Silly Reunion*. Whatever was happening in that classroom at the moment had nothing to do with the actual "R" - Reading.

Shaking my head in disappointment I left the classroom and headed to my office. I sorted through a stack of mail, tossing invitations to conferences, curriculum ads and repetitive Title 1 updates in my recycling bin. Sifting through the heap of mail I came across an envelope addressed to "Hudson Park Principal Mrs. X." I stared at the envelope confused, is this a letter that is supposed to go to the teacher, or was this my mail inappropriately addressed? Based on the fact that it said Hudson Park Principal, I opened it. It was on a school district's letterhead following up on a letter of reference written by Mrs. X. This was the last straw, I couldn't take it anymore, the parent complaints, the poor teaching, the cheating, the absences, the overuse of SSR, the impact this burnout was having on my students, and now this…posing as the principal and providing someone a letter of recommendation. What gall, I'd take on any complaint procedure, union representative, fight any contract, and hold as many courageous conversations to get this person out of the classroom. I phoned MC to discuss the next steps. Then, I walked back into her classroom, no teaching was taking place, kids were at their desks writing in journals, a prompt was written in blue ink on the whiteboard "Over the weekend I…" The same student that I spoke to before hopped up out of her seat and came over to me, "you're back, now we're doing our Weekend News" she said with a smile, I nodded. Then walked to Mrs. X's desk where she sat fiddling with papers, "meet me at the district office after bus duty, please bring your union representative" I said firmly. "Okay, what's going on?" she asked. I gripped the open envelope tightly, waving it in my hand before walking out of the room. Then, I stormed to the second grade POD to check-in with a teacher who was my building's union representative. "Can you represent Mrs. X after bus duty today, I need to ask her some questions about attendance, parent complaints, and a possible violation of board policy?" She nodded in agreement.

We sat in MC's dimly lit office, it was stuffy and humid, we huddled around a small circular conference table. Although it was 75 degrees outside, Mrs. X sat bundled in a winter coat zipped to her neckline with blue fuzzy earmuffs covering both ears. Her union rep sat with a notepad and pen, I began with questions while M.C. typed away on his IPad.

"Your attendance has been really spotty lately, can you tell me what is going on?…, I'm getting a lot of parent complaints, many requesting to move classrooms."

"I have Parvo," said Mrs. X. "Excuse me, you have what?" I asked.

"Parvo" she repeated factually "You mean the dog disease?" M.C. cross examined.

"Yes, I'm very sick, I'm suffering from Parvo." Mrs. X said, looking over at M.C.

"That's impossible, it's a disease for dogs, mainly puppies, humans can't get Parvo…this is ridiculous" M.C. harangued, he was visibly frustrated. He took a deep breath. "We need a doctor's note."

In my best HR voice, I rephrased it slowly "based on your frequent absences, we are requiring a doctor's note, stating that you have Parvo."

"Sure, I'll bring you one," she replied. The union rep scribbled frantically in her notebook.

I continued, "as you know I have several concerns, you are still not differentiating your instruction, most of the lessons that you are teaching are going over your students' heads. Last year, I paired you with our Literacy Specialist and one of our best math coaches, still no progress. I've received at least five written requests from parents to remove their students from your class. Of the fourth-grade team you currently have the smallest class size. Moving any of your students puts an added burden on the teachers in your grade level. How do you suggest we address these concerns?"

"Well, I can give them a call, but ultimately if they want to move then that's out of my control" she said a bit louder, flailing her hands in the air.

"Does that seem fair to your partner teachers? I do my best to balance each grade's class size" I quipped.

"I guess not, but you asked if I had any suggestions, well that's it" Mrs. X said arrogantly.

I bit down hard, grinding my back teeth before gaining my composure, "During our last testing window a staff member reported that you were giving one of your students answers to a state exam. You later admitted to doing so. As you know, I had to report that infraction to the Teacher's Licensing Commission. That investigation is still open, there's a possibility that you could lose your license. That puts our school in a bad light, it also puts your reputation as a teacher at risk….do you care? Is there something going on that we should know about?"

She sadly dropped her head, a brief look of shame cross her face for seconds, then it was gone. "I just sat here and told you, I have Parvo! I got it from the children" she said, raising her voice. I paused before responding, glancing over at M.C. who had one hand on his head. "How did you get it from children?" I asked.

She made a disgusting face "they have these little circles on their skin, it kind of looks like a ringworm, but it's Parvo. They're nasty little carriers of it. It's highly contagious, now they've passed it on to me!"

"Earmuffs" M.C. blurted. I clenched my teeth again, this time hoping not to snicker, I maintained a professional demeanor. The room was silent. "What's with the earmuffs?" M.C. sarcastically duplicated.

"I'm cold, the Parvo makes me cold." Mrs. X doubled down before continuing, "why do you care? It's no crime to wear earmuffs." M.C. scoffed "well it's a little weird don't you think? Cold huh, well I guess that explains the winter coat in spring" M.C. retorted.

Before she could respond, I reached in my bag and pulled out the letter, I pointed to the salutation which read, Dear Principal Mrs. X. "Can you explain this? Why does this school district think you are the principal of Hudson Park?" I inquired.

"Well, I don't know," she said quickly, furrowing her brow, then cleaning her glasses and replacing them on her nose. "May I see that," she asked in a crackly voice. She held the letter up high, squinting closely at it. "So, if I call that district, they'll say it was done in error" M.C. challenged, "cause if I find out otherwise, we got problems" he said sternly.

The union representative placed her pen on the table and said "I'd like to halt the meeting to talk privately with Mrs. X. You don't have to answer any more questions," she said to Mrs. X.

"Sure, you can use my office, it's the small space in the back corner by the restrooms, just knock on the door when you're ready to come back in" I said calmly. The trailer walls of the district office were paper thin. M.C. and I sat in silence, aghast by what had just taken place. "That lady's lost it, she can't work with kids, if we don't get a doctor's note, she's done" MC whispered.

Approximately five minutes later, there was a gentle knock on the door, then they resumed their seats. "Mrs. X has something that she would like to share with you" said the representative. "I wrote a letter of recommendation for my daughter, she just got her teaching license" she said. "You wrote her a letter, put it on a letterhead and signed off as the principal of HPE, is that correct?" I asked. "Yes, I saw no harm in it, it's just a little fib" she replied. I looked to M.C., "what do you think Superintendent Carter?" I asked, setting him up for the kill. "Well, I'm shocked, it's more than a little fib. It's a flat out lie. Besides that, you're not one of my administrators, I wouldn't hire you as one of *my* administrators. Not so sure, I even want you in one of my classrooms as a teacher, I can't trust you." He continued… "don't ever, again misrepresent yourself as one of my administrators. Am I clear?" he asked. She nodded yes, barely making eye contact with either of us. I sat silently, steaming, I was hoping for a letter of resignation to no avail.

I handed her a letter that I had typed out during the break, "I am putting you out on leave, pending a doctor's note. You have five business days to provide the district office with a doctor's note stating that you have Parvo. Otherwise, I am bringing a recommendation for termination forward to the Board based on attendance, testing impropriety and violation of the Ethical Educator law. Do you have any questions?" Neither of them had questions.

On the fifth business day one of Mrs. X's relatives stopped by the district office and handed a sealed envelope to Mary. It was addressed to me, she handed it to me in the Commons, it was a letter of resignation.

Early Wednesday morning I got a call from M.C., it was a late start Wednesday and I was commuting from my new house in Vancouver. We left Ridgefield after finding out the owners were losing the house to foreclosure for an unpaid mortgage. We had planned to buy it, but the situation with the owner was so convoluted that we determined it was best to find a new home that was drama-free. We were contacted by the bank offering us a "cash for keys" deal. If we moved out by a certain date and left the house in decent order, they would pay us a lump sum. We would have left the house in good condition regardless of the deal, but of course we weren't going to turn down the money. So, we stuck to the terms, quickly purchased a house in Vancouver, moved swiftly and collected the "cash for keys." The morning of the move a bank representative came to conduct a walk through, "looks great, I'll come back later to get keys and give you the check" he said.

I ran errands before returning to meet the representative. The house was pitch black, I flipped the light switch, nothing. Glancing in the dark we found that the light fixtures, door handles, mirrors and appliances were gone. Vacant space where the fridge used to be, no oven, a gaping hole in the island where the gas stove once lived. "They stole everything!" said the bank representative. "They jacked me for my kicks!" I replied finding two pairs of sneakers and my remaining clothing missing. "Just file a police report and move on," he said as he left.

We had moved a bit closer to Portland, which cut down on my wife and Dad's commute, it made mine about 15 minutes longer. My car Bluetooth rang, "do you know who last drove the district car?" M.C. asked. "No, why? what's going on?" I replied. "Whoever used it last, left it a mess, it was filthy, trash everywhere, it reeked like a dead body. I just paid for a car detailing place to shampoo the interior. It's better but still smells." I burst out laughing…he continued, "I'm telling you man, it's bad. Don't count on doing PLC's today, cause I need to get to the bottom of this." "Ok, see you soon" I chuckled, "I'm almost to the bridge." The district car was a red Ford Focus that M.C. purchased for staff to use for local workshops and conferences. He had a first come first serve system. If a staff member was attending a local conference they would check to see if the car was available before driving and submitting a mileage reimbursement form. If the car was available they could reserve it, carpooling with other staff, there was even a gas card available, with instructions to fill the tank before returning it. M.C. took pride in having this benefit available to staff, he kept the vehicle neat and tidy for the next driver. During the late start, he went on about the condition in which the car was left, "I try to offer this benefit to staff, and this is the thanks I get. It smelled like a dead body in there!" A few chuckles filled the air. "You think this is a joke, if you know who did this, you better come forward as soon as possible. I spent my whole morning on this, I'm not playing around." he said intensely.

Just when I thought things could get any crazier, Megan caught me in the breezeway between HPE and the Jr./Sr. High school. "Hey" she said, "I need to tell you something, it was Mrs. X." "What was Mrs. X?" I asked. She looked around nervously, "the district car, the week before she resigned, three of us were going to carpool to Northwest Regional ESD for a Benchmark Math workshop" she explained, "Mrs. X checked out the car the night before. The next morning, we waited for her to pick us up but she never came. She almost made us both late, I ended up driving us both there in my car. Later, she called me and said she wasn't going to make it to the workshop because her dog died. I thought nothing of it until I heard Michael going off today." Then she ended with, "It smelled like a dead body in there, because there *was* a dead body in there. She must've transported her dead dog in the car to wherever it needed to go. The whole thing just turns my stomach" said Megan softly.

Moments later I was knocking on M.C.'s door, "You got a moment, I found out what happened to the car." I grinned.

CHAPTER 10

When Opportunity Knocks

M.C.'s words rang in my ears, not the big fish, small pond analogy, the words "don't stay forever." He was right. My triple role was a definite learning ground, but unsustainable. We moved at a clip that would eventually wear me out. It was a circus, we were jugglers, skilled at balancing multiple plates, bowls and flat objects on long sticks. We'd become quite masterful in technique, but eventually something would drop. Our only hope was that a colleague was skilled enough to catch the item, putting it back in motion, before it shattered.

On April 5, 2014, a new addition joined the family, a beautiful little girl. She was born with a disability, Trisomy 21, known as Down Syndrome. A condition where a person is born with an extra chromosome. The additional chromosome changes how the person's body and brain develop, causing physical and mental challenges throughout their lifetime. While each person with Downs may have similar attributes, each individual's abilities are different, unique. We named her Samia, which means - exalted on high. For months, medical professionals laid out the worst-case scenarios to us, filling our mind with worry, negativity and angst. After an ultrasound a doctor told us her face may possibly be sunken, because her nose had no visible cartilage. In addition, he stated "she may never be able to walk." Brian said there's no way to tell that from an ultrasound. We switched doctors, which yielded a different opinion. She had Trisomy 21, but would be fine, she'd need a lot of love and support.

I sat between Paulie and Azaria at Legacy Hospital, when Samia came into the world. She had no visible physical impairments. A perfect bundle of joy, strong, yet fragile and delicate at the same time. Her nose looked just like Paulie's, it also resembled mine, "well she's a Coakley" I said, ever so gently touching her on the nose. Her big puffy jaws stood out making her the cutest baby I had ever seen. "Look at her cheeks, so cute," said four-year-old Paulie. He sat on the edge of the hospital bed gently holding his baby sister in his arms. She was swaddled in a white hospital blanket covered in red and blue hot air balloons. Her head was wrapped in gauze, with a clear intravenous tube visibly attached. She sat in silence, her eyes tightly shut. Grandparents, relatives and friends, holding baby gifts, balloons, cards and flowers filled the waiting room. Only immediate family was allowed in the hospital room. When Paulie got tired of holding her, I took her in my arms and held her close. God made me her father for a reason. I was entering a new season, uncharted territory. I was an earthly protector, provider, encourager, a solid foundation, these were my children. Breathing a sigh of relief, I glanced toward the heavens, our future looked bright.

COSA keeps their website updated with administrator job postings. HR Director's submits their vacancies there. By doing so, a job gets listed broadly by the organization's national affiliates. I hadn't thought about vacancies for the past seven years, I was content navigating Rainier's pond. Performing a juggling act, while the audience watched in amazement. While salary was on the lower end of the spectrum, learning opportunities, leadership experiences, and overall responsibility far outweighed the salary. I'd taken two weeks off to help get Samia settled at home. Scrolling through COSA's website, I noticed a posting with a similar title to mine, Assistant Superintendent/Human Resources Director, Centennial School District. It was my current role minus the elementary principalship. Fascinated by focusing solely on supporting the superintendent while addressing HR issues, and provide guidance to principals filled me with excitement.

Centennial served around 6,000 students in East County, located smack between Gresham and Portland. Some of the district's schools had

Portland addresses, others were physically located in Gresham. During high school, I'd bike through its residential areas, it was all Gresham to me. My old stomping ground, the community I grew up in. In my mind, Portland was Northeast the "NE", where I shopped, got haircuts, went to church - the Black area, King, Ockley Green, offshoots of MLK Boulevard. Ten years prior it was rare to see Black folks in Centennial or Gresham. Now, it was the norm, 181st straddled the dividing jurisdictions of Gresham and Portland.

The Metropolitan Area Express (MAX) was a light rail system that changed the look and feel of the suburbs. During my high school years, the MAX ran from downtown Portland through Gresham. MAX was a hotbed for crime, gang activity, fights, muggings and temporary respite for vagrants avoiding a downpour. I stopped riding in high school, after a bad experience, a group of dudes planned to jack me for my red and gray Nike Flight 89's. During the height of gang culture, daily news of drive-by shooting, senseless killings, wearing the wrong color in the wrong place, at the wrong time, I had the audacity to wear a pair of crispy bright red $100.00 attention getters. Stepping on the train in flaming red Nikes, oblivious to the world, obviously unarmed, for no apparent reason other than *looking fresh*. I was a rapper not a fighter, a feather weight, barely 140lbs soaking wet. "Hey lil' homie, I like those kicks" said a large dark skin brotha wearing a ratty khaki colored Dickie suit. LaBa and I stopped bantering, glimpsing at the group of bruisers. "Thanks" I said, peering out of the corner of my eye. "What size are they? My homeboy wanna' try'em on" he said coldly. Since eighth grade I'd been a size 11. Peeking downward at the bigfoot crew I called out a smaller number, "These? 9 and a halves" I said trying to sound believable. "Them thangs too small" grumbled Dickie suit, "...but let me see'em anyways" he snarled. His homeboy had been looking me up and down as if he knew me from somewhere, "hold up man, ain't you Mr. Coakley's son?" "Yeah" I said proud but timid. "Damn, man! Your Dad's my principal." The MAX slowed, settling at the next stop, "these lil' dudes cool, we was just playin' about the shoes, peace homie" he said before they exited the train. I smiled nervously at LaBa, "ooh, that was close!" His eyes shot daggers back at me "you almost got us killed!" While I never rode the MAX again, the rail system expanded years later extending to further suburbs Beaverton, Hillsboro, the airport, and Clackamas.

The gentrification of Northeast Portland flipped the demographics of Gresham and Centennial, Northeast was no longer the "NE" I knew and loved. Portland's families of color were quickly priced out of the Alberta, King, and Ockley Green neighborhoods. Their previous Northeast Portland digs were unrecognizable, a depiction of Jonathan Krisel's television series, Portlandia. Bike shops, cafes, book stores, food carts, trendy restaurants, and gelato creameries filled with Fred Armisens and Carrie Brownstiens as far as the eye can see. Classrooms in Centennial, David Douglas, Parkrose, Reynolds and Gresham school districts diversified. 181 street was a sea of Black and Brown faces, filling low grade apartment complexes and affordable one-story houses.

The house we owned that I had commuted to Rainier from was in Centennial. Our long-time renter was a Centennial staff member, she lived there for years, ending her lease on good terms before purchasing a home. Eventually my mother-in-law occupied the house. Frequenting Centennial's stores, business and restaurants I knew the community well. The student population was a balanced blend of Dr. Howard and Rainier. Maybe my current role as a jack of all trades would make my hiring materials pop amongst the pool of White males that traditionally held these educational leadership seats. The Jeff's, Steve's, Robert's, David's, Chris's, Mike's, Kevin's, Jason's, Matt's, and Dan's. Maybe a Paul could blend into that group of names undetected, it was nonthreatening. The "Dr. title" might set it apart from the rest, logically I'll get an interview. I updated my resume, cover letter, required essay questions and application. The Dr. Paul E. Coakley in bold black ink at the top of my resume gave it a certain panache that was missing before. I mailed it, leaving no time for second guessing.

After the job posting date passed I was called and scheduled for an interview. I notified M.C., "It's a stretch but I want to be transparent, you said test the waters, so I threw my name in the ring" I said. "Hmm, I know I said that, now I'm kicking myself, you're gonna be hard to replace" he said. "It's just a round one interview, no job offer yet" I responded. "You've got a good shot. I know the superintendent, kinda. I think his name's Sam. He's solid, a sharp shooter, young guy...about your age. He's probably hoping for a person of color" said MC. The only Oregon superintendent I knew, hoping for a person of color beside Dr. Matthew Prophet was Michael. To be honest, I wasn't even sure he was *hoping* for one, he was a people person, hoping for a good leader. Knowing him, the fact I was Black was an added bonus. An opportunity to uplift, empower and change the Oregon's educational landscape, which I greatly appreciated. He opened a pathway to the superintendency, a seat only held by a handful of Black leaders since the eighties. M.C.'s foresight and lived experiences stretched well beyond mine. Over time, he saw me as the next generation of superintendent. Planting seeds for me to pursue a doctorate. In Oregon, at the time, having a White superintendent ally vouch for your leadership track record is an unspoken rule. That coupled with a doctorate better open the damn door to an interview. It's actually questionable if it doesn't.

What I didn't know at the time was, Sam Breyer, Centennial's superintendent would've interviewed me without any unspoken requirements. He was a superintendent truly intentional about creating an educator workforce that reflected the student population. Centennial was a majority minority district, meaning more than 50% of the student population were students of color. The student demographics rapidly changed, while staff demographic slightly moved. To be expected, the staff was predominantly White. Less than five percent of staff were people of color, who were mostly classified employees.

On the interview day, I drove into Portland from Vancouver, getting a feel for what might be my daily commute. I arrived early, parking under a large maple tree facing the elementary school nearest to the district office, Lynch Meadow Elementary. Not sure why the school had that name, but I had my assumptions. I looked at the tall trees as images of strange fruit flashed violently through my subconscious. Reminiscing the fear of biking past the school's fence, reading the sign Lynch Meadows in sixth grade as I high tailed it to a friend's house. No time to stroll down memory lane, I straightened my tie through the reflection of in driver side window, tossing on my navy pinstripe suit jacket. The District office was proportionate to the size of the district. It was no double wide trailer, nor was it the behemoth tri-level in PPS. A one-story building, with office spaces, cubicles, a large boardroom, staff lounge and dual restrooms. It gave off the feel of a giant manufactured home, equipped with dark wooden paneling. The process began in the boardroom. I was unusually comfortable as I talked to a group of approximately 15 people, a mix of teachers, administrators, classified staff, and administrative professionals I'd spoken with a few times on the phone. Gazing across the faces of the panel they seemed friendly, engaged and attentive. One principal stood out a bit, James Owens, who introduced himself as the principal of Butler Creek Elementary. I'd done my due diligence, learning as much as possible about the district and Superintendent Breyer. I even found a YouTube video from years prior where he presented to Gresham's City Council about the district's goals. I took notes, ensuring my talking points were in alignment. I perused old articles, Sam was principal of Butler Creek before serving as superintendent. Butler Creek was a level five school, the only school in the district ranked in the top five percent of the state for achievement. Sam hired James as his predecessor; James maintained the ranking as a second-year principal. James wore a navy suit similar to mine without pinstripes, he had a smart look about him, clean cut, professional and confident.

After the group interview, the retiring HR Director led me in and out of tiny offices for the next two hours, meeting with small groups, discussing issues and completing a writing assignment. His office was filled with filing cabinets and storage bins brimming with papers. The left side of the office was a wall with wooden built-in shelving, every inch was covered by binders, educational resource guides, books and clipboards with papers clamped down tightly. The right side had a desk, large metal gray filing cabinets and dark diagonal wood paneling, reminding me of a ski lodge. This could be my new office I thought, glancing around the room.

The process concluded with a 1:1 conversation with the superintendent. Sam's secretary was positioned directly outside of his office. His door was closed, "Hi Paul, I've known your Dad for years, we used to work together at PPS. Tell him Connie said hello." "I definitely will," I replied. "Nice to meet you." Connie was a cheery older lady, with short silver hair, she shook my hand, greeting me with a large smile. Sam opened the door inviting me in, "Superintendent Breyer, nice to meet you," I said. "Call me Sam, I've heard a lot of good things about you, but even more about your father" he said, "every reference call, I had to clarify that I was talking about Paul Jr, not Senior" he smiled. We were about the same height and age, Sam was friendly, a wise beyond his years. I made a mental note that he had already contacted my references. I glanced at the wall, "were you in the military?" I asked. "Marine Corp" he replied. "Wow, that's major, thank you" I said. He quickly changed subjects. "So, you complete your doctorate…dissertation defense and everything?" "Yeah, last summer, I graduated in 2013." "That's major, many begin but few finish" he stated.

That evening Sam called me directly and asked if I could come back on Thursday for round two. "Sure thing." Round two was straight forward, an interview with the Cabinet. Then he invited me to a burger joint in the southeast Portland. After a bit of small talk he said "you are the front runner, I'd like to offer you the job, I'm going to write down a number" he jotted on napkin, "would you accept the job for this amount" he asked, sliding a piece of paper across the table toward me. I peeked at it like a card player with no poker face in a game of Texas Hold'Em, "Yep" I replied. "Okay…, well that was easy," he said. "I thought you'd negotiate a bit. "Nope." I said with a smile, damn, I could've negotiated I thought, a skill that I was unfamiliar with, plus I didn't want to seem ungrateful, maybe that's a cultural thing. Nevertheless, I was more than happy with the number on the paper.

My last months in Rainier were rough, M.C. and I were cool, he was genuinely excited for me to take on a new challenge. The staff on the other hand became resistant, they knew I was leaving soon. When I shared the news with staff the custodian said "you didn't stay very long." In my estimation, seven years is about the right length of time for a leader to make a significant impact before hitting a wall. We accomplished a lot, both technical and adaptive, from installing a covered playground to analyzing schoolwide data to drive classroom instruction, meeting kids' individual needs, ensuring content that's rigorous, relevant and culturally responsive. Staff diversity increased by 7%, we survived budget cuts, Swine Flu, opened an online program and school health center, both were thriving. My goal was to leave the school in a better position than it was when I first started - mission accomplished. The prior principal stayed 28 years, "staying long" wasn't my goal. Leaders build leaders, I believed Megan had the leadership skills to pick up where I left off, to take HPE to the next level of success. She applied and was runner up, so she remained the Dean of Students. In true Megan fashion she was fine with it, "the new principal has much more experience than I do, I'll be here to support her" she said. "Unless you want to come to Centennial" I remarked. "Really, it's tempting and I'm honored, but I can't leave Rainier," she said. M.C. and I stayed on good terms, "if you want to talk, I'm just a phone call away" he said. We stayed in contact, connecting during COSA workshops and conferences, laughing, joking, telling war stories whenever we saw each other. "What up M.C.? It smells like a dead body in there" I joked while pointing to a workshop presentation.

In Centennial, Sam and I picked up where me and M.C. left off, a dynamic duo. His personality was quite the opposite of Michael. An introvert, sometimes visibly uncomfortable in group settings, but only if you really know him, most people couldn't tell. He was also direct, serious, straightforward with a socially conscious, culturally competent compassionate side. I'm an extrovert, not as extreme as Dad or M.C., dialed back a notch. Somehow we balanced each other out. Sam gave me clear goals to accomplish, "your biggest priorities this year is tackling the teacher evaluation process. If you can do that, you'll make a lot of people happy. You should also start connecting with our principals and union leaders, building relationships. You're starting in July, I'll be on vacation. I'm riding my bike through California, over the Golden Gate

Bridge." "Nice, what parts of California?" I asked. I plan to leave from Gresham and go all the way through. I've mapped my pathway and pit stops along the way. I'll bike as far as I can each day, staying the night at different motels along the way, then start again the next day. My wife will meet me in San Francisco at the end of my excursion" he said. "That doesn't sound like a vacation, that's work" I said. He smiled, "it's something I've always wanted to accomplish."

In week one, I cleaned out my new office, aka the ski lodge. Discarding out-of-date binders, old textbooks and handbooks. Relocating the desk, placing generic office art with leadership quotes on the diagonal wood paneling. My version of Breakthrough Coach's *"clean your office"* mentality. In a few days' it was decluttered, equip with the bare minimum. It felt crisp, airy, as a finishing touch I purchased a classic bankers lamp. The kind that appears in almost every movie, with a brass base, green lamp shade, and patented pull chain switch. I found the lamp exuded a calming effect that was psychologically soothing. I combed through a large box, left by my predecessor labeled "evaluation process," an assortment of loose-leaf papers, scrawling of notes, old agendas held by the Educator Effectiveness Committee. The committee's objective was to bring staff together to create an evaluation system, based on continuous improvement, with clear expectations and objectives. A system that increases student outcomes, assess strengths, acknowledges growth and empowers staff. I stayed into the evening hours reviewing documents in the dim office, only lit by the emerald green glow of the bankers lamp, supposedly allowing its radiance to improve my focus and concentration.

During the summer I met each principal at their school, listening and asking questions. Learning their perceptions, the strengths and challenges of their jobs and the system as a whole. Noting their frustrations with the evaluation process, the nuances and themes of school and district culture. Building trust, getting a sense of who they are, figuring out the best way to support their needs. Part of my role was coaching, making our principals look good. I began holding monthly meetings with union leadership. The teachers union preferred meeting in my office, classified leaders preferred a nearby Mexican restaurant. We traded stories, set expectations for operating in the spirit of collaboration and transparency. We shared our hopes for the district, I spoke about improving the evaluation process. "Let's create a process that supports everyone, while strengthen their skills, ensuring the best learning experience for all students."

Every four days or so I got a text from Sam, "how are things going?" he'd update me on where he was on his journey. He even sent a few pictures, in each photo he was leaner than the one before, his beard - thicker. "Dang man, you're melting away" I texted. "I'm biking about fourteen hours a day, anything I eat is immediately used as fuel." It was motivating, but not on my bucket list. I despised driving to California, let alone biking.

In Fall, I relaunched the Educator Effectiveness Committee, passionate educators volunteering their time to help refining evaluations. We scheduled bi-monthly meetings, developed norms, setting a December completion date. The committee process would be uploaded into an electronic evaluation system that outlined and archive evaluations by year.

I studied every contract, teachers, classified, administrators, even my own. I spent time getting to know my executive assistants, Tami and Shannon. They were lifesavers, detailed wealth's of knowledge, work-a-holics, genuinely there to make the department as effective as possible. We'd grab lunch every now and then, discussing the HR strategy. Our conversations helped us get to know each other, becoming a unified team. They never took time off during non-work days. I'd encouraged them to take time off, especially during the holiday. Through winter and spring break I'd drive past the district office and spot their cars in the parking lot. Then, I'd send a text, "you guys are supposed to be decorating the tree or sipping eggnog." Tami would reply "Yeah right, people need their paychecks." The district had an antiquated timesheet system, requiring HR to track and code staff absences, calculate them, then submit everything to the payroll department, payroll went through a similar process. Payroll staff was typing away in their offices while most staff tried finding some form of work-life balance.

For educational leaders transition from working with children in school environments, to working with adults at the district level, the change can be unfulfilling. For me, it was a natural progression. Perhaps my multifaceted year in Rainier gave me a clear reality of what my job was. I delved into systems work, measuring growth, diversifying, recruiting and retaining staff, helping principals, and monitor plans of improvement. Sam was a systems thinker, great at brainstorming ideas, exploring possibilities, and providing insight. He had a keen ability for seeing the big picture. Many times, he'd shared opinions and perspectives that hadn't been considered, I appreciated that.

Racial incidents became more prevalent across the country, schools were no different. Hate speech, racial epithets and stereotypical assumptions frequently reared their ugly head in schools. The racism shouldered by Black people in America didn't slow down, it just shifted a bit. It spread, expanded to every shade of melanin, landing on anyone not of European descent. US citizens' animosity, hostility and disdain for one another was evident. The media focused its attention on daily hate crimes, racially charged attacks of local businesses, neighborhoods and community gatherings. Many school boards were fractured, with "equity" being the dividing point.

At the same time, Sam and I were determined to build a system, different from traditional systems, centered on equity, diversity and inclusion. A district where academic outcomes were not predicted by race. Where discipline data, suspension, expulsions, and special education classrooms weren't overrepresented by Black and Brown students. Where students of color could engage in Advanced Preparatory (AP) courses, while feeling they belong there. Where students experienced more than one educator of color during their K-12 journey. A district where students didn't need to prove themselves to their teachers. Where staff believe in them, meet them where they were, and supported their academic success.

This work began prior to my arrival. In May of 2013, one month shy of my doctoral graduation, the Centennial School Board was the first district in Multnomah County to adopt a District Equity Policy.

The policy clearly outlined the Board's non-negotiables for working in the district, directly citing what they believe:

1. *We believe that race, ethnicity, economic circumstance, primary language and special needs do not predict academic success; but rather*

2. *We believe culturally responsive staff and effective use of research based instructional strategies predict academic success.*

The Policy had a strong definition for educational equity: *Educational equity means raising the achievement of all students while:*

1. *Narrowing the gaps between the lowest and highest performing students; and*

2. *Eliminating the racial predictability and disproportionality of which student groups occupy the highest and lowest achievement categories.*

Before applying to Centennial, I reached out to a friend that previously worked there. He shared his insights about on district, schools and community culture, as well as his admiration for Sam's work. My main take away was that the Board had set a strong foundation for creating equity both educationally and racially. "Check out the District Equity Policy" he said. Reading the policy, I felt empowered, it gave the superintendent authority to identify and eliminate practices that led to the overrepresentation of special education and discipline disparities for students of color. Calling out graduation and advancement placement data by race resonated with me. The policy gave HR the authority to comprehensively address harassment and discriminatory practices. Calling for recruitment, hiring of a workforce representative of the student body, plans for developing, supporting and retaining staff at all levels who are responsive to racial, linguistic and cultural differences. Directing the district to empower and elevate voices, especially underrepresented voices in school planning and district decision making processes. It concluded with a language that made the policy a priority "aligning resources to attain educational equity."

I had many conversations about this type of shift, especially amongst doctoral peer, colleagues and college professors. It was refreshing to see it in policy, upheld by a school Board, this is where I needed to be. A special place, doing difficult work in tumultuous times, a significant moment in history.

Sam and I were vocal about reducing suspension rates and eliminating expulsions. We drilled home the message to our administrators in our own specific ways. During an in-service focused on implicit bias and educational equity Sam stated, "every time I sign off on expulsion it makes me sick to my stomach" a powerful statement from our Superintendent. In my one-on-one conversations with a principal recommending a student expulsion, I asked them, "What gives you the right to place this student on a pipeline to prison?" They got the message. With strong leadership centered on the District Equity Policy we quickly identify our Believers, leaving Tweeners to determine what side of the fence they'd fall on. Sending Fundamentalist heading for the hills. We pushed on Survivors until they got on board or went elsewhere. At the helm of hiring, we diversified our workforce, eventually hitting a stride, our leadership team looked different. Not every vacancy was filled with a person of color, nor did it need to be. We filled each position with a Believer, through my past experiences interviewing in Beaverton and the like, I created a process that made sure we got the right people.

As the number two, my interactions with Board members were during board meetings, providing hiring recommendations, presenting policy updates, sharing changes to contract agreements. However, the interactions became more frequent due to long range facilities planning. I served on the committee, which included the majority of our Board. Our buildings were old, outdated, in need of repairs that our budget couldn't handle. Across the state district were passing bonds, renovating and modernizing schools, creating spaces for students that inspire creativity, confidence and inspiration. The only school we had with a newer feel was Butler Creek, which was more than twenty years old. It was located in our district's most affluent corner, near Clackamas, the upscale back hills of Gresham. Our oldest building was Pleasant Valley, constructed in the 1950s, dawning original brick and historic flooring. Our schools were well maintained, the maintenance crew paid attention to detail, doing their best on a tight budget. However, key replacements were needed. The boilers were so old the parts needing replacement were no longer being manufactured. Our team bought parts in bulk, storing them for future use. While we kept up appearances, there were major issues behind the walls. Heaters, pipes, coils, vents, and roofs were in poor condition.

The planning committee understood the issues, but disagreed on how to prioritize the spending of the funds. Some pushed for new construction, while high school supporters advocated for new athletic facilities, upgrading the pool, or putting in a turf football field. Every item was important, there was no way to do it all. Centennial was a district of retirees, fixed incomes, single parent households, and renters dreading an increase. Surrounding districts had larger tax bases, more businesses, private industry partners to shoulder tax increases. For Centennial any increase weighed heavily on our families and residents.

We gave it a shot, sharing information about our plans for a bond that kept taxes low. We planned to build a new middle on a large plot of land near Pleasant Valley Elementary. We presented to homeowners associations, local Rotary and Chamber clubs, soliciting the support of local restaurants and businesses. Sam and our Business Manager went on a road show, sharing the plan and information, answering questions, providing a clear picture of our needs. The Board and I went door-to-door providing information and handouts to residents. We created a schedule for weekly meetings and weekend canvassing, trying to enlist staff participation. We were a small team of Believers, a dozen of us consistently showed up, board members, two active parents, one teacher leader, Cabinet, me, Sam and principal James Owens.

The bond plans didn't include upgrades to Butler Creek, just minor repairs and a fresh coat of paint, but James always looked at the bigger picture. He focused on the success of the district. His orientation was similar to mine as principal of HPE. We had some good principals in the district, but in facilities conversations they were squarely centered on what their school would get if the bond passed. James was a principal with specific qualities that separate school leaders from district leaders. His ability to work on a system, instead of inside it. Selflessly view the district at scale, making decisions that benefit all students, staff and community. Through this process we learn about each other. We began having conversations about where Centennial should be in five years.

During the May election, the bond failed by a small margin, dashing our hopes of facility upgrades. We caught wind that a few high school staff that were frustrated with the bond package, they spoke against the plan since it didn't include a turf football field. Centennial's had the only grass field left in the region. It was in terrible condition, crowning in the center, becoming a mosh pit of mud on rainy days. The field was a bone of contention for voters. Based on our bond surveys, the community indicated they'd vote the bond down if they had to pay taxes on a field. A small group would vote no if the field wasn't included in the bond package. Through passionate discussions the team made the decision to leave the field out of the plans. Based on the small margin we lost by, I let it get under my skin, wondering if our own staff put the nail in the coffin by having a small-minded mentality. Either way, the results were in, the show would go on. We continue doing the best we could with the cards we were dealt. Our students and staff made due with cold classrooms during winter months, patched roofs and buildings that weren't as glitzy or glamorous as the surrounding districts.

Year two had its successes, attendance was up, graduation rate incrementally moving in the right direction. Our staff was becoming a reflection of our student population. We drastically reduced suspensions and expulsions, our schools used restorative practices, partnering with culturally specific organizations, providing support during school and afterschool programs. HR was a well-oiled machine, moving forward district goals and initiatives. Sam and I hit a good stride, besides the bond attempt, everything was going well. We met monthly over pizza, planning, discussing problems, strategizing and finding solutions. After spring break, I got an unusual text from Sam asking to meet for coffee. "Sure" I responded. We met for lunch regularly, even grabbed dinner with Cabinet before board meetings, but never coffee. I replayed HR issues in my head wondering if I screwed up somehow.

I arrived early, Sam was already there sitting in the coffee shop with his beverage. He stood to shake my hand as I walked in. I grabbed a black coffee and sat across from him. As a man of few words, he cut to the chase, "I just want you to know I'm a finalist for the superintendent job at MESD." MESD is the Multnomah Education Service District, ESD's provide regional support to K-12 districts. While I didn't know all the ins and outs of ESDs at the time, I knew they provided out-of-district special education placements, technology support, offered professional learning opportunities and technical assistance to our staff. "Congratulations, … I thought you were happy here? We're really kicking some butt" I replied trying to disguise my worry. "Things have been rough at the ESD for a while now, I've been vocal about their need for improvement, so much so that someone said, why don't you do something about it? That sat with me, so I decided to step up to the challenge." "That's respectable, you'll probably get the job" I responded. "Right now things are confidential, but they'll publicly announce the finalists in a few weeks. I'll let our Board know today, which makes it tough because I may not get the job, nothing's set in stone. A few years ago, I wouldn't even consider leaving, there wasn't anyone internal I felt could take on the role. Now you're here, you're ready. Due to the timing, the Board will probably want an interim. I'd recommend you to the Board as the Interim Superintendent, then you could see if you like the job. You'd keep the momentum going. If I'm at MESD, you'd be one of my component district superintendents. We'd still talk all the time, I'd be there to support you" he explained.

I sat contemplating for a second, surprised on all accounts. "I appreciate your confidence in me, but I planned to be a superintendent much closer to retirement. The life expectancy of the job is only two years, ideally I'd be Assistant Superintendent/Human Resources for at least another 5 to 7 years." He chuckled, "you're right about life expectancy… but think about this, you have to take an opportunity when it presents itself. You could step up and lead, or wait and see who gets hired. It may be someone you work well with, or someone that you don't align with at all. Then you end up wanting to leave, or looking for another job" he said wisely.

I knew he was right, if everything played out the way Sam speculated, he'd land the gig in a month or so. Due to it being late in the year, the Board would appoint an interim. A May/June exit made it almost impossible to conduct a Superintendent search before school begins. Oregon's superintendent contacts begin on July 1st. If the doors of opportunity swing open for me, I'd best be ready to lead. Passing on my moment would be a fatal mistake. As leaders, we set goals, timelines, self-imposed deadlines trying to balance our passions, with the needs of those we serve. Sometimes our plans work out, other times life happens, changing our course, charting a new pathway. Ultimately none of it is in our control. Change is inevitable. Hold onto things with a loose grip. Be able to adjust in the moment. We can't prepare for every season, nor will we always understand the reason. We'll find out more on the other end.

"Man, you're gonna be the next superintendent in Centennial, I can feel it!" said Dad. "Don't get your hopes up, a lot would need to fall into place, I'm just letting you know it's a possibility" I replied. "It's gonna happen, I know these things. If God wants you there, nothing and nobody can stop it…get ready, you can't put the brakes on this thang!" he said in an exuberant tone.

For weeks I pondered all the angles, staying hyper vigilant on my job, crossing every "t" and dotting every "i." I thought about our principals, I had stronger relationships with all of them, I knew their strengths and challenges. I'd supported each of them in various ways. A few announced retirement, which was an opportunity to hire. The unions and I were still in good standing, the communication lines were open, we spoke regularly, proactively working to address issues.

Sam landed the job at MESD. In true Sam fashion, he downplayed celebrations and congratulatory hoopla. He wrote a heartfelt letter to staff sharing his reason for leaving, highlighting the opportunity to support all students across the region. He'd prepared our Board for his exit through 1:1 conversations. Centennial had a supportive Board, each board member was there for the right reasons. I enjoyed getting to know each of them. They came from a variety of backgrounds, collectively focusing on the right work, doing what's best for students, staff and the broader community. I couldn't think of a more ideal board situation, for an interim Superintendent.

The Board Chair was Shar Giard, a realtor, an outspoken spit-fire who deeply cared for the community. She working with students to create a food pantry out of an old school bus, which sat in our high school parking lot. She met with me soon after Sam's announcement, "I've seen your work in HR for the past two years, it's been excellent. But we need someone who can pick up where Sam left off, it's some big shoes to fill. He and several others believe you have what it takes. We're looking for an interim to get us from point A to B, then the Board will hire an agency to conduct a national superintendent search. If you're the interim, you can apply for the job. First things first, are you interested in the interim? If so, you'll need to interview with the Board soon" Shar said frankly. "Thanks for the opportunity, yes I'm interested. Just tell me when and where I need to be, I'm there" I quickly responded.

Soon I was in the hot seat…interviewing at a public board meeting in open session.

CHAPTER 11

Changing of the Guard

In the weeks that lead up to the board meeting I had several one-on-one conversations over coffee that bent more along the lines of informal interviews. Then I was publicly interviewed which was a blur, an hour of questions with onlookers. I spoke rapidly about the district's strengths and growth, as well as continuing to keep the district's positive momentum moving in the right direction. The May heat beamed through the boardroom's blinds. I took small sips of water from a clear plastic bottle to avoid breaking a sweat. I mostly spoke directly to the Board Chair, Shar and Vice-Chair Pam, but was sure to make eye contact with every board member. I got more comfortable when my eye contact was met with grins and nods of affirmation.

After the last question, the Board took brief recess for bathroom breaks, refilling logoed coffee mugs, chatting with attendees, administrators and students receiving awards. Chair Giard wrapped the gavel on the table calling the meeting to order. One member moved to appoint me as the Interim Superintendent, which was seconded by another board member. "All in favor" said Chair Giard, all seven hands went up "so moved" she stated before smiling at me and saying "congratulations, I feel good about this, we will miss Sam dearly as he moves to support us at the county level, but we are lucky to have you." Just like that, I was the interim superintendent. I was up to the challenge, felt ready, there was a long road ahead. Interim positions can be risky, but when it came down to proving yourself worthy, I was truly a master.

My position as Assistant Superintendent/HR Director was posted internally and I made quick work of the selection. At the very next board meeting, Superintendent Breyer made the official announcement "Dr. Coakley has selected James Owen as Interim Assistant Superintendent/ Human Resources Director for 2016/2017." Board members smile when they heard the news. Our district had strong administrators, every candidate gave it a good run, but James' attention to detail, articulate delivery and composed confidence put me at ease. I knew he could not only do the job, but do it well. He asked the right questions, planned his actions, knew our labor contracts in and out, and had built positive relationships with staff at every level of the organization. The Board got to know him from the time he had dedicated months prior participating in facilities discussion, canvassed neighborhoods delivering information about our bond.

At the last board meeting of the school year, Sam set the stage by delivering a strong message. Shining a spotlight on the district's accomplishments while explaining the work that lies ahead. "We're in the final stages of contact negotiations for both unions. The new interest-based bargaining process (IBB) with both teachers and classified have been completed. The IBB process took a significant amount of time. However, it allows everyone outside the process to focus on teaching, educating students… the process was really valuable." He explained that the contracts would be ratified in the summer, both were good for three years. He recognized my efforts, letting them know I co-lead the process. "This shows how much we can accomplish by working together as a community, instead of in an oppositional manner" reported Sam.

Sam shared the positive accomplishments that the district made in the last five years, from increased PLC, to literacy and math adoptions. "As superintendent, I've been vocal about the fact that our entire leadership team was White, which was all well intentioned. It's been nice over the last couple of years to have progressed in diversifying our team. Dr. Coakley has made changes to the hiring process including aggressively recruiting BIPOC candidates. We believe the changes are really benefiting our decision making, and connections with our community."

Superintendent Breyer gave kudos to the leadership team and Board for their efforts on a variety of work and commitment to students, before foreshadowing what was lying in wait just around the corner.

"Had the bond passed, we had hoped to wrestle with our school names while working on naming a new middle school. There needs to be a community conversation around the names of these three schools – Lynch Meadows, Lynch View and Lynch Wood. In the near future, this issue will either come before the Board and be forced upon you, or the Board can choose to have the conversation" he said.

"For residents who have lived in this community for a while, those names just roll without even noticing them. If you've been here historically, you know the Lynch family dedicated land, which was an amazing thing for the district, the schools are named to recognize that. For me, eight years in, it's interesting that I almost don't think twice about it anymore. However, for people new to our community, particularly our most underserved and underrepresented communities of color; the word 'Lynch' attached to the words "View, Wood and Meadows" are not heard as a name. When I first came to Centennial, I remembers thinking as an outsider about the impact of those names and how 'Lynch' hangs out there. Obviously, Lynch has a historically negative impact particularly for our communities of color. So, names like Lynch Meadows, Lynch View or Lynch Wood have significant impact; we also hear about it from our community partners, our principals have heard it from parents" said Sam. "It's quite telling that with two principal positions posted at Parklane Elementary and Lynch Wood Elementary, we had significantly more candidates of color in one of those pools than the other. I believe our Board will need to have this conversation in the future. How do we honor the history of our district while also honoring the community we serve? This is an important issue, one I intended to help the Board wrestle with, but with the failure of the bond it just didn't happen."

Superintendent Breyer concluded his report by expressing his appreciation for the staff and the administrative team; he recognized the Board's work, their clear non-negotiables and focus on student achievement. "Centennial is in a great place! We have amazing staff, they do great things every day. I know Centennial will continue to doing wonderful things!"

The room felt heavy, mixed emotion filled the space making the mood weightier than before. Gloomy due to Sam's departure, pessimistic at the possibility of changing the school names, optimistic for James and I's interim roles, apprehensive changes happening quickly. What if we're only interim? What if I applied for the permanent position and didn't get it? There was no looking back. My mind raced, thinking about the failed bond, continued issues with our facilities - cold classrooms, leaky roofs, outdated equipment, fifty-year-old brick, cafetoranaisiums, (a cafeteria, auditorium and gymnasium hybrid) even turf fields. I thought about our district leaders, our classified staff, our teachers, our new hires, supporting them, their needs, their hopes, their dreams. Most of all, I thought about our kids. How can we increase attendance? Academic outcomes? Graduation rate? Safety and security? Practices of equity and inclusion?

I thought about students who look like me, impacted by their schools name, educators' low beliefs and expectations, and the lack of staff diversity? Those who moved to East County from the NE, from a house to an apartment, from a community a color to a sea of Whiteness. I thought about the parents that scheduled meetings with me asking for hardship transfers, emphatically telling me "I don't want my kids to go to these racist schools, - why is it called Lynch Meadows?" My mind flashed on my own experiences...running from Gresham High School junior year while being chased by skinheads in a raggedy truck. They hurled rocks and racial slurs, I zigzagged, ducked, dodged though an empty field, finally making it to the Town Fair Apartments where I lost them. My mind fast-forwarded to a similar experience at U of O my freshman year. Walking back to campus after grabbing a slice of pizza with two brothas from Portland I just met. As we reached the edge of campus, a similar looking truck revved its engine, charging towards us as if to run us over. We ran deep into a field on the backside of the campus. I could hear loud racial epithets and rock landing in the distance. After a thirty second sprint, I heard the dark skin dude I was with who wore a Jheri curl and crisp white t-shirt say "Nah Cuz, we ain't running no more."

He pulled out a silver pistol from his waistband and began blasting off shots toward the truck. The truck did a quick 180, the driver put the pedal to the metal, his tires spinning in the dirt before grasping solid ground, then burning rubber up road.

Glancing around the congested boardroom I silently gave thanks. Thanking God for bringing me to this point, the opportunity to serve in this space. I wasn't a negative statistic, a blip in the data, a Black male locked in a cell, or a victim of a hate crime. Every barrier that I had encountered, I managed to overcome. So many people had helped me along the way. For every foe I encountered there were double the amount of allies, people that believed in me. People excited about my appointment to the superintendent role even if it was only interim. They put their hopes in me, expected me to do a good job, I can't let them down. I surveyed the space, eyeing the board members who exhibited their trust, humbly smiling at Sam for his support and encouragement, looking at the diverse students and families in attendance, watching the Cabinet, the team I would now be leading. Lastly, James and I glanced at each other, we were on the same page. Heading into unknown territory, entering a new season, everyone witnessed the changing of the guard.

Soon after my official announcement the news articles were released and floods of text messages and phone calls began rolling in. Congratulations from relatives, family, friends, neighbors, co-workers, acquaintances, anyone who had my phone number. Unk, Coach Hudson, LV, M.C., Dr. Adair, PPS and Rainier staff, doctoral colleagues, Nick Fish, who was now a city Commissioner, many others picked up the phone to share their excitement. I read the articles, one pointed out something that I hadn't thought about before. The article stated "When he becomes superintendent of Centennial School District July 1, Coakley will be the sole African-American superintendent in Oregon." I noticed the article left out the word "interim." I also noticed that my shoulders felt much heavier, I was shouldering the weight of the Black community. Why was I the only one? I'm sure I'd find out soon enough, I definitely wasn't in a rush to find out. I'd become used to it, I had been the only African-American in White spaces for a longtime. Having to prove myself worthy my entire life. My skin had grown thick, my will power was stronger than most. If someone told me I couldn't accomplish something, I'd fight until I did.

The summer was nonexistent, I was pleased the building was empty, it meant our staff was taking a well-deserved break. James and I were putting the finishing touches on contracts, recruiting and hiring, updating policy, planning professional development opportunities and organizing our new offices. The complaints died down during the summer, but picked right back up in the fall. The start of the year went well, we kicked off the welcome back for staff with my first opening day speech, which focused on the importance of good teachers. Well received by our staff and Board, all sitting in the front row in full support. Our Board had shifted a bit over the summer, now I had two Board members of color, an African-American female, Rhonda who stated in her interview "I am running to support Dr. Coakley" I also had a sharply dressed African gentleman with a background in education. I spent all summer perfecting my message. Public speaking didn't come naturally for me but practice makes perfect.

Hiring was going well, James picked up where I left off, continuing to build a strong team. We got the right people on the bus and in the right seat. Energetic leaders, centered on equity, collaboration, parent involvement and improving outcomes for all students. Using the systems that Sam put in place to lead the district, we meet with our administrators twice a month, the Cabinet met weekly. On Friday's I sent the Board email updates keeping them apprised of key information, upcoming events, highlighting the district's happenings. I provided a monthly newsletter to staff and community members sharing the accomplishments of our students, highlighting our staff, programs and initiatives. My executive assistant Connie was a master at managing my calendar. "I want to visit all ten schools regularly" I said. She constructed my calendar so I was able to do so. I walked hallways, met with teachers, educational assistants and union leaders, chatted with secretaries, and held one-to-one principals meetings to discuss strengths and challenges, problems and solutions.

In the first thirty days the pressure had melted away, along with the worry of having "interim" in my title. There were much bigger areas to focus on, so I put it out of my mind. The district moved at a fast clip, nothing dropped, we were doing the jobs, no time to think about the added pressures, or being the sole African-American superintendent. The district needed us to step up to the plate, James and I both did that, day in and day out.

Time flew by, in October the Board hired a search firm to spend a few months gathering information from staff and families, holding community listening sessions, conducting online surveys to see how things were going. In November there would be an opportunity for public input on the superintendent search process. At the same meeting the results of the surveys and listening sessions would be shared. The position would be posted in December and in January the firm would outline the hiring process to the Board in executive session.

At the November meeting, the Board reviewed the information gathered, then publicly determining the salary range, they met in executive session to discuss the survey results. We'd survived a harsh winter, resulting in nine inclement weather days. I'd wake at 5 am each morning in January, debriefing with transportation, texting neighboring district superintendents, gathering information from those in higher elevations. We made the right calls, always erring on the side of caution. James and I engaged our unions in conversations, finding creative ways to add instructional time back for students without extending the school year. We had a strong plan that I presented to the Board, then another snow day, sending us back to the drawing board. We ended up letting go of a few Late Start Wednesday's, to make up the last day. Our plan was appreciated by parents as well as staff.

In late January, the search firm summary concluded that things were going well, the results were overwhelmingly positive. They also outlined the details of the broader superintendent search process. Shortly thereafter, the Board decided to withdraw from conducting a national search, they appointed me to the permanent position. On February 22, 2017 my contract was ratified. I'd built strong relationships with the

Board, the unanimous vote spoke to their confidence in me, the survey results affirmed the staff was also in support. "I won't let you down" I said, shaking the Chair's hand firmly. Chair Giard read the press release issued on Thursday, February 16, 2017, announcing "Centennial Board selects Dr. Paul Coakley as district superintendent effective July 1, 2017." The news release included an overview of my administrative experience, education and current involvements. It further contained a summary of the process the Board went through to appoint me as the permanent superintendent.

At the next meeting, I appointed James to the permanent role as Assistant Superintendent/Human Resources Director and we continued moving forward. With every administrative vacancy, PPS's leaders were applying by the droves, we were building a team of superstars. Poaching the daylights out of the behemoth. After all I had gone through, it brought me a silent satisfaction. One was our new Curriculum Director, she joined the team in September immediately landing us two Federal School Improvement Grants (SIG), bringing over $2 million dollars to Centennial to improve academic outcomes at our two lowest performing schools. Both schools had first year principals of color, a Latino principal and Asian principal, they brought vigor, innovation and a new-found enthusiasm to their school communities. All three of these talented administrators came from PPS. Grant money on such a large scale was something new for Centennial staff. Centennial was fiscally sound, but dollars were tight. The SIG grants provided an avenue for making creative ideas a reality, expanding opportunities for students, and allowing multiple solutions for a variety of learning styles.

Year one was good in the eyes of many. As superintendent, my duties included participating in Gresham Chamber meetings, being a member of the Rotary Club, getting to know community members, local business owners, building relationships by attending meetings, delivering Meals on Wheels to residents and assisting at Rotary's annual Steak Fry. However, there were pockets of Centennial students and families that weren't feeling the love. James received over a dozen complaints filed regarding the Lynch school names, hardship transfers requests were increasing weekly. Our principals frequently met with upset parents of color trying to explain the history of the names, "It actually has nothing to do with lynching" a message that constantly fell flat.

With the year and the interim titles behind us it was time to stop talking about the problem and start addressing the problem. Over the summer, I thought a lot about the question Sam posed, "How do we honor the history of our district while also honoring the community we serve?"

That was the million-dollar question, and I needed to find an answer to it fast.

CHAPTER 12

Someone Should Lynch the Superintendent

When people have difficulty grasping a concept, or understand why something is a problem, raise their consciousness. I began sharing information with the Board about complaints we were receiving with regard to our school names. The number of transfer requests, the amount of time per week spend meeting with frustrated families on the issues. This information sparked many questions from the Board, which led them to asking me for more research, gathering data to find out if the names had any impact on students. My fact-finding mission led me to providing the Board with a white paper, a report that guides and informs readers on a complex issue, presenting a philosophy on the matter. The paper is intended to help readers understand the problem, solve a problem or determine how to proceed in making a decision. Interestingly enough, I wondered why it was called a "white paper." I found that governmental documents used to be coded by color, white was the color of the documents that were designated for public access.

After months of research a white paper was produced for the Board entitled "Lynch Schools Educational Impact." The paper focused on finding out if the Lynch names were having an adverse effect on educational outcomes for students of color attending Lynch Schools. Based on the information collected, the Board would determine whether or not the topic needed to be addressed. The history of the Lynch family, and how the names came to be in Centennial Schools, was clearly outlined. The paper states "While the Lynch family who donated the property has no direct connection to the term "lynching," the negative connotation of the word based on its history seems to have a negative effect on Centennial's rapidly changing, diverse population. To be clear, the perceived issue is the term "lynching" as it relates to the violent act of hanging a person in public, by the public, outside of any judicial proceeding or finding of guilt for a crime. This was particularly prevalent in the South as a tactic used by lynch mobs and the Ku Klux Klan against African Americans."

The white paper gave a brief history of lynchings in Oregon, provided data on district transfer request based on the school names, listening sessions, and district surveys. The Board was surprised to find approximately 31% of students and families felt the school names had a negative impact on their educational outcomes. "If even 1% of our kids feel this way that's too many" said a board member.

After the Board held a lengthy discussion in public session, they allocated $10,000 dollars to hire a consultant to convene a citizens workgroup tasked with further researching the issue before bringing recommendation to the Board for resolution. The Board was resolute about hiring a consultant that would use the district's Equity Lens to guide their process. The Equity Lens elevated these questions:

- Who are the racial/ethnic and underserved groups affected?

- Does the decision being made ignore or worsen existing disparities or produce other unintended consequences?

- How have you intentionally involved stakeholders who are also members of the communities affected by this decision?

In my second year as superintendent of Centennial, I unintentionally drew national attention. After our Board requested information about the impact the Lynch names had on students, the local media went into a frenzy. All it took was an article by a local paper which began with "The Centennial School District will likely change the names of three of its elementary schools that include the name "Lynch" because of the violent, racial connotations the word evokes." In my experience, reporters rarely highlight educational stories on academic growth, student accomplishments, scholarships, or community service projects that bring value and benefits to others. Those types of headlines rarely peak interest. Stories dealing with race, violence, misconduct, or lawsuits is what moves the average reader, anything that will reflect negatively on an educational systems. They ask why there is an educator shortage? Why is there a retention problem? What we should be asking, is why do people still apply for these jobs?

Using the word "likely" in the local article leads people to believe it was done in haste, no research, no process, strictly feelings. The news spread like wildfire, flaming across the region, scorching statewide before quickly igniting nationally, smoldering newsstands, radio broadcasts and television stations. The unwanted attention threw our staff into a whirlwind of angry phone calls, racist emails, violent threats, even cyber-attacks. As well as thank yous, messages of affirmation, appreciation and support of students well-being, mostly coming from parents, students and people from historically marginalized groups. Before we had an opportunity to gauge the impact, the media's push for a juicy new story, riled the old guard exposing the hidden racism, "Portland nice" went out the window, the "woke," "keep Portland weird" melting pot dismantled. Our tiny board meeting turned the city into feeling like the deep south. A community divided like Gallatin, many staff, students, families and community members filled with hope, the possibility of removing a barrier that was mentally blocking their full engagement in their district. For others, the thought of changing the names, or erasing the history as some older Centennial residents referred to it, infuriated them, exposing their resentment, their true beliefs about the students we serve in our district, which had grown to 53% students of color. "The school names are here for our community, not just students of color, people are so sensitive these days!" said an upset resident.

Our secretaries were apprehensive to answer phone calls, jittery, letting it ring before picking up with a timid hello. Unsurprisingly someone was on the other end ranting "You're too sensitive" … or curing about "that Black superintendent…" or "what'll you guys change next?!" I directed our administrators to shoulder the calls, "take the call quickly, protect your secretaries. If you are not available, have them send it to your voicemail." Board members stood strong, they were getting the same treatment, calls, emails, even approached with rude and threatening comments while grocery shopping, or when spotted with their families.

From the outset, I based any change on the number of written complaints, the feelings of students, and the impact of school culture. I served at the will of the Board, I planned to present the research, go through a process to collect information, data and share the findings. As an educational researcher, it was right up my ally, a basic qualitative research study. As the issue rose to personal attacks, social media trolls reached vocally racist heights. "Someone should lynch the superintendent" was threatened on social media. I also received a postcard with a photo of my car that read, "Watch Your Back, We're Watching You." I sat in my black leather office chair, under the glow of the banker's lamp, my inbox filled with Lynch, my voicemails full of Lynch, my mail was Lynch. I found myself once again in my space. A place very familiar to me when making a decision that isn't going to please everyone. An inner strength that trembles in my gut, forcefully pushes outward giving me a hard exterior. I was ready, no matter who you think you are, or how long you've been here, these names are changing, and there isn't a damn thing you can do about it.

The year moved forward regardless of divided feelings, teaching and learning continued, yellow school buses filled the streets, kids walked to and from school with backpacks and lunch boxes. We held meetings looking at academic growth over time, kindergarten readiness, third grade reading, fifth grade math, and ninth grade on-track data. Prioritizing everyday matters like attendance campaigns, and finding alternative methods to address suspension and expulsion. I drove from building to building, checking-in with principals, visiting classrooms, making notes of facilities issues and other needs.

Music has always aided me in stressful times, sometimes uplifting, soothing, confirming, motivating, even reflective. I'd returned to Lexus, purchased a hybrid HS. I'd become skilled at driving in a manner that maximized gas mileage. It took a few months before it became second nature. After totaling the Lex Bubble in Illinois, I had a certain allegiance to Lexus, a feeling of safety, I knew I would get one again at some point. Hip-hop had disappeared, for a while nothing piqued my interest. As I was navigating an outwardly aggressive racism, I found hip hop back in a strong place. Chance the Rapper's Coloring Book, Drake's Views, and J. Cole's 4 Your Eyez Only album. A new era of dudes slightly younger than me, taking the genre to a place it hadn't been before. There were also rappers I grew up on still making new music that influenced me, still relevant, still rough, reminiscent sounds of the 80s and 90s, like Master Ace. The Falling Season, which made me go back and listen to his passed catalog, songs that I had missed like Son of Yvonne and Juanita Estefan.

2016, rapper Malik Taylor, aka Fife Dawg of A Tribe Called Quest passed away at the age of 45 from complications of managing his diabetes. A Tribe Called Quest was my all-time favorite group. I'd been listening to them since ninth grade. They propelled me through high school with every album, People's Instinctive Travels and the Paths of Rhythm (1990), the Low End Theory (1991), quickly followed by Midnight Marauders (1993). I caught them live once at LaLuna, the old Pine Street Theater in Portland, which is now long gone. I stood front and center with my crew, about seven Portland MC's, there was Quil, Snafu, JB, Dialog, and other names that I don't remember. Next to me was the Shandog, smiling, living in the moment. Opening for Tribe was Souls of Mischief, they had just released their first album 93 'til Infinity. At the time, I didn't realize how classic the moment at LaLuna was, New York's Tribe, with East Oakland openers. My general admission ticket - less than 30 bucks with taxes and fees. The first and last time I'd see Tribe perform live, Fife had gone to a better place, leaving Q-Tip, Ali and Jarobee in search of a missing piece of a puzzle, irreplaceable. Months after Fife's passing, Tribe released "We got it from Here…Thank You 4 Your Service." A gift to fans that pushed me to the finish line.

The jazzy horns, and rhythmic eclectic sounds of Tribe, carried me through the last few months of the school year. During our June board meeting, I shared the year's highlights during my Superintendent's Report. Much had been accomplished, the boardroom was empty. I provided the information to the Board directly while the secretary took the minutes. That summer the family and I disappeared, the community uproar didn't die down. We'd endured a full year of harassment by a portion of the district that loathed change. Superintendents in neighboring districts checked on me to see how I was holding up. Sam and I met on a regular basis, he knew I'd been through the ringer. "Are you doing anything this summer? You should get away, don't read emails or the paper" he advised. I told him that we were driving to Disneyland, I planned to go to Sneakercon, the world's largest sneaker convention, which just so happened to be in Anaheim that year. Sam seemed relieved, "smart move" he said. My Board Officers expressed the same concern for my wellbeing, "Are you're taking a vacation?" said the Chair, so I shared my vacation plans." "Good, nothing's going on here, strangers are stopping me in town to gripe about school names, it's time to travel" she said frustrated.

I tried having a similar conversation with James, encouraging him to take a vacation. Nonetheless, he was dead set on holding down the fort in my absence, "have a good trip" he said. "Thanks, call me if you need anything" I replied.

Vacation was a blur, a ten-year anniversary, a drive to California, days at Disneyland, even Sneakercon, only captured by photos as evidence that it all took place. The stress of the job never left. It moved to the back of my mind, lingering as I rode rides with the kids, taking family photos in different lands of Walt Disney. Before I could blink, it was over, I was back in my office, facing an email inbox with hundreds of unread messages that had been responded to with auto reply. I deleted the sales pitches, skimmed the threats and responded to legit "work" emails.

I met with my Communications Director, Carol she'd been responding to the media all year, providing guidance to the Board, while dealing with the barrage of negativity on social media platforms. Carol updated me on what trolls were posting on the district's Facebook page. Our page was full of negative comments, untrue accusation quickly gaining responses from others. Each comment continued to fan the flames. Sometimes posts caused people to email or call the district office. It was a vicious cycle.

Summer board meetings are usually a ghost town, sparse boardroom with just enough Board attendance to ensure a quorum. A smattering of administrators who are scheduled to present, the board secretary and brief agenda. Our August meeting was nothing like the summer meetings that most districts had come to know and love. Based on the number of people that signed up to provide public testimony we moved the meeting location from the boardroom to the high school cafeteria. The media kept a close eye on our board agenda, then signaled to the public when our Board would determine the outcome. Agenda item 7.1.1 Consider the Re-Naming of Lynch Meadows, Lynch View and Lynch Wood Elementary Schools (Taken out-of-order after item 4.0 – Public Forum), bought the crowds out in droves. The cafeteria filled with people, filling in, as if they were about to watch gladiatorial bouts in an ancient colosseum during the Roman games, when teams would match up to fight to the death. One side of the cafeteria was filled with staff, students, people of color, many parents, and every school administrator attended in support of the change. The other side was made up of Old Centennial, in opposition of the change. I sat at the middle of the board's table, between Chair Giard, and a board member who was a retired teacher. I wore a navy suit, a crisp white dress shirt that was squeezing my neck, with a navy and aqua striped tie. I sipped from a water bottle, tapping my foot under the table trying to stay calm. You could cut the tension with a knife.

The number of people that wanted to speak was unmanageable so the Chair announced that she would give fifteen minutes to each side. Listening to those opposed and those in support of the change. She gave the audience time to select their spokespeople, then she set the timer. She started with those opposed, it was fifteen minutes of comments like "this proposal has been an embarrassment to the staff and the community as a whole…" and "this is not about racism, but that is what this had been made out to be." I sat in silence, taking small sips of water and watching the clock tick down. One man in the audience started pacing, yelling and screaming at the Board, he was escorted out by our school resource officer. I looked in the audience, to find my father, some close friends, and my dude - Pete, a retired Police Officer with a military background who reminded me of John Shaft. He glanced in my direction tapping his leather jacket; if something went left, he had my back.

The clock hit zero, then we heard from the group of supporters. One man stated, "The term itself is associated with terrorism -- of people who look like me, terrorism of my descendants." A student shared "I know the majority of you guys are White and it's hard to know how that word could have an effect but it does, if a simple name change could make students feel safe, then why are we holding back?"

After public comment, the board moved agenda item 7.1.1 up to the next item, Carol, Director of Communications read a statement into the minutes explaining the history of the Lynch names in detail. "On March 13, 1900, Patrick and Catherine Lynch donated an acre of their property (at what is now SE 162nd and Division) for a school to be built. The original school was named Lynch School. As the district grew, Lynch was utilized in several of the school's titles up to the present day, Lynchview, Lynch Meadows and Lynchwood."

She then delved into the growing number of concerns raised by our school community around the names our schools and the painful history of lynchings. The negative connotation of the word "lynch" and the effect it was having on our rapidly changing diverse population. She called out the gentrification of North and Northeast Portland over the past decade, families of color being forced to move into our community to find affordable housing. Many students and families come to us with feeling of displacement, resentment and hostility of being forcibly displaced due to economic circumstances. This coupled with having no idea where the "Lynch" school names originated has led to a barrage of complaints and request to transfer out of the district.

Carol outlined the process we used throughout the school year that bought us to this point. "Staff members from all three schools have conveyed the importance of changing the names based on them impeding their ability to build trusting relationships with students and families… There are more than 50 languages spoken in the district, 55% of our student population are students of color" she stated.

She closed with a strong statement, "In Centennial School District, we're building a culture of equity, which requires asking questions through an equity lens to create a meaningful space for dialogue in order to ensure that programs, policies and systems are built in a manner in which each and every student's needs are met."

One principal spoke on behalf of the administrators in the district, letting the board know they were in full support of finding a win-win solution that honors the students and families that raised the complaints. "Finding that solution will help us continue to move forward in educating our children, which is the only reason we are here!" he said proudly.

The Chair deferred to me, I reiterated that our Board listened to multiple perspectives through public forums of students, parents, community members, and staff. The question that drove our process was: "Is there a win-win solution that honors students and families complaints while also honoring the Lynch family that donated the land in 1900?" I referenced my conversation with Maggie Evans, great-granddaughter of Patrick and Catherine Lynch. She expressed concerns regarding the name change in addition to things she'd read in the paper. I shared the district's intent to create a win-win solution. We discussed the current context in which the names are used in our schools; and how possibly a different context could create a win-win. It was a cordial conversation that ended on a positive note. I closed by bringing forward a resolution to the Board to consideration renaming our schools.

Minutes later, Chair Giard called for a motion to adopt board resolution item 7.1.1, which directed the Board to rename all schools with the name Lynch, and that the school closest to the original Lynch School be named Patrick Lynch Elementary.

It was moved by our Chair, Shar Giard, and seconded by Vice-Chair, Pam Shields, "all in favor?" asked the Chair, each board member said "Aye." "All opposed?" A few loud "Nays" came from the audience. "Motion carries" said Chair Giard firmly. The Board unanimously adopted resolution number 7.1.1. Removing the institutional barriers that were causing harm to students, families and communities of color.

Swallowing the last drops from my water bottle while surveying the cafeteria, students and parents cheered, teachers and principals smiled, my dad beamed widely, Pete stood calmly, his head on a swivel. Chair Giard called for a brief recess, the crowd dispersed. Police monitored the crowd as they went to their cars, some left in celebration, others in disappointment. I had just witnessed a modern day Plessy vs. Fergusson, a Brown vs. Board moment, the removal of unwritten Jim Crow Laws. A community divided, thirty minutes of public comment on the impact of race, racism, and institutional barriers, while we ironically sat under an array of colorful flags from every country and nation representing our district's student population. The flags were displayed prominently swaying above our heads in the packed cafeteria. No more kids who looked like me would have to ride their bike past the Lynch Meadows sign while images of strange fruit violently played in their heads. Signs telling them they don't belong prominently displayed on school buildings, while teachers and staff do all they can to let their students know that not only do they belong, that they will be seen, heard, listened to, and that they matter.

Our long-time Budget Committee Chair, an older gray haired fellow that I enjoyed talking with during meetings, stormed toward the Board and tossed a handwritten letter of resignation on the table, "I will never serve on another committee in this district again" he yelled. "Good riddance" said Shar sharply, staring him dead in the face. I stood squarely towards him as he backed up then headed out the door.

The media got a quote from Shar before they left for the evening, "We are doing what we believe is right for our children. We have children of other colors and cultures, and we want to make sure they can cross the thresholds of those three schools and be comfortable in their surroundings," she said.

When the brief intermission was over, Shar called the meeting to order. The cafeteria looked like a regular August board meeting, a ghost town. The only difference was we had all seven board members present, most of our principals stayed, as well as a few staff. The three hundred plus people that filled the seats with passion just moments ago had headed home. Reporters rushed to write their stories. I gave my Superintendent's Report in a large cafeteria full of empty blue hard plastic chairs, while flags from every nation dances above our heads. At that moment, I knew the war was over. Our Board held their ground, they did what they thought was right, they remained student-centered, they brought our Equity Policy to life. I was ready to take on any ill comment lodged at me during Rotary, restaurants, community gatherings, grocery store, newspaper articles, even from sarcastic radio disc jockeys.

The schools were renamed, each new name came from a process driven by the students. Lynchwood, became Powell Butte Elementary, Lynch Meadows, dropped the Lynch and became Meadows Elementary School and Lynch View, the school closest to the land donated by the Lynch Family in 1900 became Patrick Lynch Elementary School. Changing the school to a name changed the context, honoring the family's history. A win-win, whether people agreed with it or not, there wasn't a damn thing anyone could do about it.

The coast was clear, James and I chatted at our cars before driving in opposite directions. On the way home, it felt like a weight had been lifted, a large boulder - removed, opening opportunity and access to a population of our students and community that felt unwanted and unwelcomed.

CHAPTER 13
Broad Shoulders, Brutal Pivot

With the name change behind us the Board and I faded into the background. Being on the radar as the center of the attention was never our intention. The next few years we put the good work of our staff, students achievements and learning at the forefront of every message. Intentionally over communicating, a Community Mailer was sent out annually to every Centennial Resident, in addition to the previous forms of communication. We shared information about academic goals, athletic events, programs, scholarships, highlighting student's accomplishments. It was the season of rebuilding good will within a divided community. Sharing so much good that our support would be undeniable.

Our facilities planning team studied the results of our failed bond attempt; many of the "no" votes came from a pocket of the district's two largest retirement multiplexes. We strategized, holding student performances there, winter choir concerts, jazz ensembles, delivering Meals on Wheels to sick and shut ins, giving one hundred athletic passes to residents to attend games free of charge. Staff diversity increased, hiring pools yielded more people of color, our leadership team was a representation of our student population. We'd completed another round of interest based-bargaining, contracts were settled before the end of the school year. The collaborative process proved to be effective, kept us aligned, centered on student learning, safety and academics. Two years prior I hired Pete our District Safety and Security Administrator. He assessed emergency drills, trained principals, and worked to strengthen emergency response protocols. He was the liaison between our district and police jurisdictions. The guy who could navigate both worlds, build mutual trust, helping us move in unison during emergencies.

Our biggest challenge was still our facilities. The 2017 - 2018 school year was time to begin ramping up for another bond attempt. Reopening facilities discussions were met with discouragement, teachers saying things like "we've never passed a bond in this district, that's just how it is." Principals expressed concerns "some people are still upset about the name change, they say they'll never vote to pass our bond." Even a Board member commented "Paul, I know we need one but our community, just can't afford it." It had been 19 years since the last bond passed, but the difference this time was that the bond our community had been paying on had a stepdown, dropping the amount of property taxes that people had been paying. The tax rate would drop in May of 2020. An outside firm was hired to guide our Bond Oversight Committee. The committee identified over $120 million dollars in needs, which would increase the tax rate, in surveying Centennial residents this plan would definitely fail.

The committee held late night meetings, and community forums. They discussed the identified list of needs, whittling it down to key priorities, identifying about 65 million dollars' worth of bond projects. The number identified by consultants that would allow us to keep the tax rate the same based on the projected step down. Residents would see no increase or decrease in taxes, we're only asking them to continue to pay what they had already been paying, a tax rate of $1.19 per $1000 of assessed property value for bond repayment. It was a plan that allowed us to tell our community that our bond *won't* raise taxes. If the bond was approved the district would receive a matching grant from the state for $7.5 million, to offset the bond rate. This was a bare bones bond approach, there would be no new school buildings, it was about addressing the dyer needs of the district while upgrading our current facilities.

Based on our survey, 75% of the community was in favor the plan. The results predicted us winning by a landslide, only a small portion of residents still needed convincing. Several oversight committee members wanted to swing for the fences, trying to keep up with the Jones.

Neighboring district had passed bonds, remodeled high schools, build new elementary schools, even upgraded their district offices. Our bond would be done in phases, $65 million was the estimated cost for a new elementary school, for a new middle school the floor was $80 million, which was out of the question. We had to address the critical needs, touch every building, do as much as possible with $65 million dollars, in a district with ten schools and very aged facilities. "Our plan needs the support of parents, portions of the retirement community, local business, something that resonates with everyone" said the consultants. Our plan had to be viewed as a benefit, increasing the value of property, something our residents would be proud of. My hope was that the initial survey results would hold true, our parents and supporters would vote "yes," that the last few years of spreading positivity and goodwill had moved people beyond division caused by renaming our schools. That Patrick Lynch Elementary School was seen as a win-win solution. Voters would err on the side of doing what is best for kids.

During the 2019 -2020 school year, the Oversight Committee toured all ten schools with consultants and our facilities team. They assessed issues, had conversations prioritizing projects, jotting themes on sticky notes, drawing up plans on large chart paper with red, yellow, and green dot stickers. Our consultants dug into construction costs for each project and gave us the real deal, "if this project is the top choice, you will need to let go of this one, you don't have enough funds for these larger projects." Eventually, our team came up with a plan that would touch every building. Larry David said it best "A good compromise is when both parties are dissatisfied." Well that was the best way to describe the Oversight Committee when we identified the final plan.

This was the list:

- re-purpose Oliver Elementary School as a middle school

- build gymnasiums for Meadows, Parklane, Patrick Lynch, and Powell Butte Elementary Schools

- repair roofing at all schools

- upgrade safety and security at all schools

- repave school parking lots

- update drainage systems

- modernize heating units

- repair Centennial High School Pool

"This plan isn't sexy" said one committee member, "the community wants something that they can see. Heating, plumbing and roof repairs just isn't going to cut it." Another member said "We're still the only district in the region without a turf field. What does the high school get in this plan? No turf football field, what are we doing?" The consultants piped up "the survey we tested out early let us know that your community doesn't support paying for artificial turf, we don't recommend putting it in your bond package, it could tank the level of support." Half of the committee met the response with eye rolls, mostly coming from our high school coaching staff. I talked strategy with James, and my Board Officers, we had to get a hold of this situation quickly. Any negative comments from Oversight Committee members would split our staff and parent support quickly.

I called a meeting with our high school committee representatives, James and our Board Offices the following day. "I know you were all hoping for a turf field. I want one as bad as you do, but if we can complete the projects our team identified with bond dollars, that frees up money in our general budget that is usually spent on repairs. Meaning, the turf field could be paid for internally, possible in year 2 or 3 years" I stated. James spent time explaining how this is possible, getting into the technical side of the budget, using the white board to map out future possibilities. "If I hear anyone talking negatively about our plan, we're going to have a problem. The last bond failed because people didn't get their way, we're not going there again" Shar, said fiercely. "When this meeting ends, there better be alignment, all on the same page. This is the plan," I said pointing to the chart paper with the listed projects. "Those are our only talking points. We'll address the field internally once we pass this, let's get the ball rolling, agreed" I stated directly. Everyone shook hands and left with a code of silence, either share those talking points or shut up. It was early November, when we began strategizing our plan of attack, our Cabinet would go on an internal roadshow, holding two meetings at each school, one with staff and one with parents. Then, January to May was presentations to service organizations, local business, homeowners associations, retirement communities, as well as canvassing neighborhoods and gaining endorsements.

Resistance was the last thing that came to mind when preparing to present our plan to staff. The road show began by attending each school's staff meeting, answering questions from smiling teachers, secretaries, educational assistants and active parents hoping for improvement.

Things ran smoothly until our visit to Oliver Elementary School. Years prior Oliver had been a middle school. Oliver's building was large, and had a full-size gym and lots of classroom space. Part of our bond package was to convert Oliver back into a middle school to address the overcrowding at Centennial Middle School (CMS), to reduce class sizes and provide a second middle school option.

However, many of the Oliver staff saw it as a change that impacted them personally. During the staff meetings, the questions we were getting weren't about the big picture. Things like "Will our staff be split up?" "Who will be transferred to other schools?" "What if I don't have a middle school teaching endorsement, will I lose my job?" Questions that we could not effectively answer because we were too early in the process. In situations like this, I find that it is best to be transparent. "I hear your concerns, first we have to pass the bond, then there will be a year of planning, as well as a few years of renovations. During that time HR will work in collaboration with the union to figure out the timeline and movement that will occur" I explained. "Will we be expected to teach while the building is being renovated?" someone asked. "Yes, for the schools in districts that border us, that's the way they all do it. There's really no way around that" said a board member. James gave them the HR perspective, "no one is guaranteed to teach at a specific school, as a district we can involuntarily transfer staff now. The facilities plans that we are presenting aren't based on the needs, wants or comfort of individuals. Staff members have bumping rights, there's a process built on seniority, we will cross that bridge when we come to it. To pass this bond everyone should be on the same page, we need a unified message." One lady left the meeting crying. The principal followed me out to my car after the meeting saying, "I know they're emotional but I'll work through this, they'll get on board. Your transparency helped. We'll get there" he said confidently. "I appreciate that, our staff has to be unified" I replied.

January 2020, I went to visit B and his family for the first time since they had moved to New York. They visited Portland often, but I rarely got out of Oregon due to work. Brian was a doctor at Mt. Sinai Hospital, he'd reached his childhood dream of serving as a Pediatric Surgeon. He completed his residency in Vancouver, Canada and New York before landing the job at Mt. Sinai. No longer the little kid testing out a glossary of terms that made me laugh, now a husband and father of three. I looked forward to reconnecting with my nieces, nephew, and sister in-law, but mostly I was just glad to see my brother again, especially since I was visiting on his birthday. He took me to his favorite local haunts, stores and restaurants. I hit some of the tourist attractions during the day when they were busy at work. I even got to walk my nieces and nephew to school a few times. They were up early eating breakfast when I stepped out of the guestroom, "Good morning Uncle PJ" they'd say in unison. The week prior to my visit the first COVID-19 case was confirmed in the US, in state of Washington just about a three-hour drive from my home. I remember fielding some phone calls about the case, B and I talked about "coronavirus" as we rode the NY subway, visiting stores and popular eateries. Good times, just what I needed to clear my head before holding over 30 presentations between February and May to gain support for the bond election.

In February, the Cabinet hit the ground running, completing all school staff visits, meeting with our local unions, then doubling back, holding meetings with parent groups, Parent Teacher Organizations (PTO), presenting at after school events, book clubs and parent coffees. I presented to the Gresham Rotary Club. I'd been a member for five years and had built support with the organization. Regularly attending meetings at least once a month, participated in annual fundraisers, helping man the grill at the annual Steak Fry and partnering with a fellow Rotarian to deliver Meals on Wheels to the community a couple of weeks out of the year. By the time I presented to Gresham Rotarians I knew the presentation like the back of my hand. I'd given it at least two dozen times, I had an answer for any question that could be asked. I was relaxed, confident, the presentation has serious points, timed laughter, even areas that tugged on heartstrings. Rotarians listened, asking questions while eating lunch huddled in a small backroom of a local restaurant, munching on sandwiches and salads. They voted to endorse the bond, which was huge, they spoke for a large portion of the business community. I was scheduled to meet with the Chamber of Commerce in a few weeks, hopeful they'd do the same. Carol, my Director of Communications had laid the groundwork, she has been an active member of Chamber for years, attending their early morning meetings, building relationships, keeping them updated on events, sharing Centennial's positive happenings. She also kept me up-to-date on Chamber activities, making sure I attended the key ones.

By March 7, 2020 New York declared a state of emergency, COVID-19 cases and death tolls began flooding the news. NYC shuts down over 500 events due to safety precautions. Deaths in other countries and cases across the US grew state by state.

On March 8th the number of confirmed cases in Oregon had climbed to 14 people. Hillsboro School District in Oregon announces one case that was identified at a Middle School, the superintendent announced that the school is performing a deep cleaning over the weekend and classes will continue Monday as scheduled. Two days later Portland's high school career expo was canceled due to COVID-19 concerns. Usually this event brings more than 7,000 students to the convention center. The number of confirmed cases had risen above twenty by March 12th, most of which were in Multnomah County. Consumed by worry, anxiety and stress for the safety of my family, students, staff, friends, community and me personally. How deadly is it? What if I have it… spreading it unaware? Samia had a weaker immune system, how do I keep her safe?

The night before I sat near the fireplace watching the last two Blazer games on DVR, pissed at Rudy Gobert for touching all the mics, mocking COVID-19. He was the first player to test positive in the NBA. Possible patient zero, which led to quickly ending an entire NBA season, for the first time in history.

I sat bunkered in the back of a small conference room in Centennial's District Office. Me, Cabinet and my new Head of Security, Pete, who had taped an 8 x 12 "Incident Command Center" sign on the door. In the small room we discussed whether or not to cancel after-school events, calling neighboring districts to gather their thoughts, in hopes of building a unified approach. Some Cabinet members wore masks while others didn't. We'd been crouched together all week so an exposure may or may not have already happened. "We made the decision to cancel, then began calling principals, sharing talking points and crafting a letter to send home with students. When we called the high school to notify them about the cancellation they raised the question "what about football?" "What about it? It's a national health emergency" I quickly responded. "Well, this virus supposedly spreads indoors…we were hoping to close down the weight room and practice outside. Other teams are probably still going to practice. If we cancel it puts our team at a disadvantage." "No, when we close the district it means everything, if we cancel after-school activities, it's all of them - no exceptions" I stated in irritation, quickly getting off the phone. I glance at James, "What kind of dumb logic is this?...we close everything except for football…oh, let's risk lives to win at all cost!" I sarcastically ranted. I could feel my stress level begin to rise, "I'm going to make a few calls" I announced to the group. Pacing the parking lot on my phone I called the superintendents again, "are you planning to cancel football?" It was a mixed bag, "Why? When we cancel after-school events all means all" I remarked.

For other districts it was more complicated, they had board members that were past coaches, relatives who were players, wildly entrenched in the season. Like most communities, the politics of high school football runs deep. No matter how deep, I was shutting it down in the name of safety. I was tired of the good ol' boy politics, back door agreements, handshakes and side deals. A group I attributed to the loss of a portion of our voters during the past bond attempt. The entire NBA was shut down, Lebron, Lillard, Curry, and the like were home chillin' and we're discussing whether or not to hold a high school practice. No, it's not happening…we canceled our after-school events, then sent our district office staff home at 3:30pm.

That evening, COSA called a virtual emergency superintendents' meeting using a new technology that had been around for years but was new to us, Zoom. Our technology staff created Zoom accounts, preparing our laptops for a shift to virtual meetings. We logged in, finding every superintendent and assistant superintendent in the state staring back at us in square boxes. COSA and Oregon Department of Education (ODE) leaders led the meeting providing us with data, guidance and updates. The most important was that Governor Kate Brown was announcing that all schools would be closed Monday, March 16, 2020 in efforts to prevent the spread of COVID-19. The following week was Oregon's scheduled spring break. "Health professionals expect that schools may be closed for approximately two weeks, with a plan to reconvene school on April 1st." Comments flooded the Zoom chat box, state leaders announced that another virtual meeting would be scheduled in a week, "We will take time to review your questions and concerns and provide you with more information at that time."

On March 13, President Trump declared a national emergency. Our expected two-week closure soon stretched into the unforeseeable future. We met with state leaders via Zoom listening to information about how to provide supplement learning support as the situation continued to get worse. The early COVID spring break was nothing like the winter break, peace, joy and goodwill toward fellow man was out the window. Store shelves were bare, toilet paper, over the counter medicine, gloves and cleaning supplies - gone. Paper products, produce, frozen food lockers and meat freezers - barren. Masked customers with shopping carts piled high with groceries. As an early riser I'd make the store run at 5AM to avoid the crowd. Peering over my shoulder to eyeball anyone walking too closely behind me. Trying to keep my distance double masked using my shopping cart as a shield.

It was the season of cooking meals at home or drive-through fast food joints, eating meals in cars, plus obsessive hand washing. Scrubbing intensely for at least 30 seconds under scalding hot water – lather, rinse, repeat. Pocket hand sanitizer was the weapon of choice, backups were stored in glove compartments and car door storage bins, plastic rolls of Clorox wipes rolling around car floorboards. Frequently watching the news as case numbers rise across the globe along with the death tolls. Face Timing relatives to check on them, "everybody doing ok?" Statewide curfews were mandated, shutting down restaurants, bars, businesses, beauty salons, churches and barbershops. For some, it was like being on house arrest, some families bonded, many divided, walking around with earbuds, constantly watching television on their phones. During the day, I would set up my laptop in the laundry room, using the ironing board as a standing desk. We met as a Cabinet discussing a plan for getting 1:1 technology as well as getting resources to our students. My experience launching an online program provided me insight into key resources and curriculums that would benefit our student during this shift. We organized distribution centers in front of school buildings where parents could drive through to get breakfast and lunches for their students for the week. We distributed printed learning materials sorted by grade level, deploying Chromebook, chargers and information on how to access our supplemental resources page. Our staff made a quick shift, pivoting from brick and mortar to supporting students from a distance, everyone stepped up and met the need.

In the evening, I got back to using my elliptical, watching movies with the kids while trying to reach twelve thousand steps a day. Dad was doing the same, we became accountability partners, using the fit-ness apps on our phones to track steps and screenshot a photo when one of us reached twelve thousand. It became a competition. On Saturdays I'd get up at the crack of dawn to walk the neighborhood, knocking out my steps early sending Dad a snapshot that I was done at 8 am. He once sent me notification that he was done at 6 am. A bing on my phone woke me up before my morning alarm had gone off. I got out of bed and called him. He was on the other end laughing. "I've been up since 3, just walking the living room listening to music" he chuckled.

I also got back into the hobby of brushing my hair, but not the normal kind of brushing. I'd do these hour-long brush sessions trying to get elite waves. I was obsessed with it. Ordering special wave brushes, mirrors, durags and products. Brushing consistently while listening to music. My waves were the best they had ever been. I had also been cutting Paulie and my father's hair for about two years, but other than an edge up I never really had the heart to cut my own, until the pandemic. I began watching barbers haircut tutorials on YouTube, perfecting Paulie's fade and testing out my own hair while holding a long oval shaped mirror, not bad. Each cut became more precise. Like many of my colleagues James was growing long hair and a really thick beard, after one month of COVID lockdown he looked much different. Each Zoom meeting more facial hair, "man your hair grows fast" I said when he turned on his screen. "I can't get haircuts, how are you maintaining yours?" he asked. "I've been cutting my own hair, maybe when this is over, I won't need to go to the barbershop anymore." My cutting skills were constantly getting better, Dad was loving it, taking full advantage of the situation. I'd get an early morning call, "Hey Dude, can you swing by later today and give me a cut?" Just five years prior he would go to the barbershop of a friend of mine. The shop was first come first serve, so he would wait in line for about an hour and get a haircut once a month. When I told him I could cut his hair, he stopped going to the shop, I'd cut him up every two weeks. Now, during the pandemic when no one is going anywhere, all of a sudden he wants a cut every week. "Didn't I just cut you up a few days ago?" I joked. "Man please. Hook a brotha up" he responded. I always did, it was a reason to get out of the house, check on my parents and let them see their grandkids. Paulie also joked "Papa, what are you cutting, there's not much hair up there, every cut looks the same" he giggled. Mom and I laughed, Dad responded with "Man please."

The role of the superintendent changed from being proactive to reactive. The role had always been isolating, but the pandemic pivot to virtual hit different, beyond isolation, you're deserted. Only able to connect by phone with a small group of trusted colleagues. As a superintendent, I've always worked to build a trusting, supportive relationship with my principals and staff. I began regularly giving pep talks to groups of teachers virtually, using Zoom 1:1 to check-in with principals, we began adding a theme during our virtual administrator meetings, like "crazy hat day", or "tie-dye shirts" just to break the monotony. I poured everything into keeping people's spirits lifted, across the nation record breaking retirements were projected, a national poll amongst teacher showed that 68% were seriously considering leaving the profession, the teacher shortage was larger than ever, growing by 10% the year prior, teachers and classified staff were quitting daily, principals and superintendents were dropping like flies. There was too much unspoken trauma, too much hiding behind the surface, family illness, death, financial woes, marital issues and fear of the unknown. Still we show up and try to take care of others.

The bond was getting closer, I was trying to remain hopeful, we switched the roadshow to virtual meetings. We cut the number of presentations back because many of those groups weren't meeting. The supporters, consultants and Oversight Committee switched our strategy from delivering the message door-to-door to mailers, email blasts, and social media posts. We also had a citizens committee made up of parents, board members and participants of the oversight committee, they fundraised by hitting the phones for donations. Businesses were permanently shutting down, many parents, and community members lost their jobs during this time, but it was too late to turn back. Several committee members asked me if we should send out a preliminary survey again, to gauge the support, letting me know that the number would probably be much lower. "All that will do is make us more timid, or maybe take the wind out of our sails. It's too late to turn back, we don't need another survey. Besides, this is the only year we have a step down in the last bond's payment, it's now or never" I said.

I was holding it together, putting up a good front, but I was living in a house divided. My wife had moved to her mom's house six months prior, before getting an apartment. We were "co-parents" working to support the kids during the day. Paulie completed assignments on his Chromebook next to me, while I typed away at emails. For Samia, it was much rougher, beside listening to books, alphabet and counting song, it was basically a period of learning loss. A lot of marriages ended in divorce during the pandemic. That was definitely the case amongst my circle of friends. Ours was no different, but we remained adult about the situation, promising to always do what is in the best interest of our kids.

CHAPTER 14

No Time to Celebrate

n April, everyone was working at top speed providing education at a distance. During virtual board meetings we focused on highlighting strengths, increasing collective efforts, working together as a unit.

We recognized our student based non-profit, Food for Families, they were serving nearly 300 families weekly distributing pre-packaged meals. Our cafeteria staff continued providing meal distribution district-wide, but was in need of additional volunteers due to the demand.

Every virtual meeting I talked about giving students "grace before grades." Urging everyone in the district to show grace to each other. Grace meaning unmerited favor during these unprecedented time. I shared a PowerPoint illustrating the breakdown of closures across the country. Sharing information on how governors of western states plan to gradually lift stay-at-home orders. We urged employees to remain home, discouraging staff from reporting to the building to access materials, or teach virtually from their classroom spaces. Keeping everyone healthy was our top priority. "Schools will eventually open but it's dependent on reducing the spread of the virus" I stated.

We sent newsletters to our community asking them to learn and grow with us as we transition to educating students in a new way. Distance Learning involved converting lessons and materials to Google Classroom for asynchronous learning, shifting grading and attendance policies, providing virtual meetings for synchronous learning, live lessons. We continued distributing meals, high school students and staff planned for a virtual graduation. Centennial School District was pouring love into the community day in and day out.

On May 19, 2020 during the throes of a global pandemic, the community poured their love back into the district by passing Measure 26-208, our bond issue, on the May 2020 ballot. The first in 19 years, yet in despair, distant learning, fear of safety, closing of businesses, loss of jobs, rising cases, the death toll at an all-time high, our bond passed by 53.37%. Much lower than the percentage our preliminary survey indicated before the pandemic, but it didn't matter. It was a $65 million dollar win for Centennial! We celebrated through phone calls, emails and text messages. The next day was our regularly scheduled virtual board meeting, "We want to thank voters for supporting the bond measure on yesterday's ballot. We're grateful for everyone who helped spread our message, make phone calls, encouraging others to get out and vote! Special thanks to our Oversight Committee, and citizens group - Yes for Centennial Kids, for their hard work, commitment to fundraising and enlisting supporters. Thing became much more challenging due to the pandemic, but our work made a difference. I am hopeful for the future and looking forward to the work ahead of us."

Being at the helm of the bond initiative may have been the biggest accomplishment of my career. A collective effort worthy of reflection, recognition and merit. Unfortunately, the moment quickly disappeared because I witnessed a murder. We witnessed it together, in Minneapolis, Minnesota on May 25, 2020 a White police officer kneeled on a 46-year-old unarmed Black man's neck, by the name of George Floyd. The man uttered the words "I can't breathe" a few times, gasping for air. The officer calmly applied more pressure continuing to kneel on the man's neck for 8 minutes and forty-six seconds. Until he cried out for his mother, and took his last breath.

To many Americans it was an eye opener, observing such inhuman brutality at the hands of police, caught on camera for all eyes to see, witness and hear. For many Black Americans, including myself, it was no surprise. Our lived experiences with police officers made almost any potential scenario, a situation that could possibly result in the death of a Black civilian. Speeding tickets, routine traffic stops, noise violations, things normally classified as minor all had the potential to go left, at any moment. It happened time and time again. Before the killing of George Floyd many perished at the hand of police, Breonna Taylor, Elijah McClain, Jacob Blake and so many others. In Portland alone thirty-nine people had been killed by police between 2003 and 2020, of that number the majority were Black. The difference between those situations and this one, was that this was caught on camera, everyone had to acknowledge it.

The brutal action fueled a valid reaction. Cities were destroyed, the national guard was deployed in more than thirty states. The news highlighted the destruction in Minneapolis, Chicago, New York, Washington DC, Los Angeles, and Portland. Downtown Portland drew thousands of demonstrators into the city, gathering at City Hall, giving speeches on the waterfront, wearing Black Lives Matter t-shirts, holding signs with "No Justice, No Peace," "I Can't Breathe", and "Black Lives Matter."

Witnessing a murder heightened the trauma we were already experiencing, the pandemic had now taken the lives of 103,000 Americans, leaving more than 40 million without jobs. Students, staff, community, and especially people of color were hurting. A Presidential address in efforts to bring the county together never came, only threats of crowd control through tweets and brief interviews adding fuel to the fire. What started as demonstrations, quickly shifted to riots, looting, arson, destruction, tear gas. Saddened at the destruction of our city but in unison with the cause, I watched the news intently. Crowds of people throwing rocks and racial slurs, masked and unmasked, while the number of confirmed cases grew along with the death toll. People of color were dying rapidly for a myriad of reasons, which the media categorized as *underlying conditions.* Underlying conditions in medical terms are risk factors such as diabetes, high blood pressure, heart disease, obesity, cancer and kidney disease. In non-medical terms, the risk factors of being a person of color in America, dealing with the trauma of racism, police brutality, slavery, desegregation, impacts of gentrification, generational poverty, stereotypes and cultural appropriation.

While the drama ensued, like most cities Portland's downtown area became unrecognizable. A wasteland of closed business, boarded up buildings, broken glass, spray paint, mounds of garbage, entryways, and hovels full of tents of unhoused people. Schools continued pushing forward. Superintendents, principals and school leaders sent messages of support, encouragement, resources to deal with trauma, death and grief to their school communities. In Centennial we held virtual spaces for students and staff to connect with counseling services, mental health supports and virtual resources. Our distribution centers began providing Covid-19 testing, masks and sanitizer along with meals.

In June we had our first ever drive-up graduation ceremony, a safety plan was created through thoughtful conversations between students and staff. The Board and I sat in chairs socially distanced six feet apart facing a stage on the edge of the track. We applauded as graduates and their families drove up towards the stage. Students exited cars to give their principal an "air high five" receiving their diploma following all social distancing protocols. Their families stood near their vehicle taking photos. Once they drove off, the next graduates car approached. It was categorized by last name. While it took the majority of the day to complete, it was the best plan we could provide while ensuring safety under the circumstances. Graduates and families were pleased. While untraditional, it felt like a graduation.

After graduation, the school year usually winds down as we transition into the summer. I thought we'd made it through the most intense potions of the year, when I was blindsided by union leadership. Folks I'd collaborated with for the past six years, met with on a regular basis, used interest-based methods to bargain contacts and MOU. I thought we'd created a culture of solving problems at the lowest level, but I was wrong. They moved an issue they had with me to the highest level, the media.

A year prior the Board reviewed superintendent compensation data across the region, finding that I was the lowest paid superintendent compared to district of similar size. Making thirty thousand dollars below eleven other superintendents. Based on this information they used a calculation to raise my salary within the median range of comparable districts over a two-year period. When the issue was raised in the Fall of 2019, way before the pandemic, while I thought it was a noble gesture, my response to the Board was "you don't have to fix this, the perception might be off." As a rule, once a superintendent's contract is in place, it almost is what it is. You need to negotiate everything upfront, because almost any change or adjustment is met with opposition. Personally, I've found it difficult to negotiate with people who are hiring you. Especially coming from an interim role to a permanent position.

In recent years the more savvy superintendents, or the ones that have been burned badly as I have, bring in a consultant or legal counsel to negotiate their contracts. When I was offered the job, I took the contract with little to no negotiation at all, not knowing I'd be locking myself into a base salary. Ultimately, the decision to increase a salary is up to the Board, in being satisfied with my performance they upped it in the hopes of retention. They followed all the proper procedures, the increase was voted on in public session receiving no questions or resistance from the union, who were present at the Fall meeting in 2019 when the raise was approved.

But now, in the midst of a city in chaos due to racial injustice, police brutality, the pressing trauma of living through a pandemic, the union took issue. I had no problem with that, the problem I had was that after years of positive relationship, we got no questions about my salary. Only questions from the media about the concerns raised by the union. Personally, I've always taken issue with the media, they failed to ask me about any of these things:

- Passing a Bond after 19 years

- Distributing more than 3,000 Chromebooks to students

- Distributing Instructional Materials to students

- Transitioning to a Distance Learning Model

- Getting our Seniors to Graduation

- Providing more than 165,000 meals to students

The phones lit up to see why a superintendent was receiving a raise during a global pandemic. To that end, emails, calls and accusations directed at the Board and I were based on assumptions. "It must be because he passed the bond," someone said. An anonymous Facebook post insinuated that my salary was being paid with bond dollars, or that the raise would result in a reduction in staff. All of these concerns could have easily been answered if we were offered the decency of a simple conversation, the way we had done things for the last five years. Instead, the teacher's union president went on the news expressing her concerns. She shared the possibility that districts could be facing budget reductions due to the pandemic. My Board Chair, Pam Shields responded to news stations to set the record straight "let me correct you, it's not a pay increase in the middle of a pandemic, this was approved last year, far before the pandemic…in particular our Superintendent Dr. Coakley was the lowest paid in the metro area."

The following week we held our virtually scheduled board meeting. I felt like I was on trial for a crime I didn't commit. The week prior I received an outpouring of support from community partners, district leaders and organizations including Black Lives Matter wanting to protest the allegations of the union. They felt I was being targeted as the only Black male superintendent in the state. They expressed the way the story was portrayed in the media felt racist. They wanted to attend the board meeting, but I discouraged each group and individual I spoke with. I'd always looked at Centennial School District as a family, when families have issues I felt talking through them was the best way to find resolution. It saddened me that our district was airing its dirty laundry for all to see and judge, determining whether or not we were a district worthy of serving our community. My Board was really taking the heat, fielding calls, refuting email and allegations. Stressful unfounded assumptions defaming their good work as public volunteers, who dedicated so many hours giving back to their community. Once again, they stood their ground. They'd done nothing wrong and were prepared to set the record straight.

Here I was once again positioned to prove that I belonged in my seat. The feeling brought back the post-traumatic memories of my elementary school, middle school and high school years. The SEI jacket that never materialized, my Portland Teacher Program experience, Portland Public's Aspiring Administrator Program, being falsely accused of forgery, being runner up time and time again for administrator jobs but never actually landing a gig. M.C.'s words to Paulie rang in my ears, "don't join the union kid." Not that he actually had any issue with the union, he was basically saying that when money becomes scarce people play dirty, relationships are tossed out the window. Reminiscent of my father's experience in Gresham-Barlow, Dad called me before the meeting. "Hey P, in these situations when you know you are right, all you can do is stand. Stand, make space for yourself, you've got nothing to be ashamed of. You're the leader of that district for a reason. God put you there, you're in the right seat, no one can take it from you. So just stand!"

I decided that I wasn't going to explain anything, or prove myself to anyone. Every year I let my actions speak louder than my words. When people take the low road, I'd take the high road. I began my Superintendent's Report "I want to thank our staff for their extraordinary efforts in rising to the challenge of educating and supporting our students through the distance learning model due to the Covid-19 pandemic." I highlighted all we'd accomplished throughout the school year, then ended my report with, "districts around the state are standing together to advocate for full funding of K-12 education. At the state and county level we've been busy meeting with legislators to lobby for adequate K-12 funding, sharing stories, explaining the impact of the inadequate funding projection. We've made a lot of strides this year, during this turbulent time, kids need us now more than ever. I want to call on our unions tonight to join us as district leaders in lobbying for fully funding K-12 education."

Those were my last words for the night, then Chair Shields called on James to present the budget which was based on the state projection, my salary adjustment was part of the budget proposal. The actual numbers were unknown until mid-August. As James spoke, I felt relieved, assured, empowered and unblemished. Assistant Superintendent James Owens was my personal Johnnie Cochran, only younger, White and a district administrator. Every question posed to our Board the week prior, he answered. Every email concern shared with us, he addressed. He left no stone unturned, explaining every detail with a fine-tooth comb. It was Texas Hold'Em, our accusers had gone "all in" unaware that James was sitting across the table with pocket aces.

When James finished speaking you could hear a mouse walk on cotton. I watched the Zoom participants' number dwindle from double digits to much lower numbers, leaving only the Board, my Cabinet and the die-hard union leaders waiting for their turn to speak. They had written statements to read, the statement asked questions that James had already answered in his budget report. When the last comment was read, our Chair asked the Board if they had any comments before they voted on the proposed budget. My Vice-Chair Rhonda Etherly, the only African-American female on the Board, was the strong silent type. She was a Centennial parent dedicated to serving her community. Through-out the name change, the pandemic, and the killing of George Floyd, she would call me and express her support. She spoke up when she felt the need, and when she spoke people listened. "I don't speak on every issue, but I felt compelled tonight to speak, Dr. Coakley is an effective leader, he never brought up his salary. Pay equity legislation would have required his increase. To those who thought he should continue to be significantly underpaid, shame on you! For obvious reasons I will not ask Dr. Coakley to be paid less than his White colleagues performing the same work. The audacity of those who spoke to Dr. Coakley in an insensitive manner shows a lack of professionalism. If Dr. Coakley was White, would we be having this conversation? The time to dispute contracts has passed. The work of our entire staff is appreciated. Let's focus now on what should be our priority, our students."

Before voting Chair Shields said "this process has been difficult, and laws must be followed. I appreciate our employees. I have 40+ years of union experience in a number of capacities, I'm a union member at heart even though I'm the Board Chair. I will never break a contract with a union, a principal, an administrator or a superintendent. The budget process is not designed to force a salary freeze, furlough day or other decreases that have been deemed equitable. A teacher's union leader contacted me with a 17% miscalculation of the superintendent's salary. I asked her to reconsider the incorrect characterization of our superintendent's raise. His contract was written and approved more than a year ago. As your Board Chair my character was challenged. I was blamed for not answering questions about the incorrect information quick enough. I appreciate Dr. Coakley, the heart he has for this district, the person he is, and I will do everything I can to retain him. I'm voting yes, I don't want people to believe that I'm doing this to break a contract, freeze salaries or set aside the voices of our staff. If I can't break an agreement with our union members, I can't break a contract with our superintendent."

Then, Chair Shields took a roll call vote on the motion to approve the budget. The vote passed and the budget was approved 6 to 1.

CHAPTER 15

When One Door Closes

Since visiting B in college, I've always wanted to attend Harvard. A dream I thought I'd never attain, especially as a single Dad running a school district. The pandemic shifted my mindset, this could be an opportunity to reinvent myself. K-12 students adapted to online learning, colleges also adjusted, it was the only option. To take advantage of the situation I applied for Harvard's Advanced Educational Leadership Program. Why not go for it while programs were offered online? I got accepted and began taking online classes.

Fall 2020, we opened Centennial Virtual Academy (CVA), transitioning our alternation high school, known as Centennial Park School into a fully accredited virtual school. Reminiscent of Rainier, we used a similar model tracking time worked virtual, coupled with 1:1 staff check-ins, utilizing Zoom as a drop-in space. Statewide districts were dealing with rapidly declining enrollment. Rolling out distance learning left many students and parents frustrated. Many left districts to attend virtual schools. By surveying Centennial parents, we knew that by providing our community a fully virtual school option we'd meet the needs of a large portion of our students, at least temporarily throughout the pandemic. The majority of the summer we planned the virtual school launch, reshuffling staff, updating students and families, providing trainings, gauging interest and enrolling participants.

By September the new Centennial Virtual Academy had over 500 students K-12, more students than several of our elementary schools. 500 students that would have potential left without a virtual school option.

The school could serve students from anywhere in the state. There was only one stipulation to enrolling, once a student enrolled they were making a one-year commitment. Student weren't allowed to transfer back and forth from CVA to traditional school until the following year. This allowed for stable enrollment and proper staffing for the year. There was a strong possibility that school buildings would open back up in the near future and many CVA students would want to go back in-person. Based on this logic the Board approved the new online school for one year, with plans to assess the program mid-year and determine whether it will continue after year one.

In January 2021, every district in the county collaborated with Sam's team at Multnomah Education Service District including Health Professionals in launching a mass vaccine distribution clinic held at the Oregon Convention Center in NE Portland. The Governor planned to get vaccines distributed to the entire state as fast as possible, requiring that nurses and doctors be on-site in the same location rather than having people schedule appointments to visit their regular physicians' offices. Hospitals had limited parking, space or bandwidth to deal with the multitude of people in need of vaccination. This effort would take Portland's four largest health providers Kaiser Permanente, Providence, Legacy Health and Oregon Health & Science University pooling their resources together to serve all Multnomah County Residents. Shortly thereafter, the federal government announced the release of all vaccine doses a few weeks into the New Year. Governor Brown laid out her plan for the eligibility of vaccine recipients. Those 65 and older were prioritized first, followed by educators and child care providers. It took several weeks before the state had enough vaccines to provide them to everyone who qualified. Once educators received their first dose, schools would reopen their doors to students. The Governor stated "getting teachers and school staff vaccinated will help make our learning environments as safe as possible. We need to make sure our kids know they come first" Brown said.

As superintendent, I focused on planning for an orderly reopening and vaccine rollout, breaking staff into categories by age and position, prioritizing those working directly with students. HR worked diligently ensuring every staff member had a day, time and clear understanding of how to access their vaccine. At the time the options were Pfizer-BioNTech, or Moderna. The mass vaccine clinic opened its door at the Convention Center in late January, ushering educators and residents 65 and older through quickly. My parents got their vaccines, both received Pfizer, reporting they had no negative reactions. Those who received their vaccine shared their experience on how their bodies responded with colleagues, friends and relatives. We weren't only dealing with providing access, we were also dealing with anti-vaxxers, staff refusing to be vaccinated, a small portion of staff applied for a religious exemption. Addressing exemptions case-by-case basis, being thoughtful about how to utilize those staff in a way that prioritized the safety of all. It was an ongoing process, in late February our last group of educators, mostly administrators including James and I got our first dose of vaccines along with several other superintendents. A small index card provided proof of vaccine, indicating the date, vaccine manufacturer and administering health professional's signature. Like my parents, I received Pfizer having no reactions other than a light sniffle for about 24 hours. Scheduled for a second dose about three weeks out.

March of 2021, Oregon schools reopened doors with a new learning model - Hybrid Learning. A week made up of in-person school days and days where students were working from home. Students were split into cohorts by grade level, in Centennial we used an A/B schedule. On days when cohort "A" was in-person, cohort "B" worked from home on assignments built into Google Classroom. The cohort model reduces student numbers, allowing schools to follow all safety protocols, social distancing desks, tables and lines of students. We required masks, frequent hand washing was part of the daily routine, schools were provided sanitizer and boxes of masks for those needing them. We closed school to all guests, the parents picked up and dropped off procedure moved to outdoors as well. Temperature checks were conducted before students entered the building, school nurses and health assistants diligently checking students, contacting parents, running isolation spaces where students with symptoms were quarantined and picked up by a parent. Frequent messages were sent on how to protect yourself and others from spreading the virus. Our custodial staff cleaned buildings frequently between the change in A and B cohorts, deep cleaning anytime there was a confirmed Covid-19 case. Staff were contact tracing, notifying families when a child was in a location that may have exposed them to the virus. All students possibly exposed were required to quarantine for ten days. Students had the option of continuing to work from home in Google Classroom if they chose.

Health guidance and protocols continued shifting, learning in the moment, building the plane while flying it, modifying and adjusting. The virus itself continued to morph, strands changed, spiking at times, sometimes showing periods of decline. As superintendent, safety was the driver of all decision, I relied heavily on experts and health professionals, soaking up information and providing clear communication to staff and community was my job. Our staff remained flexible, stepping up to support each other when people were out with symptoms, or quarantined due to exposure, pivoting and adjusting with each change or requirement. Our schools functioned with half our students in-person, half learning virtually. Educating masked, socially distant, build relationships, maintaining a healthy culture. The most difficult time to be an educator in American history.

Sam and I met on a regular basis, discussing all that was going on. My divorce, co-parenting, the pandemic's impact on relatives and friends, its effects on the educational system. In December 2020, Sam informed his Board and staff that he'd was leaving MESD at the end of the school year. He had served in the role since July of 2016, when I took the interim spot at Centennial. He'd mentioned I should consider applying for the position, the position was posted in March. "What are you going to do next?" I asked. Not sure, take some time off" Sam replied. "Are you retiring early?" I asked. "No, just stepping away" he said. "I wish I could do that, I don't see time off in my foreseeable future" I joked.

I thought long and hard about apply for the job. When faced with tough decisions, I usually consulted my father. He was an encourager, gave sound advice, he loved imparting wisdom. "Sam's right, you should apply. Think about it, you'd be leaving Centennial on high note, your work there is done. You're leaving the district in a better place than you found it. You diversified the staff, changed the school names, passed the bond during the pandemic, opened an online school, got staff vaccinated and back in the building. Plus, you're leaving them in good hands with James, he can take it from here. Step aside and give him the opportunity to lead, you know he's ready. You've got the support of the superintendents' group, you been collaborating with them for the past five years." "Hey Dad, you're forgetting one thing, I have to actually interview and get the job first" I smiled. "Hey, that ain't no thang...you tell me where they're gonna find a Black superintendent with a doctorate in educational leadership, about to get another from Harvard University, you don't grow on trees. Besides, after this last stunt the union pulled, I'd tell'em sayonara!" he said loudly.

Dad was right, Sam had also left MESD in a better place than where he found it. Sam boosted morale, restored relationships with the component districts, built comradery amongst superintendents and increased systems of support across the region. I held high admiration for the MESD staff. They supported the toughest, most vulnerable student populations, from alternative settings to hospital programs, juvenile detention centers, prison programs, during the pandemic they were ever-present. They provided school nurses and school health assistance regionally, without them there would be no Hybrid Model. I liked the idea of conveying the Superintendent Council meetings, working collectively, supporting their systems behind the scenes. The more I reflected, the more excited I became. I applied, but first I met with James over lunch, sharing the news. James was supportive, but had a lot of questions. "First I have to interview," I said. "Right, but you're probably out of here" he replied. "If I do get the job, I'll recommend the Board consider you for the gig" I said.

MESD's hiring process was virtual with several components. Once I advanced to round two, I notified my Board Officers, Pam and Rhonda. They were surprised but also understanding of why I was looking. The process dragged, Zoom meetings with teachers, students, educational assistants, administrators, board members and superintendents. I interviewed in my laundry room, standing in front of the washer, the folding ironing board housed my MacBook Air.

In mid-May I was offered the position, I accepted after negotiating my contract a bit. I felt relieved, proud of my work at Centennial, one door was closing, another was opening. I shared the news with the Board and administrators, then Centennial staff, in the nick of time before media printed articles. The local headlines read "Centennial superintendent Coakley tapped to lead MESD" and "MESD Board Votes Unanimously to hire Dr. Paul Coakley as Superintendent." While excited about the opportunity, I committed to finishing the year strong at Centennial, setting the stage for the future. No one was more excited than Dad, he called relatives across the country, sending local articles to everyone he knew, constantly repeating "what'd I tell you! I saw the writing on the wall." His texts stirred up a barrage of congratulations emails, texts and calls.

The Centennial Board accepted my resignation at the next board meeting and stated that due to timing they'd consider filling the position internally. Graduation was held outside, a traditional graduation ceremony, with social distancing and masks.

I started at MESD on July 1, 2021. Sam and I met prior to ensure a smooth transition. I got keys and toured the district office with my kids and parents. The building was empty, the photos in the main lobby displayed the diverse Board that hired me. The upper hallway had photos of past superintendents who served from 1950 to present day. I was the first superintendent of color added to the wall. We parked it in my new office for a bit. "I'm just taking it all in P, this is amazing, you're serving students across the region. I'm so proud of you! You went out on a high note" said Dad. "Maybe seven's my lucky number, I worked in PPS for seven years, Rainier was also seven, then seven in Centennial. Yeah, I run my course in about seven years," I joked. "Here you're just starting, what'll you do after seven years here?" Dad asked. "I don't know, maybe get some sleep," I said.

On Sunday, July 18, 2021 I pulled in a parking lot directly across the street from my new office. It was our designated location for exchanging the kids. Their Mom was parked in her usual spot when I arrived. I updated her on what the kids had for lunch. During our brief conversation, I missed a call from Brian, while saying goodbye to Paulie and Samia I missed B's second call. "Hey, I've gotta go, this could be an emergency" I said. We drove in separate directions, my phone rang, I answered on Bluetooth "PJ, where are you?" said Brian's wife Shema. "I'm in Portland, near PDX, why?" "Get to your parents' house quick, I think your Dad passed away" she said. "What?!, How?! I just spoke to him this morning." I heard her crying on the other end. "I'm on my way" I said before hanging up.

My parents' house is a twenty-minute drive from MESD, but it took an eternity to get there. Everything moved in slow motion, I drove dazed, in a fog, my mind raced. "I just spoke to him this morning...Shema must be mistaken... am I dreaming? Maybe this is a nightmare, someone wake me up" I thought. I called my mom twice, no answer. Finally reaching my parents driveway spotting unfamiliar cars. I expected to see Dad, maybe laying on the floor, instead I saw Herb, a long-time family friend from the old neighborhood where I grew up. He answered the door, his wife was consoling my mom who was sitting on the couch. "Have you heard what happened?" asked Herb. "Not really, but I think so." "Your Dad passed, he was driving from the store, he started swerving, then slowed down and waved for help. He pulled over in my neighborhood, we were there with him, we prayed for him, he didn't struggle. Paramedics came, they tried, but he was already gone" said Herb.

I sat with Mom, stunted, heartbroken, shocked, unable to move. Etched on the outside of the large living room window above Mom and I's heads were two angel wings that had never been there before, no idea how they got there.

Days went by before I broke the news to Paulie, he asked a few questions. At Mom's house he broke into tears, "I keep thinking that Papa is hiding, and he is going to come out" he said, reminiscent of their games of hide and seek. "Yeah, me too," I said before hugging him. Soon Brian arrived from NY, followed by his family, then relatives from Tennessee, Detroit and Atlanta. Dad's funeral was attended by hundreds in-person and virtually by live stream. Mt. Olivet Baptist Church building was closed due the pandemic; they'd conducted service virtually the past year. The church leadership team met, "we'll open it for Paul" they said. Mom asked me to speak at the funeral, I spent the next few days crafting my thoughts, what should I share? What's too personal to share? What would make Dad smile? How would he want his funeral to be? This is what I decided to share:

"Thank you all for coming. I'm Paul Edward Coakley Jr. I spent a lot of time talking to people and listening to their stories. Many of my friends were raised in single parent households, many of their fathers for whatever reason, weren't there consistently to raise them. So many kids, especially kids of color were raised by their amazing mothers, their glorious grandmothers, their dependable relatives, or their great guardians. I want to recognize and commend all of those mothers, those grandmothers, those relatives and guardians who raised children without fathers. So many of my friends had fatherless stories but they strived, they made it out of whatever their circumstances were regardless. Some of them used that fuel, that feeling inside them, that curiosity of why their dad may not have been there. They motivated themselves to succeed out of the circumstances that they were given. I want to commend every single one of the men and women listening to me today if that's your story, because that is really tough on a kid.

But that's not my story because I was blessed with a father, not just a father, a wonderful strong Black father, who was always there. Matter of fact, I can't think of a time when he wasn't there. Not a birthday, not a holiday, not a graduation, not a year, not a week, not a day. He always picked up the phone, he always cared. He always encouraged me, he always believed in me.

My Dad was many different things to different people. For some of you, he was your principal. For some, your mentor, your coach, your colleague, your uncle, your brother, your teacher, your neighbor, your grandpa, but to me he was my rock. He was my encourager, he was my

252

confidant, he was my Dad. I believe that people come into our lives for a reason and for a season. Sometimes that reason is short, then that season is over. My dad blessed people during his season for 67 years, for me, since the day I was born we took 45 laps around the sun. But last Sunday, that season ended, but that reason will go on forever. During those seasons we made a lot of amazing memories and stories. I could go on and on telling you about different stories, but instead of doing that I'm just going to go back to last Saturday. My Mom and Dad came over and spent a day at the house with the grandkids. Dad was really excited because he wanted to watch Space Jam 2. He called and texted, he said "hey, it's coming out on HBO Max, I don't have HBO Max, do you have it?" I said "I don't know, I don't watch HBO Max", but I found out I actually had it. So, I called him back and let him know, he said "Oh, it's gonna be on, it's gonna be on!" So, they came over, watched the movie and my 7-year-old daughter Samia sat in his lap sucking her thumb, just cuddled up to him as they watched. He was laughing and playing with her. My 12-year-old son Paulie sat right by him, bouncing and playing around with who he calls Papa. At the end of the movie the son looks at LeBron and says "I love you Dad" and LeBron says it back. My Dad looked at my son Paulie, he said "Paulie, you got something you wanna say to your Dad?" Paulie looked at me and said "I love you Dad" and I said it back. Then, Paulie looked at me and he said "Dad, you got something you wanna say to your Dad?" I looked at my Dad and said "I love you Dad" and he said it back. He had a huge smile on his face, after the movie they went home. When he got home, he called me saying "today was a fantastic day, I really enjoyed spending time with my grandkids, I just wanted you to know that."

All throughout my life he would call or text and he would say "what you got going on today?" He was a real early riser, and so am I. We'd be up, I kinda got that from him because I grew up watching him, observing him as a role model. He'd ask about my day and I'd say today I've got this or that…I have several meetings. Then he'd say "handle your business P." That's the only way he'd let me get off the phone. Each morning I just hop up, it's ingrained in me from my Dad to handle business. After this Sunday, it's been a lot tougher, sometimes I don't feel like handling business. But I hear his voice saying "handle your business P." That's all I need to get up.

He was there for each of you in some capacity, everyone in here has their own stories of what he meant to them. What he meant to me, is who I am today. So, I'm gonna continue to handle business because that's the way that he and my Mom raised us. That's the way he'd want it to be. I love you all, thank you for coming."

That July, Portland lost a living legend. An outpouring of love, stories, testimony and comments about Paul Coakley Sr, were shared on social media pages, explained in written letters, preached about in sermons, honored in reports. The impact he left spread far and wide, much farther than any of us could've imagined. That July was the end of our season. That month I almost lost my stride, again I saw my life stretched in front of me. A large puzzle laid out on a flat surface. The far end of the puzzle was unfinished, the past was tightly put together except there were more holes than before, representing loved ones who passed away. My Uncle James, my Uncle Bobby on my mother's side, missing pieces representing close friends, neighbors and colleagues. One portion of the puzzle had a gaping hole full of missing pieces, full of memories, stories, sayings, wisdom, love, pride, and impact. The hole was illuminated by light, a bright beam shined through the empty spaces of the puzzle, so beautifully bright it's impossible not to recognize it. The sense of loss, grief, sorrow and mourning left me in a fog. Melancholy to the light that lit up my life, radiating far beyond my puzzle, farther than my scope of thought.

In July, I completed Harvard's Advanced Educational Leadership Program, earning the program certificate. I don't remember how the program ended, I don't even remember completing, finishing or submitting the final assignments. Although the large certificate with Paul Coakley printed on it, dawning the official Harvard seal, signed by the College President, and Graduate School of Education Dean, was evidence that I finished on autopilot.

I began my new job as Superintendent of Multnomah Education Service District. I don't remember setting up my office, writing my introductory messages to staff, meeting my new Cabinet, or preparing for the opening of the school year. Nonetheless, it all happened, documented by email, video, message of appreciation, letters of support and people sharing their hopes for the future.

After Dad passed, I spent a more time with Mom once Brian traveled back to New York. He took a chunk of time off, helping her get things in order. I helped her around the house, cleaning out Dad's closet, donating and giving away his possessions. In the back of his closet, Mom found his SEI letterman's jacket. The once butter soft sleeves were rougher and drier, the collar and cuffs, tattered and frayed. The backside dawned the large patch with the SEI logo in whitish puffy varsity style knitting, with red stitching surrounding the patchwork of a basketball hoop in the distance suspended in the clouds, with an up-close image of a hooper's hands on a ball. In small red lettering it said "life without education is a long shot." The front right pocket had "Coakley" embroidered in white. The jacket took me down memory lane in a more positive way than it had in the past. Memories of my Dad's years as the principal of Harriet Tubman, the way he walked the halls larger than life interacting with students, staff and parents. Building relationships, promoting learning, creating a healthy school culture where everyone is seen, valued, heard, celebrated, where each individual matters. "He'd want you to have this," said Mom, handing me the jacket. I smiled, "maybe I'll get it framed."

His closet also had two pairs of unworn Adidas Ultra Boost, stored in their original boxes. Over the past six months, he and I were in heavy competition to reach 12,000 steps a day. Holding each other accountable through calls and text messages. In June, Dad's competitive text messages slowed down, becoming almost nonexistent. I'd call checking on him, he'd say "I just can't do it today P, my feet hurt." I told him about my Ultra Boost, the shoes I used for walking. "They're one of the most comfortable shoes out there, get a few pairs so you can get back to doing your steps, you don't want to lose momentum." He tried on a pair in the store, pacing back and forth. "Yeah, this is it, it feels like I'm walking on a cloud," he said.

I didn't realize at the time that he was actually tired. He'd given all he had to everything and everyone. He'd run a good race, positively impacting every place and person he came in contact with. As a retiree, he constantly subbed in schools across the city for principals, he mentored principals and vice-principals, he was frequently called, consulted, requested and sought after. He never said no to anyone in need of a helping hand. He was tired of overt racism, institutional barriers, gang violence, police brutality, crime, pandemic trauma, extreme cases of homelessness, poverty, politics, and the media. He'd poured every last drop of his life into a system that constantly takes, rarely every giving back. Taking your time, your energy, your peace, your leadership. The system of education can give you hope, joy, and fulfillment. It can also easily chew you up and spit you out. A reality that we both knew first hand. Pushing people aside, crippling them, and ending their livelihood as if they never existed.

He'd given me and Brian all he knew, everything he had before God called him home. I imaged God saying something along the lines of... leave the Adidas Ultra Boost in their original boxes. You've fought the good fight, you've finished the race. You've kept the faith. It's your time to walk with Me in the clouds.

Leaving a Legacy:
Lessons for Leaders

It's been a few years since my Dad passed. I still meet people from all over that tell me stories about how he influenced them. They begin sentences with "If it wasn't for your father…" and "he was my principal" or "he was my mentor"... "I would call him for advice and…" During his years as an educator, I knew he was well liked, made a difference and left a positive influence on the community, but I had no idea to what magnitude. Just a few weeks ago I received a call from a school district in Oregon, letting me know that they were going through the process of renaming a school. I immediately began to think this person reached out to ask me questions about the process that I conducted in Centennial for remaining our schools. Instead, I was pleasantly surprised to find out that they had conducted a process which yielded five names, and my Dad's was one of those names. I am sure that all five of the individuals left a long-lasting legacy and impact deserving of being honored in this way. In my estimation, I can't think of anyone more deserving than Paul Coakley Sr, only time will tell.

Rarely do we get to give educators their "flowers" while they can still smell them. Sharing our appreciation and gratitude with those who removed barriers, imparted wisdom, provided guidance, support, inspiration and encouragement. As I reflect on my own personal journey, I've faced many barriers, and continue face them, as I serve in the role of superintendent. This memoir is only a brief snapshot of my experiences.

What resonated most with me is that for every stumbling block I faced, someone was there to help me overcome that specific situation or hurdle. Sometimes it was a person of color, other times a White ally, people who believed in me, opened doors, shattered glass ceilings, removed chains, and created hope.

The section is for educational leaders who are working to leave a legacy. I've had the opportunity to work with many amazing people along my journey. I've also served in a variety of roles, holding different positions throughout the educational system. I believe that the key to leaving a legendary legacy as an educator regardless of title, position or job classification, comes down to a few key factors.

Wherever you serve, leave it better than you found it. Successful leaders aren't people who create problems to address, or change things just because they're in a new role, hoping to be different than the person serving before them. Successful leaders actually spend time learning about the culture, context and system in which they serve. They assess what is working well and what needs improvement. They get to know their staff, students and community. They look at the big picture from all angels, and make student driven-decisions. They find out what barriers are impending success by listening, observing, gathering information and assessing. Then, they clearly identify the problem, raise people's consciousness of the issues, and gain supporters to thoughtful help them craft a plan of action plan.

Apply the equity lens at the beginning of your process, using these key questions as a guide:

- How does this policy, program, practice, or decision increase access, equity, and inclusion?

- Who is being impacted by this decision? Has everyone involved been able to participate in this process?

- What are the barriers to more equitable outcomes for all? Does this decision advance on worsen the outcome of marginalized groups?

Center your conversation on racial inequities, using the questions to help you understand the impact of the decision, issue, practice or policy has on your system and those you serve. Examine the unintended consequences on underserved groups, barriers that impede achievement and mitigating negative impacts. Your staff will gain a deeper understanding, making decisions that advance your district goals. Soon, it will be like second nature, a community of leaders who are grounded in advancing equity.

Understand your why, use it as fuel and know when it needs to be shifted. Keep your "why" student-centered. As a superintendent, my "why" is creating a school system that yields high-quality learning experiences for students. Experiences more engaging than providing an "invitation to learn." Meaning I want to remove barriers, pitfalls and stumbling blocks that I experienced as a student of color. Many times, the negative experiences were due to teachers who held low expectations and beliefs based on race or stereotypes. Other times it was traditions, systems and policies with embedded biases, systems that cater to White culture only, leaving non-conforming learners on a failing path. As a superintendent, my "why" drives me to elevate marginalized voices, build on the strengths of systems, remove barriers that impede success and dismantle practices that allow Fundamentalist to work with students. Students need caring adults they connect with, people that encourage and believe in them. As I think about the needs of students, as well as my past experiences, those thoughts fuel my "why." Many of the same barriers I faced as a student still persist in our school systems today, posing issues for K-12 students. As an educational leader, I am driven to address and remove these barriers. Just because something is a tradition, doesn't mean it's good for kids. Stay focused, not only on improving students' outcomes, but also their experiences.

We'll all face low points in our careers, times where we feel unmotivated. In my role, I find that many issues brought to me are based on the problems of adults, staff conflicts, contractual issues, poor relationships, etc. This can be draining, feel unfulfilling and take leaders away from the real work that needs to be accomplished. When faced with this, I use the phrase, "it's not about us, it's about them." I share this phrase with educators, staff, and especially leaders. When I say "us" I mean adults, and when I say "them" I mean students. It brings people back to reality, reframing the context, letting them know that the work we are doing should be centered squarely on students. There was a situation in this memoir where I felt I was at my lowest point, dealing with an issue based on the insecurities of adults. To push through it, I dug deep into "why," centering myself in the fact that I am here for a reason, I'm here to represent for all students.

Stay connected to schools, programs and students. A healthy culture can only be accomplished through building trusting relationships. Many educators struggle with making the transition from classroom teacher, to building administration, or from principal, to district office administrator. With each of these moves, you are less connected to students, in some cases you go days without interacting with kids. It is important to stay visible, frequently visit school and programs, and create systems that elevate students' voices. In your new role actively work to improve students experiences, creating ways to make things better though expanding access, opportunities, and partnerships. During visits, actively listen, ask questions, and learn about the strengths and challenges of each program. Get to know the staff, create systems that elevate staff's voices. Empower those from underrepresented groups to participate in decision making processes. Assess each school and program's culture. Find out what factors contribute to the school or program culture in a positive or negative way. Be thoughtful, transparent and collaborative in your approach to finding solutions.

Build a team of believers, and stick to your non-negotiables. As a superintendent and former Human Resource Director I've spent a lot of time hiring. Getting the right people on the bus and in the right seat. As a matter of fact, hiring may be one of the most important components of a superintendent's job. For the past ten years there has been an educator shortage. The shortage has led to increased recruitment and retention efforts. These are critical areas to focus on, especially recruitment. Hiring provides an opportunity to expand the organization's group of Believers. People that believe in the students, families and community you serve. Educators that exhibit the ability and passion to work beyond providing an invitation to learn.

While retention is also important, I believe that not everyone should be retained. Exemplary educators are the ones who love what they do. They have a passion for their work, they dedicated themselves to becoming an expert at their craft. Author Malcom Gladwell states that it takes 10,000 hours of intensive research to gain mastery of a complex skill. I see many people leaving the field of education well before they reach mastery. There's an unlimited number of mitigating factors that play into with their decision to leave the profession. As an administrator, I've had coaching conversations with educators, which led to them giving me a letter of resignation. The majority of the time, the key reason is that they never fell in love with the job. They don't enjoy what they do, a job without passion isn't sustainable or what's best for students. We have a tendency to throw money at the problem, which can be a temporary fix, increasing specific positions in pay, improving job descriptions, and decreasing individuals workloads. More often than not, I've found that if the person in the position is not passionate about the work they are doing, these technical fixes are not going to retain them for long.

When leaders get the right people on the bus, in the right seat, stay student-centered and create a healthy culture, retention rates increase. In one of my opening addresses to school leaders I added "I'm driving the bus, if your aren't on the right bus, and you don't want to push on equity, you don't what to remove barriers, if you don't believe in the work that we are doing, ring the bell and I will let you off at the next stop."

If you are in a position to hire folks, kick down doors, eliminate past practices that limit diversity, put processes in place to actually assess your candidates skills, values and beliefs. Your staff should be representative of your student population. Hire leaders that don't just talk about the importance of diversifying the workforce, they actually do it. Regardless of what role you are working in an organization, take advantage of opportunities to influence decisions, serve on committees, and participate in processes. Don't underestimate your influence, you are more important than you think you are.

Help your team reach their goals, and support them in reaching their dreams. You're only as strong as the weakest member of your team. As a leader, you have to know your team well and utilize their strengths and skill set. Set aside time to identify your team's goals for the year. As a superintendent, be transparent and ensure that your Cabinet members are not working in isolation. Decisions that impact more than a specific department should be made collectively.

It's also important to know your team as individuals, their goals, their hopes and their dreams. If they are leaders you believe in, help them reach their next level of success, even if they'll be hard to replace. Never hold someone back from achieving their goals. Don't be afraid of letting them spread their wings. Don't allow your leader, to impede the dream of those they supervise. Gatekeeping needs to be dismantled, it creates resentment, and builds a negative district culture. Provide opportunities to build relationships, celebrate successes, and build trust. You will not always have the opportunity to handpick your team. Meet people where they are, have a clear vision and provide them with support, without micromanaging or doing their job for them. Hold them accountable to the work they were hired to do.

Take care of yourself so you can take care of others. Work-life balance is important, but educators and school leaders don't actually know how to accomplish it. Most passionate, dedicated educators are workaholics. Many are also perfectionists. They spent time planning for the future, working on projects, looking at data and responding to emails late at night or early in the morning. It took me quite a while to begin figuring out how to take care of myself. I am by no means an expert. In terms of work-life balance, there is no specific plateau to reach. It's a circle, something you work on each day, by intentionally prioritizing it. I've become much better at it than I was in the past. It is a never-ending cycle that begins by setting a weekly goal. A non-negotiable for when you will stop working each day. Base it on your calendar and determine an end time. Your stopping point for work-related phone calls and work emails. Trust me, the work will be there in the morning, and unless there is a crisis, it can wait until tomorrow. If you are traveling, vacationing, or utilizing a non-workday, put on your email auto-reply. What does a healthy work-life balance looks like for you? What will take for you to accomplish it? It may be that you want to incorporate exercise, increase family time, or just carve out personal time to decompress, relax, read or enjoy a hobby or sport. Whatever it is, document it, identify your action steps and put it in place at the beginning of the week. At the end of week, assess whether or not you met the goal. If you didn't accomplish it, ask yourself, why? or why not? Then set the same goal for the following week, but adjust your behavior and action plan so you improve you outcome. Once you have mastered that goal, keep it going. After a month it should become a habit. Then, add a second work-life balance goal, incorporating it into your routine just as you did the first one, soon, you will reap the rewards.

Since my Dad passed, I have really focused on creating a healthy work-life balance. I began with the goal of incorporating time into my schedule for daily exercise. In thinking about how to actually accomplish this, I realized I needed to wake up an hour earlier. I began setting my alarm an hour ahead of my usual time. I started each day by drinking water before using my elliptical, which has been collecting dust. The first week was tough but after about thirty days, I formed a habit. Soon I looked forward to starting my morning on the elliptical. Since then, I have added more goals, incorporating weights, stretching, and healthier overall eating habits. I've lost over 70 pounds, a transformation that I feel good about. I have more energy, feel healthier overall and have reduced the risk of many underlying health conditions. All of which allows me to perform more effectively as a superintendent. My routine may not work for everyone, it's just an example of how I prioritize work-life balance.

Lead by example. Leading by example is important for superintendents who build systems where race, gender, primary language and economic circumstances do not predict student success. Holding ourselves and others to high standards while leading for equity means centering the work on educational excellence, culturally responsive practices and removal of institutional and systematically racist policies and practices that prevent success.

The best leaders strive to inspire others by believing in all students. They are always looking for new ways to increase opportunities and access. Don't ask others to do something that you are not willing to do yourself. Sometimes superintendents need to be boots on the ground, other times it is more appropriate to delegate and provide support to the right group of people. Be the change you want to see. As a leader, just know that you are not going to please everyone, center your leadership on what you feel is in the best interest of student. It takes courage to lead for equity, courageous decisions inspire some and disappoint others. A wise man once told me "if everyone's happy, you're not doing your job as a leader."

Give people their flowers while they can still smell them. Think about the individuals in your life who helped you along the way. Those who influenced you as a student, motivated you in the beginning stage of your career. People who helped you achieve your goals, those who opened your eyes to opportunities. Unlocked doors that you thought were closed to you, broadened your horizons. People who coached you, told you when you were wrong, gave you the real deal, listened to your problems and offered solutions. Those who made a lasting impression on who you are today. If any of those people you thought about haven't heard how they left a positive impact on you directly, reach out to them and share your story. Let them know how much you appreciate them. Give them their flowers while you can. Think about what they've done for you and be sure to do the same for someone else. Extend your hand to others and help lift them up. Always remember that someone did the same for you. For me it was many people, too many to name. Some of the most influential people in my life were highlighted in this story, although many were not. I appreciate each and every one of you that have helped me along the way, friends, family, relatives, colleagues, neighbors.

Best wishes to all of you, inspire, encourage, and lead, our students need us now...

ONIE COAKLEY MY GREAT-GRANDMOTHER AND MY GRANDFATHER,
PAUL COAKLEY MY GRANDFATHER. CIRCA 1060S DETROIT, MI.

BABY PAULIE AND PAPA, A BOND BETWEEN GRANDPA
AND GRANDSON, RIDGEFIELD, WA 2009

Unk, me, Brian "B", and Dad

Principal Coakley, Roosevelt HS, Portland, OR

Dad posing and I, my college/Nike days...

Marques (LaBa) and I, Troutdale, OR 1983

Paul Coakley Sr graduating from Gallatin High School, 1971

Carlus Coakey (mom) college graduation photo

MOM AND DAD ON THEIR WEDDING DAY

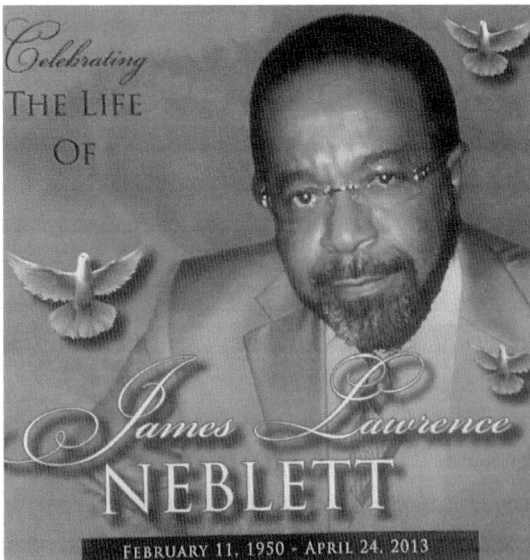

MY UNCLE JAMES, THE ONE AND ONLY

Paul Edward Coakley Sr.

AUGUST 8, 1953 – JULY 18, 2021